WAS
CHRIST
GOD?

WAS CHRIST GOD?

A Defense of the Deity of Christ

John 1:1-17

Spiros Zodhiates

AMG
PUBLISHERS

Chattanooga, TN 37421

Was Christ God?
A Defense of the Deity of Christ
John 1:1–17

ISBN 0–89957–504–8

Printed in the United States of America
03 02 01 00 99 98 –D– 6 5 4 3 2 1

PREFACE

The question, "What think ye of Christ?", presents a dilemma to any thoughtful person. If Jesus was not all that He claimed to be, then He was mentally unbalanced or He was the greatest deceiver who ever lived. Either we must accept Him as God made manifest in the flesh or reject Him as one who claimed to be what He was not, and to accomplish what only God could do. This book is intended to help you make this all-important decision. You owe it to yourself to examine the evidence and decide for yourself.

Intellectual honesty requires that you study the record carefully and without bias. One of the most important sections of that record is John 1:1-18, the portion of Scripture under consideration in this volume. If this section is understood, the rest of the New Testament record about the pre-existence of the Child of Bethlehem, His life, death, resurrection, ascension, and post-ascension ministry will be more clearly comprehended.

Since this record was originally given in the Greek language, we have endeavored, in as much detail as we thought feasible, to explain and illustrate almost every word in these eighteen verses from the Nestle's Greek Text of the New Testament. This study is not meant to satisfy the professional theologian and Greek scholar, who may have the ability to delve deeper into these verses and draw fuller truths and applications from them. Originally these messages were given over the special religious radio network known as "New Testament Light," heard across the United States and beyond its borders. They were published in twelve booklets, with a circulation of many thousands of copies. Now they are presented in book form with the prayer that they will help unbelievers to acknowledge the Lord Jesus

Christ as co-equal and co-eternal with God the Father and God the Holy Spirit, and will help Christians to give Him His rightful exalted place in their hearts.

—SPIROS ZODHIATES

CONTENTS

CHAPTER 1

IS THERE A GOD?

"No man hath seen God at any time; the only begotten Son, which is in the bosom of the Father, he hath declared him" **(John 1:18).**

Some of the most axiomatic and authoritative statements of the Word of God are contained in the first 18 verses of the first chapter of the Gospel of John. They tell us of the revelation of God in Jesus Christ. The rest of the Gospel of John, from the 19th verse of the first chapter to the very end, is simply a series of incidents given to illustrate the statements made in the first 18 verses. In these studies we shall limit ourselves to the examination of these important doctrinal statements, without necessarily resorting to the illustrative incidents.

Take, for instance, the statement in the 4th verse, "In him was life." In the original Greek, this verse actually declares Jesus Christ to be not only the possessor of life, like you and me, but the originator and disposer of life. In John 10:18, Jesus said of His own physical life, "No man taketh it from me, but I lay it down of myself. I have power to lay it down, and I have power to take it again." No human being in his right mind would dare to make such claims. Either Jesus Christ was God or he was insane. He could not have been a mere human being, as the whole Gospel of John illustrates. But what He said in John 10:18 was declared succinctly in John 1:4.

The main purpose for which John wrote his Gospel was to demonstrate that Jesus Christ was and is God. Therefore everything

1

he has to say bears a relationship to his fundamental conviction concerning the deity of this historic person called Jesus Christ. He does not begin his Gospel with the birth of Jesus Christ on this earth, because he does not consider that to be the beginning of His existence. His purpose is not to tell us only about Jesus the man, although he does that very adequately, but about Christ the God, who became Jesus the man, to save men from their sins. Therefore he starts his narrative with the concept of Jesus Christ as the revelation of God to man from the very beginning of things. We are interested in Him not merely as man, but also as God.

Emperor Theodosius, in the 4th century, denied the deity of Christ, as do many in this 20th century. When his son Arcadius was about sixteen, he decided to make him his partner in the government of the empire. Among the great men who assembled to congratulate the new wearer of the imperial purple was Bishop Amphilocus. He made a handsome address to the Emperor and was about to leave when Theodosius exclaimed, "What! Do you take no notice of my son?" Then the Bishop went up to Arcadius and putting his hands upon his head said, "The Lord bless thee, my son." The Emperor, roused to fury by this slight, exclaimed, "What! Is this all the respect you pay to a prince that I have made of equal dignity with myself?" Amphilocus replied, "Sire, you do so highly resent my apparent neglect of your son, because I do not give him equal honors with yourself. Then what must the Eternal God think of you when you degrade His co-equal and co-eternal Son to the level of one of His creatures?"

Yes, we believe that the greatest offense against God the Father is the affront that so many bring against His Son, the Lord Jesus Christ, when they affirm Him to be anything less than God. That is why John sets out in a masterly fashion, in a series of unparalleled statements, to declare that this Jesus Christ who walked the streets of Palestine was the God of Heaven.

It is the author's personal conviction that the Apostle John wrote the narrative part of his Gospel first and then came back and

2

summarized it all in these important statements found in the first 18 verses. Try reading the Gospel beginning with the 19th verse of the first chapter, and when you have finished the entire narrative, go back and read the first 18 verses and see if you do not agree with this conclusion.

However, in order to understand the first 18 verses, and indeed the entire Gospel, we must begin with the 18th verse, which reads, "No man hath seen God at any time; the only begotten Son, which is in the bosom of the Father, he hath delcared him." Here we have two statements made about God: (1) that He is invisible to the human eye; (2) that someone made Him visible. (That is the implied meaning of the Greek word *exeegeesato,* translated "declared" in this verse.)

The first statement is one that could be made by both believer and unbeliever. Here is common ground for agreement between the two, strange as it may seem. The human mind by its own efforts can only suppose God. It is impossible for the finite even to conceive of the infinite. The whole ocean cannot be contained in a glass, nor can the infinite God be contained in the finite mind of man. Since all around us we see only finite people and things, we must logically conclude that the aggregate of things finite has had something greater than their totality to cause them and create them.

A young preacher once called upon an old infidel who was constantly arguing against the existence of God. He found him sitting in his sawmill just over the lever that lifts as the saw leaves the log. As the old man began to denounce the Deity, that lever sprang, catching him under the heels and flinging him backward and downward into the stream. As he plunged, however, he shrieked as loudly as he could, "God have mercy!" The preacher ran around, waded into the water, and drew the struggling man ashore. Said the pastor, "I thought that you did not believe in a God." As soon as the infidel stopped strangling, he said in a subdued voice, "Well, if there is no God, there ought to be, to help a man when he can't help himself!"

3

As we look around us, if we think at all, we must come to the conclusion that there is something above us which is beyond us. That's how far the mind of man can carry him, and those who have not gone that far, at least in their thinking, can hardly be said to have thought at all. And those who doubt that which is beyond them are easily swallowed up by that which is around them. The circumstances of life prove to be too much for them to handle, because they do not have within them the God of the circumstances.

The fact of God is presupposed by John. That is clearly indicated by the way he begins the 18th verse. Literally translated from the Greek it would read, "God no one hath seen at any time." The statement, then, about the invisibility of God begins with the assumption of God as existent. The existence of the visible world leads us logically to the thought that someone must have made it. We can then arrive at the conclusion that what we are and what we see must be "creatures," the direct or indirect product of a Creator. This Creator in the Bible is called "God."

A business man once gave his reasons as to why he knew there was a God. He had been frankly facing the wonders of the stars and planets, their system and order. Then he said, "It takes a girl in our factory about two days to learn to put the seventeen parts of a meat chopper together. It may be that these millions of worlds, each with its separate orbit, all balanced so wonderfully in space — it may be that they just happened; it may be that by a billion years of tumbling about they finally arranged themselves. I don't know. I am merely a plain manufacturer of cutlery. But this I do know, that you can shake the seventeen parts of a meat chopper around in a washtub for the next seventeen billion years and you'll never make a meat chopper." That's just simple common sense. Man is the only one of God's creatures who can come to the conclusion that God exists, because he is the only creature who has been given the power of reasoning. And yet he refuses many times to use this power to deduce the very existence of the One who gave it to him. I am here; therefore there must have been a mother at some time who gave

4

birth to me, whether I ever saw her or not. The fact of motherhood is inherent, not in the fact of my having seen her with my own eyes, but in the fact of my own existence.

One of the greatest atheists of the past was Robert G. Ingersoll. In spite of his atheism, he had for a friend the famous preacher, Henry Ward Beecher. In the preacher's study was an elaborate celestial globe, which had been sent him with the compliments of some manufacturer. On the surface, in delicate workmanship, were raised figures of the constellations and the stars which composed them. The globe struck Ingersoll's fancy one day when he was visiting the preacher. He turned it around and around with admiration. "That is just what I want," he said. "Who made it?" "Who made it, do you say, Colonel?" repeated Beecher. "Who made this globe? Why nobody, of course. It just happened." Well, we all know better than that. We know that things don't just happen but that they have a cause, and that there must be a First Cause of all things. But that is as far as the mind of man will take him. He can arrive at the conclusion that there must be a God.

During the French Revolution, Robespierre, himself an inhuman monster, quickly saw that the renunciation of religion would soon bring about the dissolution of all society. He thereupon began to speak in favor of religion, though he admitted that he had been an indifferent Catholic. He ended his first speech in that direction with the words, "If God did not exist, it would be necessary to invent Him." But God has to reveal Himself to man in order for man to know Him fully. He has promised to do this through His Word. As unregenerate man reads the Gospel story for himself, with an open heart and an open mind, praying the Holy Spirit to lead him into all truth, it can be the beginning of a new life for him.

CHAPTER 2

HOW CAN GOD BE KNOWN?
"No man hath seen God at any time"
(John 1:18a).

"God no one hath seen at any time." This is the first statement that arrests our attention in the Gospel of John. It tells us that God is invisible. For further knowledge about God, we must allow Him to speak to us through His revelation in His Word, in the Bible. We want to know who God is and what He is. As we look at this verse in the original Greek, we see that the word *theos*, "God," has no article before it. It is not "the" God, but simply "God." Are we, then, to arrive at the conclusion that John is speaking about "a" God and not "the" God, the God of the Bible, the unique Creator of the world? Further study will show that there is a special reason why John was directed by the Holy Spirit to leave out the definite article before God. One of the ways to stress the special qualities of a person or thing spoken about in Greek is to omit the article. (A. T. Robertson, *A Grammar of the Greek New Testament in the Light of Historical Research,* Doran, p. 794.) Here John wishes to tell us that God cannot be seen by human eyes in the totality of His special attributes and qualities. God is primarily a Spirit. We have an illustration of this truth in the 4th chapter of John's Gospel, where we read of the encounter of the Lord Jesus with the Samaritan woman. Here is what Jesus Christ said to her, "God is a Spirit: and they that worship him must worship him in spirit and in truth" (v. 24).

It is because John wants to stress the basic quality of God as a Spirit that he mentions His name without the definite article. It is

6

not that he wants to refer to one of two gods or many gods, but to the only true God in His principal characteristic as a Spirit, a Spirit who cannot be seen by human eyes but is nevertheless real.

The famous English deist, Anthony Collins of the 17th century, met a plain countryman one day while out walking. He asked him where he was going. "To church, sir." "What are you going to do there?" "To worship God." "Is your God a great or a little God?" "He is both, sir." "How can He be both?" "He is so great, sir, that the heaven of heavens cannot contain Him; and so little that He can dwell in my heart." Infidel Collins later declared that this simple answer from the countryman had more effect upon his mind than all the volumes which learned doctors had written against him. This simple countryman had indeed the right concept of God, the God of the Bible, who as a spirit is the Creator of all things and yet indwells the heart of His believing creatures in the person of Jesus Christ. But when John says, "No man hath seen God at any time" (1:18), he is referring to the great God of the universe as He is in Himself and not to God as He appears in various forms and dwells in us and among us.

This point is further substantiated by one of the greatest grammarians of the Greek language, William Edward Jelf, who in his *Grammar of the Greek Language* says, "The effect of the omission of the article is frequently that the absence of any particular definition or limitation of the notion brings forward *its general character.*" (Vol. II, John Henry and James Parker, 1859, p. 124). This leads us to believe that not only the quality of God as a Spirit is stressed by John, but also His general character. In His general character, no man has ever seen God. And this is fully understandable.

A third reason for the absence of the article before the word *theos,* "God," may be found in this same reference work. Jelf goes on to say, "Some words are found both with and without the article, and seemingly with but little difference; but without the article they signify the general notion conceived of abstractedly, and not as in actual existence; with the article the objective existence is brought forward, as *theos,* the Divinity; *ho theos,* the God we worship." John, therefore, does not speak here of the particular concepts that we as human beings may have of God, nor of the occasional theophanies, or appearances of God, but about God in His complete substance as divinity. The abstractedness of God refers to His presence everywhere as a Spirit and not to His particular appearance and existence within the souls of men or in particular areas of our physical world. God, in His full essence, omnipresence, omnipotence, and omniscience, cannot possibly be seen by man. That is what John means by his statement, "God no one has seen at any time."

We have discovered new worlds in the splitting of the atom. Democritus, the ancient Greek physical philosopher, who coined the word "atom," would never have believed it. With our telescopes we find a system in every star, but with our microscopes we find a world in every atom. There surely must be more things that we don't know of than those things we do. It is logical, then, to concede that we cannot know the God of the universe in His full essence.

A little boy, on being asked "How many Gods are there?" replied, "One." "How do you know that?" "Because there is only room for one, for He fills heaven and earth." And he was right. How, then, can puny little man expect to see Him in all His majesty and glory?

Very interestingly, in his First Epistle (4:12), John makes a similar statement about the invisibility of God. And in this epistle he also begins the statement without the definite article, with the same purpose and effect. "God no one has ever seen." He wants us to understand that he does not have in mind here an appearance of God within time and space, but God in the fullness of His nature.

A youngster returning from Sunday school sat by a man in a bus one day. The man, apparently an unbeliever, seeing her Sunday school paper, decided to make fun of the child and said to her, "Tell me where God is and I'll give you an apple." The little girl thoughtfully turned to her fellow passenger and said in return, "Sir, you tell me a place where God isn't, and I'll give you a basket of apples."

There is a mystery, indeed, about the nature of God which goes beyond the comprehension of man. It is the omnipresence of God, which is but one of His characteristics. It is only natural that man cannot see God in His omnipresence, because that which the whole universe cannot contain would have to be concentrated in one place at one time. That which is beyond the limitations of time and space cannot be limited by them at any time or in any place. And yet God manifests Himself as a person at different times and places.

An infidel, who was also an invalid, sent his little daughter to live with friends, who taught her to read. She proudly told her father when she came home, "I have learned to read." "Well," said he, "Let me hear you read that," pointing to a board at the foot of the bed on which he had printed in large letters, "God is nowhere." Carefully she spelled out the words in the way that seemed right to her, "God is now here." The unbelieving father was startled and arrested, and God blessed that new reading to the salvation of his soul. God in His full nature cannot be contained nor seen, but He chooses to manifest Himself within time and space. He cannot be seen in the fullness of His glory, but the glory in which He can be seen is sufficient for man. It is only logical that God who is everywhere cannot be contained anywhere in His fullness. The understanding of this principle explains the mystery of this declaration by John that "God no one hath seen at any time."

CHAPTER 3

CAN MAN SEE GOD?

"No man hath seen God at any time" (John 1:18a, continued).

Although John in his Gospel tells us that "No man hath seen God at any time," we have to understand that this refers to the fullness of His glory. Our little cup could not contain Him, which is why we can only "know in part" (I Cor. 13). This principle also explains the various theophanies or appearances of God to man. One that is mentioned in the Old Testament is the encounter which God had with Moses. In Exodus 33:11 we read, "And the Lord spake unto Moses face to face, as a man speaketh unto his friend." Here we are told that God made Himself, not necessarily visible to the physical eye of Moses, but audible to his physical ear. This is further brought out in Numbers 12:8, "With him will I speak mouth to mouth, even apparently, and not in dark speeches; and the similitude of the Lord shall he behold." Here the voice of God is heard, but only a "similitude" of God is seen, not God in the fullness of His nature. Therefore there is no contradiction at all between what John declares and the experience of Moses.

And even before Moses, we have God appearing and speaking with Adam and Eve, but that again cannot possibly be interpreted as their having seen or conversed with God in His full essence. It was simply another theophany, for if God in His totality made Himself exclusively visible and audible to Adam and Eve, He could not have been anywhere else, and nothing in and beyond this universe can be sustained without God.

We saw that Jesus Christ, who is the fullest revelation of God given to us, has told us that God is Spirit. The word "Spirit" indicates the nature of God and not His personality. Someone who was asked to give his idea of the eternity of God replied, "It is duration without beginning or end; existence without bound or dimension; present without past or future. His eternity is youth without infancy or old age; life without birth or death; today without yesterday or tomorrow." And this is just one of the characteristics of the nature of God. God is something immaterial, not subject to the limitations of time and space. The essence of God, then, is not matter, but Spirit.

But a spirit can only be perceived by another spirit. The spirit animates matter, but never subjects itself to matter, nor is it perceived by matter. That is why nothing physical can know God. Only the spirit of man can know God. Well did Paul express it in I Corinthians 2:9, 10, "Eye hath not seen, nor ear heard, neither have entered into the heart of man, the things which God hath prepared for them that love him. But God hath revealed them unto us by his Spirit: for the Spirit searcheth all things, yea, the deep things of God."

There must be a correspondence between the receiver and the transmitter. When we listen to a radio broadcast, there are many sound waves all around us, but the only way for us to become aware of them is to have an appropriate receiver able to catch them and make them audible. We would never know that anyone was talking to us from a distance if we expected our watch to catch the sound waves.

There is only one way in which man can know God and that is through man's own spirit. God is a Spirit and can be known only by a spirit. We must not expect to be able to smell God, or feel Him with our fingers, or see Him with our physical eyes. It cannot be done. Yet that which can be perceived only by the spirit of man is just as real as that which can be perceived by his physical senses.

In a newspaper there once appeared the following: "Edison never saw a soul, and so does not believe in a soul. He believes in electricity, however. When did he see it?" Electricity is a reality

11

which is known by its results, which are physical. God can be known by the spirit of man; and the results of this knowledge of God, when it becomes part and parcel of our personalities through faith in Jesus Christ, can so transform our physical lives that others can really see and feel the difference, even as we who appropriate the unseen power of God.

A beautiful illustration of how God does speak to each heart is seen in the life of Helen Keller, who though blind, deaf, and mute has yet been a profound student, not only of facts, but also of abstract truth. Her teacher had felt that it would be impossible to teach her of the great and all-loving Spirit. It was a subject impossible to explain to one whose only sense was that of touch. But when Helen was fourteen, the teacher felt that she must make an effort to give her some glimpse of spiritual truth, so she tried to tell her of God, His infinite love and protecting care. With her sensitive fingers placed on the lips and throat of her patient teacher, Helen followed the words with a face that began to glow and shine more and more until she said, "Oh, I am so glad you told me His name, for He has often spoken to me!" How marvelously and mysteriously God reveals Himself!

Following the word *theos*, God, in the 18th verse of the first chapter of John, we have the negative pronoun *oudeis*, meaning "no one." Actually the pronoun is made up of the adverb *oude*, meaning "and not" (*ou*, "not"; *de*, "and"), and the numerical pronoun *heis*, meaning "one." Thus the emphasis here is on the fact that "not even one" has seen God in His fullness at any time. Now, in the King James Version, this word is translated "no man." This is not a literal translation but rather an inferred one, because the word "man" does not occur in the original Greek text. It is true that the negative pronoun is in the masculine gender, which would allow us to use the word "man" in the translation. It would, however, be more accurate to translate it "no one," because then the exclusion would embrace not only humankind, but also angelic creation.

But the big question which immediately arises from this statement is whether Christ also is excluded as having seen God in His fullness. No, we do not believe He is meant to be excluded in any way. It is true that *oudeis*, "no one," is totally exclusive—with a single exception. This may seem like a contradiction, but actually it is not. It is rather a form of speech for the sake of emphasizing both the exclusion and the solitary inclusion. We use this form of speech in our daily language. For instance, a preacher may say, "No one, absolutely no one, is permitted to come and disturb me in my study except my wife." Here we have a total and all-inclusive exclusion, and yet an exception. Such an expression emphasizes primarily the special privilege and authority of the wife. It is thus with Jesus Christ, of whom John is about to speak in the second part of John 1:18. It is as if he is saying, "No one, not even one, has ever seen God in His fullness, except the only begotten Son, Jesus Christ." There is an effort on the part of John to concentrate our attention upon Jesus Christ, for He is the center of all that he is about to say concerning the revelation of God to man. John speaks this way in order to focus our attention on the uniqueness of Jesus Christ as the only person who has seen God as He really is, and who consequently unveils Him before all as a man would unveil a statue to a curious audience.

As we study the life of Christ we see that it is unique in the history of the world. That is why John has given us an account of it. He recorded just what was necessary to demonstrate that Jesus Christ was God the Son, and only as such could He see God the Father. We are not propounding a theory but calling attention first of all to an historic fact, the fact of Jesus Christ, His life, His teaching, His death, His resurrection, and His assumption. If sinful man does not accept Him as God, he will face an inexplicable dilemma. It is far easier and more logical to accept Him as God than to try to explain in any other way what He was, what He said, and what He did.

John is not proud of the depravity of man and his inability to see his Creator in all His majesty and glory, but mentions it first in order to emphasize it as the basis for the need of the redemptive revelation of God. If man could see God in His fullness, then there would be no need for Jesus Christ to make God known to man. Although John's first note is a somber one, its sadness disappears with the second note concerning the redemptive revelation of Jesus Christ. John is obligated to pronounce man's sentence before he pronounces the forgiveness that is in Jesus Christ. Sin cannot escape condemnation. Here, then, we have humankind sentenced to death because of sin, followed by the wonderful news of redemption and forgiveness.

CHAPTER 4

HOW MUCH OF GOD CAN MAN HAVE?

"No man hath seen God at any time" (John 1:18a, continued).

It is only human to want to see, to feel, to touch those whom we love, and it is not surprising that man sometimes has this feeling about God. "Oh that I knew where I might find him! that I might come even to his seat!" mourned Job (23:3). But John says in the 18th verse of the first chapter of his Gospel, "No man hath seen God." In the original Greek, the word translated "has seen" is *heeoraken,* which is the perfect tense of the verb *horaoo,* "to see." John declares that there has never been any particular time in history when anyone has had a full vision of God. This is what we call an extensive perfect of broken continuity. (A. T. Robertson, *A Grammar of the Greek New Testament.* Doran, pp. 893, 896.) It extends as far back as possible and declares that no one at this or that time has had a vision of the fullness of God. The perfect tense refers to a complete action of the past, the results of which are felt in the present. We believe there is a reason why the perfect tense is used instead of the aorist here. John speaks of the fullness of God, not merely of a partial manifestation of God. He also speaks now, through this perfect tense, about the inability of man to see God in His fullness. It is possible for man to have a glimpse of God, but never to see Him fully, even through his own spirit.

That's what Moses had the privilege of seeing, a glimpse of God in a particular manifestation. As God does not make Himself fully manifest, man cannot fully see Him. There has never been any time in the history of heaven and earth when either angel or man has fully and completely seen God. There have been partial visions of

15

certain manifestations of God, but never full visions by any created being. But we should not feel that this revelation of God in Christ is insufficient for you and me as human beings.

A little girl came home from Sunday school in much perplexity. "Mama," she said, "our teacher said today that we must come to Jesus if we want to be saved, but how can we come to Him when we cannot see Him?" "Did you not ask me to get you a drink of water last night?" said the mother. "Yes, Mama." "Did you see me when you asked me?" "No, but I knew that you would hear me and get it for me." "Well, that is just the way to come to Jesus. We cannot see Him, but we know that He is near and hears every word we say, and that He will give us what we need." As we try to see Jesus by faith, He will become real to us. Only through Him can we get a vision of God.

The verb *horaoo*, "to see," is in the active voice, which would indicate that no man of himself, in his own power and of his own volition, has seen or can see God. God must at all times take the initiative in revealing Himself, and man becomes a recipient of this revelation. This Greek verb has three distinct meanings. The primary one is "to see with the eyes." A vision of the fullness of God with one's physical eyes is impossible. As we have said previously, there must be a correspondence between the transmitter and the receiver. Only the spirit of man can perceive the Spirit, God.

"Johnny," said a man, pointing his finger at a boy who was taking care of the store while his master was out, "you must give me an extra measure; your master is not in." "My Master is always in," said Johnny very seriously, and he was right. His Master was God, apparent to the boy because he had spiritual perception, but not to the man, who could see only through his physical eyes.

The second meaning of the verb *horaoo*, "to see," is "to see with the mind, to perceive, to know." Let us not forget that the verb is in the perfect tense, and that the object to be seen is God in His fullness. John tells us that even with our spirits we cannot see the

16

fullness of God. A full and complete perception of God in His majesty and glory is impossible by man. In vain does man seek God with his human spirit. We can only perceive the idea of God, that there must be a First Cause of all things, that there must be a Creator; but to know Him in His fullness is impossible for us.

The third meaning of *horaoo*, "to see," is "to become acquainted with by experience, to experience." That also is impossible for man to do on his own, through his own initiative and power. It is only through Jesus Christ that man can become fully acquainted with God and experience His presence within his very soul and life. Anyone or anything else that stands between man and God will hinder our vision of Him in our human experience.

When Alexander the Great visited Diogenes the cynic at his bath, he asked what Alexander could do for Diogenes. The cynic answered that there was only one thing which Alexander could do for Diogenes, and that was to abstain from standing between him and the sun. There are many great and mighty people who like to stand between God and man, but they only obscure man's vision of God. Only Jesus Christ, God incarnate, can bring God as the regenerating and transforming Spirit into our experience.

"God no one hath seen at any time." As the last word of this most momentous declaration, John adds the word *poopote*, meaning "ever, at any time." This supports our statement that the perfect tense of the verb *horaoo*, "to see," is of broken continuity. It refers to all the extent of past time and it extends to all time. It does not merely refer to the impossibility of seeing God in His fullness in the past, but now and ever. This is what the Apostle Paul says, as he speaks of Jesus Christ as fully God, "Who only hath immortality, dwelling in the light which no man can approach unto; whom no man hath seen, *nor can see:* to whom be honour and power everlasting" (I Tim. 6:16). Thus we can conclude that John does not only make an historic statement, that this has never happened, that no one has ever seen God, but also includes the fact that no one ever can fully see and experience God in His fullness.

17

In order to make the positive truth stronger, John speaks of its opposite negative truth. After telling us that no one at any time has seen God, he says that there is one exception. That brings us to the second clause of John 1:18, "The only begotten Son, which is in the bosom of the Father, he hath declared him."

There is a great deal of controversy concerning this most important statement. There are different readings taken from various manuscripts, but it is generally conceded by scholars that the most accurate text is the one given by Nestle in his critical New Testament, which reads *monogenees theos,* "only begotten God." Thus is Jesus Christ designated, of whom John has already spoken in the first verses of his Gospel. Let us review the whole verse, so that it may be clear in our minds: "God no one has seen at any time; only begotten God, who being in the bosom of the Father, that one revealed him." This is a little more accurate literal translation, from Nestle's text.

Taking this preferred manuscript and the first expression of the second part of the verse, we arrive at certain conclusions. The first is that only God could reveal Himself to the world. The richest man in the world, Croesus, once asked the wisest man in the world, Thales, "What is God?" The philosopher asked for a day in which to deliberate, and then for another, and then for another, and another, and another—and at length confessed that he was not able to answer, that the longer he deliberated, the more difficult it was for him to frame an answer. The fiery Tertullian, the early Church Father, eagerly seized upon this incident and said it was an example of the world's ignorance of God outside of Christ. "There," he exclaimed, "is the wisest man in the world, and he cannot tell you who God is. But the most ignorant mechanic among the Christians knows God and is able to make Him known unto others." If God is to be revealed at all, He has to reveal Himself, and He has done so through Jesus Christ. That is what John declares, and he calls Him the Word and also the only begotten of the Father. God came down to earth so that we might see Him.

18

That is why the Lord Jesus said, "He that hath seen me hath seen the Father" (John 14:9). Of course, our finite minds cannot possibly understand the infinity of God nor the workings of His revelation. We must understand that infinity cannot be tolerant of test-tube experimentation by its finite creation. If the discovery and proof of God by man were possible, then there would be no need of revelation.

The late Dr. Clarence Edward Macartney, when a theological student, was visiting in the home of an infidel. The infidel's argument was as follows: "If a man tells me that he has a horse which can trot a mile in three minutes, I tell him to bring out the horse and prove it. If you tell me that there is a God, I ask you to produce God and prove His existence." Macartney replied, "No Christian claims to know God, nor would want to know Him, in that way. By that kind of searching we cannot know the Almighty to perfection. The Christian believer does not say, 'I know God,' or 'I see God,' or 'I think there is a God,' but 'I believe in God.' " And that is what Christ came to enable us to do, to believe in God.

If we were to draw a parallel from the physical world, we might illustrate it this way. Here is the ocean. It is impossible for us to see the ocean fully and at one time in all its immensity. But it is possible to draw a supply of water from the ocean and bring it into a swimming pool. In a way, we can say that we have brought the ocean home. Truly, every bit of the water that we possess is the same as the water which is still in the wide ocean, and yet we could not possibly claim that we have enclosed within our boundaries the entire ocean. Yet what we have is the ocean, nevertheless.

CHAPTER 5

THE RELATIONSHIP OF JESUS CHRIST TO GOD THE FATHER

" . . . the only begotten Son" (John 1:18b).

When our Lord Jesus Christ came to this earth, He took upon Himself the form of a man, because that was the only way He could be seen by our physical eyes. But that does not mean that He ceased to exist as Spirit, nor was God as Spirit in His totality limited to the human form of Jesus Christ. Nor can we say that God, by coming down to earth, ceased to exist in heaven as a nonmaterial God. It is only as we remember this essential fact of the impossibility of the limitation of the Godhead to any physical form that we can understand this declaration by John about the only begotten God, who being in the bosom of the Father has revealed Him.

This expression, "only begotten God," is unique. It does not appear elsewhere as referring to Jesus Christ. It provides unquestionable proof of the deity of Jesus Christ. But why mention the word "only begotten"? In English it would be very difficult to convey the meaning of the original Greek word here. It is *monogenees,* which according to the *Great Lexicon of the Greek Language* has three meanings: (1) the only one born, i.e., the one who does not have brothers or sisters, as in Luke 8:42; (2) the only one of its kind, unique; and (3) of the same nature, related. (D. Deemeetrakou, *Lexicon Tees Hellinikis Gloossees* [Lexicon of the Greek Language from Greek into Greek], Vol. 6, p. 4741.)

We believe that, in the first 18 verses particularly, this word *monogenees,* "only begotten," has the third meaning above. It should therefore not be translated "the only begotten" at all, but "of the same nature." We are told here that Jesus Christ is God and as such He is as incomprehensible as His Father God. In a company of literary gentlemen, Daniel Webster was asked if he could comprehend how Jesus Christ could be both God and man. "No, sir," he replied, and added, "I should be ashamed to acknowledge Him as my Saviour if I could comprehend Him. If I could comprehend Him, He could be no greater than myself. Such is my sense of sin, and consciousness of my inability to save myself, that I feel I need a superhuman Saviour, one so great and glorious that I cannot comprehend Him."

John wants to emphasize here that He who came to dwell upon the face of this earth in the person of Jesus Christ was of the same nature as God Himself. Though He took upon Himself human flesh, He never ceased to be the eternal Spirit. The word *monogenees* actually is a compound of the word *monos*, "alone," and the word *genos*, "race, stock, family." Here we are told that He who came to reveal God—Jesus Christ—is of the same family, of the same stock, of the same race as God. He is in no way less God than His Father.

There is ample evidence in the Scriptures that the Godhead is a family made up of God the Father, God the Son, and God the Holy Spirit. We should not feel that it is an insult to our intelligence to expect us to accept this revealed truth of Scripture. Let us be as open to the truth as that converted Indian who gave the following reason for his belief in the Trinity: "We go down to the river in winter and we see it covered with snow; we chop through the ice and we come to the water. Snow is water, ice is water, water is water; therefore the three are one." We have parallels of the Trinity in the physical world; why not, then, in the supernatural world?

John declares that the Father and the *Logos*, the "Word," Jesus Christ, are of one and the same nature; the one is no less God than the other, irrespective of the fact that the Son took upon Himself a limited human form so that He could be made visible to

21

us. He was nevertheless God, of one and the same nature as the Father. Jesus Christ Himself declared the same truth when He said, "I and my Father are one" (John 10:30). Jesus Christ, then, has always been perfect God, even when He became a perfect man; and while He was a perfect man, He never ceased to be perfect God.

We note that the word "God" here does not have the definite article before it. Therefore, as we saw previously, it refers to God as a Spirit, to the general character of God, and to the objective divinity of God rather than the subjective feeling of a power outside ourselves. Jesus Christ, who became the revelation of God to man, is all of that. Thus we can very well understand the verb *heooraken*, "has seen," here. John tells us that this God who is of the same nature and family as the Father "has seen" God. It takes one of the same character, of the same nature, of the same race, to see God. Here, then, we are presented with two personalities within the Godhead who are absolutely of the same nature, and it is only as such that they can see each other.

A Chinese Bible woman was preaching Christ to the scholar of a market town. He heard her courteously and after a little said, "Madam, you speak well, but why do you dwell on Jesus Christ? Let Him alone and tell us about God." Whereat she replied, "What, sir, should we know about God if it were not for Jesus Christ?" How true, and this is precisely the meaning of the second clause of John 1:18.

"In the Rospigliosi Palace in Rome is Guido Reni's famous fresco, 'The Aurora,' a work unequalled in that period for nobility of line and poetry of color. It is painted on a lofty ceiling, and as you stand on the pavement and look up at it, your neck stiffens, your head grows dizzy, and the figures become hazy and indistinct. Therefore the owner of the palace has placed a broad mirror near the floor. In it the picture is reflected and you can sit down before it and study the wonderful work in comfort. Jesus Christ does just that for us when we try to get some notion of God. He is the mirror of Deity. He is the express image of God's person. He interprets God to our dull hearts. In Him God becomes visible and intelligible to us. We cannot by any amount of searching find out God. The more we try, the more we are bewildered. Then Jesus Christ appears. He is God stooping down to our level and He enables our feeble thoughts to get some real hold on God Himself." (Frank M. Fairchild in *Can We Believe It?*)

There is a reason why Jesus Christ never included Himself with us when referring to God as our common Father. To Jesus Christ, God the Father was not a Father in the same sense that He is to us. That is why we find Him saying to Mary Magdalene, during one of His post-resurrection appearances, "Touch me not; for I am not yet ascended to my Father: but go to my brethren, and say unto them, I ascend unto my Father, and your Father; and to my God, and your God" (John 20:17). True, when we accept Jesus Christ as our Saviour, we become the children of God and He becomes our Father, but we do not become gods.

But what if we take the alternate reading of this verse? What would be the relationship of Jesus Christ to His Father if it read "the only begotten Son," with the understood verb "has seen God"? The meaning of the adjective *monogenees* would still be the same. It would be "of the same nature, of the same family and race." It would still declare that Jesus Christ is to be known as the Son of God, but that He would be in no way inferior to the Father; He would be of the same nature. He was ever the Son of God, co-equal and co-eternal with the Father; but we become the sons of God within the realm of history, as John 1:12 says, "But as many as received him [Jesus Christ], to them gave he power to become the sons of God, even to them that believe on his name." Let us remember, therefore, that while Jesus Christ was here on earth, He never ceased for one moment to be in heaven also. That was the very characteristic of His deity.

"Are you happy, my dear girl?" asked a visitor of a young friend who seemed to be drawing near her latter end. "Yes," she

23

said, "quite happy." Raising her hand, she pointed to a Bible which was lying by her bedside and again repeated, "I am quite happy. I have Christ there" (Luke 24:27). Then laying her hand on her heart she said, "And I have Christ here" (Eph. 3:17). And again pointing heavenwards to where her faith, hopes, and affections were all centered, she repeated, "And I have Christ up there" (Col. 3:4). The greatest miracle of all is that God the Creator, the omnipresent and omniscient One, comes to dwell within our hearts through Jesus Christ His Son, without ceasing to be everywhere and know everything.

CHAPTER 6

GOD REVEALS HIMSELF

". . . which is in the bosom of the Father" (John 1:18c).

Since God is omnipresent, His appearance in any one place and at any one time, in a very special way or in any special form, does not steal away from Him the quality and characteristic of omnipresence. Over 1900 years ago, God made His appearance upon the face of this earth in the form of a human being named Jesus Christ.

This personality has been the unique revelation of God to mankind. Through His appearance on earth, man was privileged to see God. God's revelation to man prior to the coming of the Lord Jesus was made through the inspired writings of the prophets of God. The appearance of the Lord Jesus as the Messiah was foretold and was eagerly expected. It was just like reading about a person and then suddenly seeing him. The coming of the Lord Jesus into the world was the greatest and most mysterious event in history. We cannot fully understand it, but nevertheless we have to face this historic person called Jesus Christ.

John calls this person both "God of the same nature as the Father" and "the Son of the same nature, of the same stock as the Father." That is what the word *monogenees,* commonly translated "only begotten," actually means when it refers to Jesus Christ, as we saw in our previous study.

And then John goes on to tell us where this Jesus Christ is. He says about Him "which is in the bosom of the Father." John wrote these words after the Lord Jesus had ascended into heaven. He was no longer physically present on earth. Thus in one sense we could take this clause to mean that in His physical form He had ascended unto the Father. But these statements which John makes in the first 18 verses of his Gospel transcend the ephemeral, the temporal considerations and deal with the eternal. We believe that he was not thinking just of the time he was writing, but of all time, that Jesus Christ as *monogenees theos,* "fully God," has always been in "the bosom of the Father" even while making His physical appearance on earth. It is impossible to think of God in terms of the temporal limitations of the physical world. There was no time while the Lord Jesus was down here on earth that He was not God.

A professor of theology once asked his students to get a sheet of paper and divide it into three columns. In the first column they were to write every passage where Christ is spoken of as God-man; in the second column all the passages where Christ is spoken of as God alone; and in the third, all the passages where He is spoken of as man alone. The papers were badly balanced. The first and second columns filled right up, but as to the third column, no one found a passage speaking of Christ as man alone. There just is no such passage.

This clause of John 1:18, "which is in the bosom of the Father," starts with the definite article *ho,* "the," and the present participle of the verb *eimi,* "to be." The literal translation is "the one being in the bosom of the Father." John does not simply refer to the past, because then he would have said *hos een,* "who was." He did not say that, because Jesus Christ as *monogenees theos,* "fully God," never ceased for one moment to be with the Father. In the fullness of the Godhead, Father and Son have never been separated. All the fullness of God simply manifested itself in the person of Jesus Christ. Nor does John say *hos esti,* "who is," which would refer only to the present time, while John was writing these words.

Grammatically and contextually, therefore, it is safe to arrive at the conclusion that this is actually a timeless participial predicate and, as the Greek grammarian Winer says, "*Oon* (being)

26

signifies who (essentially) is in Heaven, who appertains to Heaven. It would almost coincide in sense with 'he who came down from Heaven.' " (G. B. Winer, *A Treatise on the Grammar of the New Testament.* T. & T. Clark, Edinburgh, 1882, p. 429.) In other words, it denotes the timeless quality of Jesus Christ. It is a characterization of Jesus Christ. It denotes the inseparableness of these two persons of the Godhead. They have always been together and yet separated, as far as we are concerned. As far as the Godhead is concerned, however, it has always been intact. Our taking a little water out of the ocean to put into a swimming pool hardly depletes the amount of water in the ocean, but at the same time it enables us to have the ocean near us, to enjoy it and understand something of its nature.

We are told, then, that Jesus Christ in His full deity has always been in the bosom of the Father. What does that expression mean? The Greek word for "bosom" is *kolpos,* which usually refers to something physical. It is the upper part of the body in the general area of which the heart is located. The heart is always considered as the seat of our affections. We also saw that God is Spirit and must not be conceived of as a physical personality. Yet it is sometimes necessary for us physical beings to use physical expressions to understand spiritual realities. Therefore, in this instance, the bosom is used as an expression of love and constant intimate communion of the Son with the Father. It does not mean that God is like us, with a body and a bosom. We are told, for instance, that when the poor man of Luke 16 died he was brought to "Abraham's bosom." That means to the place where Abraham was, into close communion and fellowship with Abraham. Thus here we are given an idea of the close intimacy of the Son with the Father. And this follows perfectly, since through the term *monogenees* we have full deity ascribed to Jesus Christ, the same nature as the Father. Because of this, He knows the deepest secrets of the Father, and the love between Them is unbroken and unique.

A Jewish soldier had been attending services where he heard

much of the character and teaching of the Lord Jesus Christ. He went to his rabbi and said, "Rabbi, the Christians say that the 'Christ' has already come, while we claim He is yet to come." "Yes," assented the rabbi. "Well," asked the young soldier, "when our Christ comes, what will he have on Jesus Christ?" What, indeed, since Jesus Christ was fully God?

There is some misunderstanding by certain commentators about the preposition *eis*, translated "in." They say that it should be translated "into," denoting motion, since otherwise the Greek proposition *en* would have been used. This is entirely unfounded, for these two words in the New Testament and in later Greek have been used interchangeably. (See A. T. Robertson, *A Grammar of the Greek New Testament in the Light of Historical Research.* Doran, pp. 535, 586, 591.) The preposition used here with the participle *oon*, "being," denotes a place and not motion. We have Jesus Christ eternally with the Father, and not merely a human being who was able to approach the bosom of the Father and make His resting place there. There was no time when the two were separated. And since persons and not locations are spoken about here, this preposition must refer to the communion and union between the two. We must never imagine Jesus Christ as apart from God the Father. The two were inseparably united, and it was an eternal union, not one accomplished in time.

"A six-year-old tiptoed softly up to the little low crib where one of this world's very latest hopes was lying throned and swathed in the coverlets that love had sewn for its coming. Big brother's face was gravely intent, his eyes bright and shining. He stooped far over and gazed down at that wrinkled, peevish bit of a face. 'Now, baby brother,' he whispered into one tiny red ear half hid by the clustering black hair, 'tell me about God before you forget.' " The brother thought that the tiny baby had a message from God. There was one Baby who did. He was born in Bethlehem. But His existence did not begin at the time of His physical birth. He had a message for us from God the Father. It is found in the old familiar

28

words of John 3:16. "For God so loved the world, that he gave his only begotten Son, that whosoever believeth in him should not perish, but have everlasting life."

CHAPTER 7

CHRIST REVEALS GOD AS A FATHER

". . . he hath declared him"
(John 1:18d).

———

God has revealed Himself to man in many ways, but supremely in His incarnation in the Lord Jesus Christ. "The only begotten Son" revealed God as a Father. In His first and last utterances, Christ calls Him "Father," which we believe is very significant. The first recorded words of Jesus are those spoken to His mother and foster father Joseph, when He stayed behind in the temple in Jerusalem. His mother said to Him when He was just 12 years old, "Son, why hast thou thus dealt with us? behold, thy father and I have sought thee sorrowing." When His mother called Joseph His father, Jesus lost no time in correcting her by saying, "How is it that ye sought me? wist ye not that I must be about my Father's business?" (Luke 2:48). And He certainly was not referring to Joseph's business, but to God's business, for that was what He was talking about in the temple. Thus, in the first record we have of Jesus speaking, He refers to God as a Father.

And in His last utterance, when He gave the great commission to His disciples to go and preach the Gospel to every nation, He spoke of God as a Father. "Go ye therefore, and teach all nations, baptizing them in the name of the Father, and of the Son, and of the Holy Ghost" (Matt. 28:19).

Our Lord came into this world to reveal to us that, when we accept Jesus Christ as our Saviour, God becomes our Heavenly Father. We have this important declaration clearly stated in John 1:12, "But as many as received him [Jesus Christ], to them gave he power to become the sons of God, even to them that believe on his name."

30

In the Old Testament God is not primarily known as a Father, but Jesus Christ came to reveal Him first of all as a Father to those who will make Him such by accepting His Son. The reason Jesus Christ emphasizes His own Sonship is to show us that God can become for us that which He is for Him. There is no other way in which God can be known and experienced as a Father but through Jesus Christ. Listen to the very words of Jesus, "I am the way, the truth, and the life: no man cometh unto the Father, but by me" (John 14:6).

Thus in Christ and for Christ's sake God can become the Father of all who come to Him. Just think of what a privilege this is! In the physical world we cannot choose our earthly father, but here in the spiritual realm and in our spiritual birth we can choose God as our Father.

But, someone may say, who is our Father before we believe on the Lord Jesus? One day this question came up while Jesus Christ was speaking with some who were opposing Him, saying that He was human and not the Son of God. He said to them, "Ye are of your father the devil, and the lusts of your father ye will do" (John 8:44).

As a Father, God thinks of us, loves us, works for us, cares for us, protects us, provides for our future. To reject this opportunity of making God our Father is the greatest folly in the world. "Father" is the most endearing appellation by which He is made known to us. "I should have been a French atheist," said Randolph, "had it not been for one recollection; and that was when my departed mother used to take my little hands in hers, and cause me on my knees to say, 'Our Father which art in heaven.'"

"This little word 'Father,'" says Gurnall, "spoken by faith in prayer, by a real Christian, exceeds the eloquence of Demosthenes, Cicero, and all the famous speakers in the world."

As we come to the final clause of John 1:18, we find the words, "He hath declared him." In the Greek the pronoun here is not merely "he," but an emphatic demonstrative pronoun, *ekeinos*, which means "that person, the person there," referring, of course, to the One who was "in the bosom of the Father." And immediately following these words we find the emphatic announcement, "that person there declared him."

It is as if John wanted to dispel from our minds the possibility of anyone else having done it or having been able to do it. Jesus Christ is the only complete revelation of the nature and character of God. He, being the Son, so intimate with the Father, of the same nature as the Father (*monogenees*), was the only One who could reveal Him.

The verb "declared" in Greek, *exeegeesato,* is indeed beautiful. This verb was constantly used by ancient Greek writers to indicate the interpretation of divine mysteries. It was an explanation to men of something divine that they could not understand by themselves. That is what Jesus Christ came to do, to help us limited human beings to understand the unlimited and invisible God. Unfortunately, this word has no English equivalent as a verb, which is why we must use the Greek form, "to exegete" the Scriptures, i.e., to bring out their hidden meaning. The word actually is made up of the preposition *ex*, meaning "out of," and the verb *heegeomai,* which means "to lead." Therefore its basic meaning is "to lead out." The idea is that of God, the invisible God, in a hiding place. He was inaccessible to man. Jesus Christ, who has always been with the Father, who is God Himself, brought Him out and made Him visible to all. He explained God. He was the exegete of God. In fact, the word "exegesis" in English comes from the verb *exeegeomai.* Exegesis is bringing out the meaning of something that is difficult to understand. Thus we can say that in Jesus Christ God is made understandable, and only in Him is He understandable. There is no other way in which anyone can know and see God. Our Lord was absolutely right when He declared, "He that hath seen me hath seen the Father" (John 14:9).

The tense of the verb *exeegeesato* is the historical aorist, which would indicate that this bringing forth of God for the world to see

32

was done once and for all. It is not to be repeated. Christ came once as the revelation of God to mankind. He will come again, not as the exegete of God, but rather as the instrument of God's justice upon the earth. Jesus Christ will not give in to the whims of individual unbelievers who want Him to reappear if they are to believe on Him. He appeared once and for all to reveal God to you and to me, and it behooves us to believe on Him and thus become the children of God.

Actually, in the Greek, there is no object for this verb. The literal translation of "He hath declared him" would be "that person declared." He declared (or brought forth) whom? Him of whom John spoke in the first part of the verse, the invisible God. The exegesis of God has been made. The invisible has been made visible. If any man fails to see God, it is his own fault. Perhaps he has looked for Him in some persons or systems other than Christ. God has discharged His responsibility in making Himself accessible to us. The opportunity to appropriate Him is now ours.

CHAPTER 8

WAS JESUS CHRIST IN EXISTENCE BEFORE HE CAME INTO THE WORLD?

"In the beginning WAS the Word" (John 1:1a).

Jesus Christ was born in Bethlehem of Judea some 2000 years ago. But was that the beginning of His existence? This is an important question for us to consider, for if He was not in existence before He was born, then He cannot be eternal and is not much different from other human beings.

The Apostle John in the 18th verse of the first chapter of his Gospel declares that God in His full essence and majesty is invisible, but that Jesus Christ, who is of the same nature as the Father God, brought Him out into the open for every one of us to see and know. This verse is divided into two sections, the first of which speaks of God the invisible, and the second, of God becoming visible through Jesus Christ. Freely translated, these sections state:

1. That no man has seen God at any time.
2. That the only-begotten Son, or God, the only One of the same nature as the Father, who is in the bosom of the Father, He it is who brought Him out of His hiding place.

There are two other verses in John's Gospel, each of which corresponds to one of these two sections of the 18th verse. John 1:1 corresponds to the first part of verse 18, and verse 14 corresponds to the second part of verse 18. Let us put these in order for greater clarity. We shall quote from the King James Version, although the translation is not all that could be desired.

"No man hath seen God at any time" (1:18a).

34

"In the beginning was the Word, and the Word was with God, and the Word was God" (1:1).

These statements speak of the eternity of Jesus Christ, who is designated by the name "the Word." They refer to His preincarnate existence as God. He is referred to as God and therefore as the First Cause of creation.

And then we have God made visible in the incarnate Christ.

"The only begotten Son, which is in the bosom of the Father, he hath declared him" (1:18b).

"And the Word was made flesh, and dwelt among us, (and we beheld his glory, the glory as of the only begotten of the Father,) full of grace and truth" (1:14).

That is the relation which exists between verse 18 and verses 1 and 14. Verse 1 speaks of the eternity of Jesus Christ, and verse 14 speaks of the historicity of Jesus Christ. This person called Jesus Christ holds no interest for us if He was only a man, though granted a little better man than you and I. The fact that His claims were proven by Him in His life ought to induce us to study the period before His birth and after His death. Jesus Christ could have been either God or an impostor. But how could an impostor rise from the dead and perform miracles such as no one ever did before or after him? The examination, then, of the evidence as to whether Jesus Christ was God is of basic and paramount importance to the Christian, for if He was not God, then the Christian religion is no different from any of the other religions of the world. It would be merely a natural religion. But if Jesus Christ was truly God, if He was really existent before His birth as a human being in Bethlehem, then the Christian religion is a supernatural religion. How well a certain Chinese Christian explained the riddle of Christ to those around him when he said, "Jesus is the invisible God, and God is the visible Jesus." Here, indeed, is the whole Christian religion succinctly put.

As we study the life of this unique person called Jesus Christ, as we listen to Him speak and observe Him in His daily walk, we must surely acknowledge that He is different from anyone else who has ever lived. Count Zinzendorf, the founder of the Moravians, was converted in an art gallery in Dusseldorf by the contemplation of a painting of Christ on the cross which had the inscription, "I did this for thee. What hast thou done for me?" This picture had been painted by an artist three hundred years before. When he had finished his first sketch of the face of the Redeemer, this artist called in his landlady's little daughter and asked her who she thought it was. The girl looked at it and said, "It is a good man." The painter knew that he had failed. He destroyed the first sketch and, after praying for greater skill, finished a second. Again he called the little girl in and asked her to tell him whom she thought the face represented. This time the girl said that she thought it looked like a great sufferer. Again the painter knew that he had failed, and again he destroyed the sketch he had made. After meditation and prayer, he made a third sketch. When it was finished, he called the girl in a third time and asked her who it was. Looking at the portrait, the girl knelt down and exclaimed, "It is the Lord!" That alone makes the coming of Christ meaningful to the world—not that a good man came, not that a wise teacher came, not that a great sufferer came, but that God came — Immanuel, God with us. If a person does not believe that, he cannot be counted a Christian, nor his religion a Christian religion.

There is a beautiful correspondence between the three parts which make up the first verse of John 1 and the three parts which make up verse 14. We have three most meaningful parallels of the eternal Christ and the historical Jesus. Let us place them side by side:

"In the beginning was the Word" (1:1a).

"And the Word became flesh" (literal translation of 1:14a).

"And the Word was with God" (1:1b).

"And dwelt among us, (and we beheld his glory, the glory as of the only begotten of the Father)" (1:14b).

"And the Word was God" (1:1c).

"Full of grace and truth" (1:14c).

In the first three statements of verse one, we have a clear declaration of the preincarnate existence of Jesus Christ. As we shall see later, when we examine every word in its minutest detail, what they say is that if we go back to the very beginning of things we shall come to realize that behind this beginning there must have been an intelligence, a mind which created everything.

"In the beginning was the Word." Correctly translated, this should read, "Before there was a beginning, there was the Word or Intelligence personified."

But here John speaks of two of the three Persons responsible for the creation of the world. These are the Word, i.e., God the Son or Jesus Christ, and God the Father. This reminds us of the account of the creation in Genesis 1:26, where we read, "And God said, Let us make man in our image, after our likeness." Why "us" and "our"? Because there were two personalities involved other than the One who was speaking. (See also the plural pronouns in Genesis 11:7 and Isaiah 6:8). In John 1:1, the Apostle speaks of two of these Persons of the Triune God—God the Father and God the *Logos,* or Son. The fact of the Trinity of the Godhead is unmistakably manifested on the occasion of the baptism of the Lord Jesus Christ (Matt. 3:16, 17), where we find Jesus Christ baptized, the Holy Spirit descending upon Him, and the Father speaking. And the last words of Jesus in His great commission refer to the Father, the Son, and the Holy Spirit (Matt. 28:19).

In the three declarations of verse 14, we have three distinct messages about the Christ in human form. First, we have the *fact* of the incarnation, "And the Word became flesh"; second, the *purpose* of the incarnation, "and dwelt among us, (and we beheld his glory, the glory as of the only begotten of the Father,)"; and third, *the character of His person,* "full of grace and truth."

What blessings await us as we study these great basic truths of the eternity and historicity of Jesus Christ. Far too many people reject Jesus Christ before they become acquainted with Him. It is not fair to Him, and it is disastrous to them. An infidel who had just finished lecturing to a great audience invited any who had questions to come to the platform. After a short interval, a man who had been well-known in the town as a hopeless drunkard, but who had lately been converted, stepped forward and taking an orange from his pocket, coolly began to peel it. The lecturer asked him to propound his question, but without replying to him the man finished peeling his orange and then ate it. When he had finished his orange, he turned to the lecturer and asked him if it was a sweet one. Very angrily the man said, "Idiot, how can I know whether it was sweet or sour, when I never tasted it?" To this the converted drunkard retorted, "And how can you know anything about Christ if you have not tried Him?"

CHAPTER 9

IS THERE ANYTHING BACK OF THE BEGINNING OF THINGS?

"In the beginning WAS the Word" (John 1:1a).

As we enter upon the examination of the first parallel of the Gospel of John, which is made up of the first part of verse 1 and the first part of verse 14, we shall uncover many basic truths.

"In the beginning was the Word" (1:1a).

"And the Word became flesh" (literal translation of 1:14a).

The first important word to consider is the verb "was" in the first statement. This is in the imperfect tense. It is unfortunate that we do not have a true imperfect tense in English, and therefore it is difficult to translate the Greek imperfect. The Greek verb *een,* "was," holds the key to the understanding of John's statement. This is what we call the durative imperfect of the verb *eimi,* "to be." And what does that tense convey to us here? It speaks of a time before the beginning of things. In other words, John tells us that this *Logos,* this Word, was in existence before the created world. Therefore we would be fully justified in translating this first clause, "Before there was a beginning, the Word had been."

We must recognize the inherent limitations of our minds when we try to think about infinity and eternity. God has had to speak to us in human, understandable language. It is true that He has endowed us with reason and wants us to use it. He says to us, If you use your reason, you will arrive at the conclusion that everything has had a beginning. But we must also recognize that the finite can never fully comprehend the infinite.

A young skeptic said to an elderly lady, "I once believed there

39

was a God, but now, since studying philosophy and mathematics, I am convinced that God is but an empty word." "Well," said the lady, "I have not studied such things, but since you have, can you tell me where this egg comes from?" "Why, of course, from a hen," was the reply. "And where does the hen come from?" "Why, from an egg." Then the lady inquired, "Which existed first, the hen or the egg?" "The hen, of course," rejoined the young man. "Oh, then a hen must have existed without having come from an egg?" "Oh, no, I should have said the egg was first." "Then I suppose you mean that one egg existed without having come from a hen?" The young man hesitated: "Well, you see—that is—of course, well, the hen was first!" "Very well," said she, "who made that first hen from which all succeeding eggs and hens have come?" "What do you mean by all this?" he asked. "Simply this: I say that He who created the first hen or egg is He who created the world. You can't explain the existence even of a hen or an egg without God, and yet you wish me to believe that you can explain the existence of the whole world without Him!" And thus the old lady's common sense sent the young man's philosophy packing. Everything finite must have had a beginning. But the important issue is, what is behind every finite beginning? Is it self-begun, or is there an infinite and eternal mind, a personality, behind it, the same personality which is behind every finite beginning? This personality John chooses to call *ho Logos*, "'the Word."

What was foremost in the mind of John as he wrote this statement? To what question did it constitute an answer? Not to the question, "Who existed before there was a beginning?" but to the question of time, "Since when has this Word, this *Logos* existed?" The answer to the first question is obvious; it is God, the First Cause of all things.

> *There is no God? Then tell me, pray,*
> *Who started the sun on his golden way,*
> *Who paints the flowers and tints the sky*
> *From a palette of color of secret dye?*

Who is it that tells in early Spring
The flowers to waken, the birds to sing,
The ice to thaw, the river to flow,
And tells sleeping things to rise and grow?
Who is it that set the stars in their course?
Just natural law commingled with force?
Is it that which brings comfort in hours of pain
And soothes a tired body to sleep again?
The sea and the valley, the plains and the hills,
The mighty rivers, the sparkling rills;
The primrose, the holly, the goldenrod—
All of them symbols. Is there no God?

The War Cry

The Apostle John, then, is not interested primarily here in *who* created the world or who existed before the beginning, but *since when* has this *Logos* or Word existed? His subject is the eternity of the Word. The emphasis is not on the Word but on the time element, "in the beginning," and that is why it is placed at the beginning of the verse and of the whole Gospel. If this *Logos*, Jesus Christ, of whom he is about to speak, did not exist before there was a finite beginning, then the whole foundation falls. Whatever he says will be sheer nonsense. The verb *een*, in the durative imperfect, takes the Word far back of the created world, farther than can be imagined by our finite minds. In it there is the concept of eternity. Eternity is timelessness. But we as limited human beings can only think within the limited concepts of time and space. It is hard for us to imagine anything or anybody not bound by them. Yet God, who is free of these boundaries, has to use human language to make us understand His thoughts, as far as that is possible. But the very humanity of the language blurs the divinity of the thought behind it. With God there is neither past, nor present, nor future. God is timeless, yet whatever He says to us has to be put within the periphery of time. He has to give us a starting point, and that starting point He calls "the beginning." But we must remember

41

that God Himself is not limited by the beginning of which He makes mention. What John actually implies here is that, when there was no time, the Word was; when no human mind existed, the Word was.

Someone asked Augustine where God was before the heavens were created. Augustine replied, "He was in Himself." He is indeed that only self-contained Being; for He is the only Infinite One. And when Luther was asked the same question, he answered, "He was creating hell for idle, proud, and inquisitive spirits like you."

"Mother, who made God?" "That's a hard question, Jimmy. Why don't you go out and play for awhile?" answered the puzzled mother. But when Jimmy insisted on an answer, the mother was inspired to take off her ring and hand it to her little boy, saying to him, "Here, Jimmy, show me the beginning of it and the end of it." After careful examination Jimmy turned to his mother and said, "But, Mother, this has no beginning and no end." "God is the same way, Son. He has no beginning and no end." That actually is the meaning of the durative imperfect verb *een*, "was," in this first clause of John 1:1.

When John later speaks of John the Baptist and of the coming of the Word to the world in human form (verse 6), he uses an entirely different verb, *egeneto*, meaning "became" or "came," which definitely refers to a particular time in an historic setting, for it is the second aorist of the verb *ginomai*. In other words, there was a time when neither John the Baptist nor Jesus the man were in existence. But there was never a time when Christ, as the Word, the *Logos*, was not. The verb *een*, then, found in verses 1, 2, 4, 8, 9, and 10, indicates continuous existence; while the verb *egeneto*, found in verses 3, 6, 10, and 14, refers to a limited existence. There is a wealth of knowledge in just understanding the distinction between these two verbs in this important passage of John 1:1-18.

CHAPTER 10

WAS JESUS CHRIST THE RESULT OR THE CAUSE OF CREATION?

"IN THE BEGINNING was the Word"(John 1:1a).

One of the most important statements of the Bible about the person of Jesus Christ is that made by John in his Gospel: "In the beginning was the Word." If we correctly translate that verb "was" (*een* in Greek), then the clause should read "Before there was a beginning the Word had been."

But we are interested in discovering what John meant when he used the expression "in the beginning." This immediately calls to mind the very first words of the Bible, in Genesis 1:1, where we are told, "In the beginning God created the heaven and the earth." Here Moses starts with a most logical assumption, that there can be no result without a cause. God's revelation is never contrary to reason, though it is often far beyond it. "Who made you?" someone asked a little girl. She replied, "God made me that much," indicating with her two hands the ordinary size of a new-born infant, "and I growed the rest myself." The little girl said this in her simplicity, but profound thinking must surely lead us to the same conclusion — that God had something to do with us. We may be tempted to think that we have done a great deal for ourselves, but we must admit that originally He made us, for He made all things.

But where does Jesus Christ fit into the whole picture of creation? John designates Jesus Christ as the Word, the *Logos*, and he says, "Before there was a beginning, the Word had been." The Greek word used by John to speak of this beginning is *archee*, a word so important in the New Testament that we ought to examine it thoroughly. An understanding of its full meaning will help us to determine whether Jesus Christ was merely a creature or the Creator. This is basic to the whole concept of the supernatural nature of Christianity and its consequent uniqueness. There are some people today who do not believe Jesus Christ was the Creator but simply a creature, though they may go so far as to admit that He was the first creature and then the instrument through which God created the rest of the world. But this is contrary to the teaching of the New Testament, although these people say they base their teaching especially on this Greek word *archee,* meaning "beginning," used by John at the very outset of his Gospel. A careful examination of the Greek text will show us whether they are right or wrong.

In one Greek lexicon, probably the largest (*Mega Lexicon Tees Hellinikis Gloossees,* Deemeetrakou, Vol. II, pp. 1009, 1010), we are given a total of 18 meanings for this one Greek word, which in the King James Version, unfortunately, is almost uniformly translated "beginning." This has led to much confusion and misunderstanding. It is not our intention, of course, to consider all the various meanings of this Greek word, but we should at least examine those that are most pertinent in the understanding of the several crucial passages where this word *archee* is used in connection with Jesus Christ.

First of all, we should note that this word is used both absolutely and relatively, and which is meant in a specific instance can be determined by the context. When used absolutely, it refers to "the beginning, the origin of all things." Here in John 1:1 it has the absolute meaning, for there is nothing specific to qualify or limit its meaning. John does not say, "Before the beginning of this, that, and the other thing," but "Before there was a beginning." The *Logos,* or Word, "was" before the origin of everything finite. And as we saw previously, the question John has in mind and is answering here is "Since when has the Word been?" He is concerned with Jesus Christ's eternity.

Here are some additional texts in which the word *archee* is used with the absolute meaning: Matt. 19:4; 24:21; John 8:44; I John 1:1; 2:13; 3:8; etc. When used in a relative sense, it means "the beginning of the thing spoken of." An example of that is John 6:64, "For Jesus knew from the beginning who they were that believed not, and who should betray him." John refers here to the beginning of the time when Jesus began to gather His disciples together.

The most important distinction, however, is that made by nearly all lexicographers—that in the absolute sense the word *archee*, "beginning," can be either passive *or* active. Whether it is one or the other has to be determined by its context. When it is passive, we are to understand its meaning as "the result of another force," and when it is active, we have to take it as meaning "the cause of all things." When used in connection with the creation, it can mean either the beginning of the created world or the first cause of the created world. The word *archee*, "beginning," then, can mean either the result or the cause of something. The beginning of a line, for instance, can mean either the point where the pencil first touched the paper, or the person's decision or intent to draw the line. Let us look at some passages other than John 1:1 which throw light on the subject. One of the most important of these is Rev. 3:14, "And unto the angel of the church of the Laodiceans write; These things saith the Amen, the faithful and true witness, *the beginning of the creation of God.*" Does John here refer to Jesus Christ as the first result of the creation of God or as the First Cause, the Creator? By virtue of other Scriptures, we are forced to adopt the active meaning of the word *archee*, that Jesus Christ was the Cause of God's creation and not the first result of it.

There are two passages of the New Testament that make this crystal clear, John 1:1-3 and Colossians 1:15, 18. "In the beginning was the Word." Is the word "beginning" used in its passive or active sense? Let us look at the context and we shall dispel all uncertainty. John 1:3 tells us, "All things were made by him; and without him was not any thing made that was made."

Verse 3 explains verse 1. And surely the word "all" is so inclusive that it can admit of no exception. It includes Jesus Christ, the Word. It is a declaration of the self-existence, the self-creation of Jesus Christ, and therefore of His deity. The word "beginning," then, used in the first and second verses of John 1, undoubtedly is used in the active sense. It refers to Jesus Christ, not as the first result of the creation by God, but as the First Cause of it, as the Creator. He could not have been the first creature, if *all things,* including Himself, were made by Him, and there was nothing created that was not created by Him. These are inescapable and logical deductions that any thinking man must make if he accepts the full and absolute inspiration of the Word of God.

Now let us look at Colossians 1:15 and 18. "Who [speaking of the Lord Jesus Christ] is the image of the invisible God, the firstborn of every creature." The word "firstborn" here in the Greek is different from *archee,* which is the word used by John which we have been considering. Therefore we shall not enter upon a full discussion of it here, although we may examine this passage from the original Greek in the future. Suffice it to say that the word *proototokos,* translated "first-born," in this case refers to Jesus Christ's priority to all creation and His sovereignty over all creation. As Lightfoot says, "This is not inconsistent with His other title of *monogenees, unicas* (only-begotten), alone of His kind and therefore distinct from created things. The two words express the same eternal fact; but while *monogenees* (only-begotten) states it in itself, *proototokos* (first born) places it in relation to the Universe." (J. B. Lightfoot, *Colossians and Philemon.* Zondervan, p. 147.) Verse 16 clearly explains verse 15, "For by him were all things created, that are in heaven, and that are in earth, visible and invisible, whether they be thrones, or dominions, or principalities, or powers: *all things were created by him, and for him.*" And then the 17th verse tells us that He is not only the Creator of all things, but also the Sustainer of them. "And he is before all things, and by him all things consist." In the 18th verse, both words under discussion (*archee*, "beginning," and *proototokos*, "firstborn") are used. "And he is the head of the body, the church: who is the beginning [*archee*], the firstborn [*proototokos*] from the dead; that in all things he might have the preeminence."

In His high-priestly prayer, the Lord Jesus Christ Himself told us that He was before the beginning of the created world. He said in speaking to His Father, "And now, O Father, glorify thou me with thine own self with the glory *which I had with thee before the world was*" (John 17:5). There can be no doubt, then, that Jesus Christ was before the beginning of the world. That's what John declares. Therefore the expression *en archee*, "in the beginning," "fixes the beginning point absolutely, without reference to its relation to the time following." (Cremer, *Biblico-Theological Lexicon of New Testament Greek.* Fourth Edition with Supplement. T. & T. Clark, p. 114.)

It was Augustine who said, "Christ is not valued at all unless he be valued above all." Augustine caught the spirit and the meaning of the statement, "In the beginning was the Word." We can only think of the beginning of our world. That beginning must have had a cause. That cause is Jesus Christ, we are told in the Scriptures. And that Cause, the *Logos,* the Word, Jesus Christ, goes back into infinity. The miracle is that this absolutely inconceivable Cause of all things came down to dwell among us.

A native of interior China wanted to become a Christian but couldn't understand how Christianity was superior to Confucianism and Buddhism. One morning he came to the missionary in a happy mood saying, "I dreamed last night, and now I understand. I dreamed I had fallen into a deep pit where I lay helpless and despairing. Confucius came and said, 'Let me give you advice, my friend; if you get out of your trouble, never get in again.' Buddha came and said, 'If you can climb up to where I can reach you, I will help you.' Then Christ came. And He climbed down into the pit and carried me out." He had the right idea. It takes the Creator of

47

man to do that. For only a Creator could recreate. Only a Creator could reach so low as to save a sinful soul like yours and mine.

CHAPTER 11

WHY IS JESUS CHRIST CALLED THE WORD?

"In the beginning was THE WORD" (John 1:1a).

In the Scriptures Jesus Christ is called by a variety of names, depending on the particular qualities that the author wishes to bring forth. John wrote his Gospel in order to present Jesus Christ, not from the time of His birth in Bethlehem of Judea, but from eternity, as the Creator of all things. John knew the Old Testament, for he was a Jew, a converted Jew, a Christian Jew. He wrote part of the New Testament, but only as that New Testament was the fulfillment of the Old. Many times he must have read—probably in the Septuagint, which is the Greek translation of the Hebrew Old Testament—how God created by the word of His mouth. "And God *said*, Let there be light: and there was light" (Gen. 1:3).

Throughout the Old Testament we find the expression "the word of the Lord" used to designate the message of Jehovah. The name Jehovah, translated "Lord" in the King James Version, referred to God as the God of promise, the God of the future revelation of grace. The Old Testament was pointing forward to the fulfillment of this promise in the person of the Messiah, Jesus Christ. It is indeed very significant that in the Old Testament it is nearly always "the word of the Lord [Jehovah]" and not "the word of God," as we commonly find it in the New Testament. There are three exceptions in the Old Testament where in the Septuagint translation we find "the word of God" instead of "the word of the Lord," and these are in Judges 3:20, I Chronicles 25:5, and Psalm 56:4, 10. And the uncommon designation in the New Testament of the Old Testament as "the word of the Lord" occurs only in Acts

8:25; 13:44 (in the variant reading), 48, 49; 15:35, 36; 16:32; 19:10 (Nestle's text); I Thess. 1:8; II Thess. 3:1.

Why is it, then, that in the Old Testament the expression "the word of the Lord [Jehovah]" is used more commonly, while in the New Testament we find "the word of God" more usual? It is because the Old Testament contained a word of promise, while the New Testament contains a word of fulfillment, a word of grace, a message of salvation. Whenever the expression "the word of God" is used in the New Testament, it is used primarily to emphasize the Gospel, the good news of salvation in Jesus Christ. It refers to the Lord Jesus as the realization of the promise of Jehovah. Jesus Christ is the Word of God. It is through Him that Jehovah God spoke most clearly to us. Jesus Christ is found in the Old Testament concealed in prophecy, but in the New Testament we find Him clearly revealed as the Messiah, the Son of God, the One who is of the same kind as the Father (*monogenees*). Jesus Christ in the New Testament becomes the Exegete of God.

Therefore, in the New Testament, the term *logos* (word) becomes a technical one, which when used in its absolute sense signifies the Second Person of the Triune God. The only places where it occurs in this absolute personal meaning are John 1:1 and 14. Jesus Christ, then, is conceived of by John as the Word of God *par excellence*. He is the final Word of God to man and not merely "another word" on the same plane as all the others spoken before. He is the crowning and sealing of God's revelation to man. There can be no other. Christ is the final and most authoritative word God has ever spoken or ever will speak to man. He is "the Word"—the Word of salvation, the Word of the Gospel. There is no other name under heaven by which we can be saved (Acts 4:12).

But why is it that John chose this term to express the idea of the eternity of Jesus Christ as the Creator and not the creature? Words are used to express ideas. When you say to a child, "Give me a glass," he knows what you are talking about. The word "glass" is associated in his mind with an object. Philosophers like Kant tell us

50

that before we have the phenomenon, i.e., that which can be seen or felt by the senses, we have the noumenon, i.e., that which is conceived of by intellectual intuition. In other words, the object's image is first formed in the mind, and then it is produced as an object. We see a table. It is beautiful. We admire it. But more than that, we accept the fact that behind that object there was a concept in the mind of someone. Or consider the Empire State Building. Before it was erected, it took form in the mind of an architect, who transferred his thoughts to paper as a blueprint. Only then could the building be put up for everybody to see.

John wants to tell us that Jesus Christ existed before the beginning of the world. The Creator was before the creature. And the first thing that occurs to him, as a logically thinking man, is that this Creator must have been possessed with intelligence, with a mind. How could he express that? Where could he find an adequate word? He could find it only in the Greek words *"ho Logos,"* which cannot be translated adequately in any other language.

The term *logos* was in common use when John wrote his Gospel. One Jewish philosopher in particular, Philo, born in Alexandria, Egypt, in 29 B.C., employed it profusely, which made some believe that John had borrowed from him. We do not believe John did anything of the sort. Undoubtedly, what John had in mind was the Hebrew word *memra,* translated in the Septuagint as *logos.* In using the Greek word *logos*, he did it with its Jewish background in mind.

Logos has two primary meanings. First, it means "speech," that which is uttered by the mouth. It is the form of communication between two people. An unbeliever once asked a preacher why John called Jesus Christ "the Word." It seemed a strange appellation to him. The preacher answered, "It seems to me that as our words are the means that permit us to communicate with others, John used it to show that Jesus Christ is the only means whereby He chose to communicate with man." Jesus Christ, then, is God's speech or discourse to man. It was He who said, "I am

51

Alpha and Omega, the beginning and the end, the first and the last" (Rev. 22:13). *Alpha* is the first letter of the Greek alphabet and *omega* is the last.

But a distinction should be made here between this word *logos* and another Greek word, *lalia*, which also means speech or utterance. *Lalia* is the mere articulation of words without necessary reference to what is behind them or their content. That which is uttered by a parrot or an animal is *lalia*, but that which is spoken by a thinking man is *logos*. In other words, *logos* is the inward thought as well as the outward expression of that thought. *Logos* as speech must have thought or intelligence as its necessary prerequisite. An animal utters sounds, but a man expresses himself. Of course, from the way that some men talk, we wonder whether there is any thought behind the talk. But human speech is supposed to be reasoned speech. Of one thing we are sure; John was trying to convey the idea that not only was Jesus Christ the speech of God, but also in that speech there was reason and intelligence. After all, thought and speech are one. Thought is inward speaking, and speech is audible thinking. Thinking and speaking, spirit and speech, are necessarily associated in the word *logos* used by John. Have you ever seen reason or intelligence so closely connected with the spirit? No. Have you ever seen God? No. But does that mean He does not exist?

A skeptical young man confronted an old Quaker with the statement that he did not believe the Bible. The Quaker said, "Dost thou believe in France?" "Yes, though I have not seen it, I have seen others that have; besides there is plenty of corroborative evidence that such a country exists." "Then you will not believe anything you or others have not seen?" "No, to be sure I won't." "Did you ever see your own brains?" "No." "Ever see anybody that did?" "No." "Do you then believe you have any?"

Let us not be so foolish as to believe that there is nothing behind that which we hear. *Logos* means speech, speech that has intelligence behind it, reason that no one has ever seen. The vein of thought here is the same as that in John 1:18. The invisible God as Spirit becomes visible, or rather audible, as the speech of God to man. The thought of God receives expression in the appearance of Jesus Christ on this earth.

CHAPTER 12

THE PERSONALITY OF INTELLIGENCE

"In the beginning was THE WORD" (John 1:1a).

"In the beginning was the Word."

It is a sign of intelligence to ask questions about the things we see. Here are the flowers, and the mountains, and nature in all its splendor and beauty. How did they all come about? By chance or by intelligent creation? Which is more reasonable for us to conclude—that what we can see, feel, and hear are the result of chance and self creation, or of an intelligence that planned it all and brought it into being? In using the word *Logos* for Jesus Christ, John wants to demonstrate to us that intelligence is back of the created world, and not chance. *Logos* is the Greek word from which we derive the English words "logical" and "logic." A logical person is one who can make the right deductions, who can use his mind, invisible and immaterial though it may be.

In other words, John says that before all things that exist came into being, before time and space were created, was the *Logos,* Intelligence, which he equates with the person of Jesus Christ. Existing things are not the result of chance. What he says makes sense, for no one ever saw a rude heap of bricks dumped from a cart onto the ground arrange themselves into the walls, rooms, and chimneys of a house. The dust and filings on a brassfounder's table have never been known to form themselves into the wheels and mechanism of a watch. The types loosely flung from the founder's mold never yet fell into the form of a poem, such as Homer, or Dante, or Milton would have constructed. Only an illogical person could believe that nature's magnificent temple was built without an architect, her flowers of glorious beauty were colored without a painter, and her intricate, complicated, but perfect machinery constructed without an intelligent mind. That man gave the atheist a crushing answer, who told him that the very feather with which he penned the words, "There is no God," refuted the audacious lie. It takes logic to come to the conclusion that there must have been a *logos,* an intelligence behind what we see. We don't even need to open the Bible to learn that. Both Moses, in Genesis, and John, in His Gospel, take this for granted, because they knew that you and I were created in the image of God, and as He is intelligent so are we. Our intelligence is what distinguishes us from the rest of creation. Yet many refuse to use this special gift which the Creator gave them to come to the conclusion that behind this universe of law and order there must be a living intelligence. Before the beginning of time and space, John declares, was the *Logos,* the Intelligence.

But no one has ever seen intelligence outside of a personality. The words "reason" and "intelligence," which are the primary meaning of the *Logos,* are not like sound waves in the air. They are incorporated in personalities. We cannot stretch out a hand and catch intelligences floating in space. The Greek philosopher saw nothing more than an abstraction in thought, but a Jew like John could not divorce thought from the thinking person. Thus, when John speaks of the *Logos,* he does not speak of the abstract intelligence, but of the person of Jesus Christ as the active Intelligence which was the Creator of the world and not merely an impersonal creative power. Behind the intelligence there is the intelligent one, behind the thought there is the thinker. Let us never make the mistake of thinking of God or of Jesus Christ as simply an impersonal idea or power. They are true personalities, although we should not think of them as corporeal personalities similar to ourselves, within the limits of time and space.

John wants us to understand fully that, before Jesus Christ came into this world as a human being, He *was,* and that His personality was not material. That is why he designates Him in His eternal state as the *Logos*. The primary nature of the *Logos* as intelligence is spiritual, is immaterial. This fully agrees with the first part of John 1:18, which speaks of the invisibility of God as Spirit. In His eternal state, Christ was Spirit, not matter, as He later became in His historical appearance upon this earth. And yet His immateriality does not in any way rob Him of his eternal personality. The Scriptures speak of many immaterial personalities, such as Satan, the demons, and the angels. Thus, Jesus Christ in His eternal state was different from what He was in His temporal state, but in His temporal state He never ceased to be all that He was in His eternal state.

The fact that the *Logos* refers to a personality is evident from the demonstrative pronoun *houtos,* translated "the same," with which the second verse begins. It is in the masculine singular, the correct translation of which is "this person," not "this idea," or "this thing." If it were something impersonal, it would be *touto,* "this thing." The *Logos*, then, is a personality.

Another reason why Jesus Christ in His eternal state is designated as the *Logos,* "the Word," is that John wanted to show us that Christ can be seen and known only by the immaterial spirit of man and not by his physical senses. There must be a correspondence between the transmitter and the receiver, as we saw previously. Let us not forget that, as Jesus Christ in His eternal state is Spirit, so man in his essential state is spirit, and it is with his spirit, as that spirit is activated by the Spirit of God, that man can know God. "But there is a spirit in man: and the inspiration of the Almighty giveth them understanding" (Job 32:8). "The spirit of man is the candle of the Lord" (Prov. 20:27). "For as the body without the spirit is dead, so faith without works is dead also" (James 2:26). Jesus Christ, then, is designated as the *Logos* because the primary thing that He is interested in is the salvation of your spirit and mine, for it is our spirits which will be with Him eternally, even as was the spirit of Stephen, the first Christian martyr (Acts 7:59).

There is yet another reason why Jesus Christ in His eternal state is designated by John as "the *Logos*," which is immaterial personality, and that is to show us that, even in His preincarnate eternal state, He was in communion with the spirits of men. Jesus Christ did not wait until after His incarnation to begin His spiritual work, but His Spirit has always striven with the spirits of men. We find Him appearing many times in the Old Testament as the Angel of Jehovah (Gen. 16:7-13; 22:11-18; 24:40; 31:11-13; 48:15, 16; Num.20:16; Zech. 1:12, 13, etc.). And then He appears as One other than the Angel of Jehovah (Gen. 18:1-33; 32:24-32; Ex. 24:9-11, etc.). John wants us to understand clearly that the saving work of Christ began far before His incarnation, for He has ever been the eternal *Logos.*

Jesus Christ was not merely "a" *logos* but "the" *Logos.* He was the Intelligence behind everything that was created. He is the Person responsible for the creation of the world. That is why the definite article is used before the word *Logos.* He is the Master Mind of all creation, so to speak. Let us never make the mistake of classifying Jesus Christ as one of many intelligences or as one of many spirits. He is *the* Intelligence, the Reason, the Spirit, above, beyond and responsible for all creation. He is "the" *Logos.* There can be no one like Him. He is absolutely unique.

And as we have said, the other basic meaning of the term *Logos* is "speech," speech with content, speech with thought behind it. We may find it extremely difficult, if not impossible, to read the thoughts of our fellow human beings. The only way in which we can know them is when they are externalized by speech. Speech is the expression of thought. Despite the fact that we are possessed with God-given spirits, we cannot know what is in the mind and heart of God unless He uses human speech. And that is what Jesus Christ, the eternal One, became to us—He became God's speech. He became man so that He could speak to us in language we could understand. And thus He brings the thoughts of God to us in clear and understandable fashion. He makes the inaccessible accessible.

CHAPTER 13

THE INFINITE BECOMES FINITE

"And the Word BECAME flesh" (John 1:14a).

No greater and more mysterious words were ever written than the simple clause which begins the 14th verse of the first chapter of John's Gospel, "And the Word was made flesh." This Word had been identified by John in the first verse as being beyond and above the creation of the world, transcending time and space. It had been presented as the Infinite Intelligence responsible for the creation of the universe.

This eternal, infinite Word became flesh. Now flesh is finite. Therefore what we have here is a statement that the Infinite became finite. And this from the very outset poses for our finite minds the greatest mystery that we could ever face. To understand how this came about is impossible. But just because we cannot understand something does not make it untrue or impossible. In fact, even in the physical world in which we live, there are far more things that we do not understand than those we do.

The story is told of a blind tortoise which lived in a well. Another tortoise, a native of the ocean, in its inland travels happened to tumble into this well. The blind one asked of his new comrade whence he came. "From the sea." Hearing of the sea, he of the well swam round a little circle and asked, "Is the water of the ocean as large as this?" "Larger," replied he of the sea. The first tortoise then swam round two-thirds of the well and asked if the sea was as big as that. "Much larger than that," said the sea tortoise. "Well, then," asked the blind tortoise, "is the sea as large as this whole well?" "Larger," said the sea tortoise. "If that is so," said

58

the other, "how big then is the sea?" The sea tortoise replied, "You have never seen any other water than that of your well. Your capability of understanding is small. As to the ocean, though you spent many years in it, you would never be able to explore the half of it, nor to reach the limit, and it is utterly impossible to compare it with this well of yours." The tortoise replied, "It is impossible that there can be a larger body of water than this well; you are simply praising your native place in vain words." This is only a Mongolian myth, but one that can teach man a great deal concerning his prejudiced view of the enormity of his knowledge even of the natural surroundings of his life, let alone the supernatural, and still more the Infinite Creator of all things. Can any mortal understand how the Infinite can become finite? No, of course not. But it would be folly to reject this fact, even as it was folly for the well tortoise to disbelieve in the enormity of the sea. If you and I deny the Infinite the power of making His appearance in human form within the limitations of time and space, we deprive Him of the main characteristic of His infinity, omnipotence.

Thus we have here a statement of fact which is inexplicable but entirely feasible for our logical minds to accept. It would be harder and more illogical to reject it than to accept it. Its rejection presents insurmountable problems, while its acceptance provides the solution to all that is unexplainable regarding nature and its Creator.

Remember all these basic considerations as we enter upon the examination of this unique statement made by John that the *Logos*, the eternal God as the Second Person of the Trinity, became flesh and dwelt among us. This is possible because everything is possible with Infinity and Omnipotence.

The first thing to note in the exegesis of this unique statement, "And the Word was made flesh," is that the King James Version has definitely mistranslated the Greek verb *egeneto*. It is not in the passive voice, but in the middle voice. It does not indicate that someone from without exercised his coercive force and molded this *Logos* into human form. As the translation stands, it would give rise to the serious misconception that Jesus Christ was subordinate in His nature and essence to someone else, and therefore He would not be, He could not be, God co-equal with the Father. It is easy to see, then, how a mistranslation of just one verb can lead to a fundamental heresy concerning the central Person of our most precious faith. We should correct our English Bibles, whatever translation we may have, and never again say "the Word *was made* flesh," but "the Word *became* flesh." He became flesh of His own volition and power, without the exercise of any outside power or coercive force. The Infinite took on a finite nature of His own accord and in His own power. Otherwise He would not have been the Infinite; He could not be called *ho Logos*, "the Word."

This verb is used previous to verse 14, in verse 3 of this chapter, in reference to the creation of the world. It means "to become" or "to begin to be." When it has a predicate, as is the case in John 1:14, it has a relative meaning. It means "to become something." Here that something is "flesh." The *Logos* became "flesh." The immaterial *Logos* takes on matter, flesh. He who was previously invisible to our physical eyes can now be seen. In His flesh Jesus Christ becomes the Exegete of the invisible God, bringing Him out of His hiding place, so to speak. Here is the evidence of God's interest in man, so plainly presented that no one may have an excuse for not knowing.

But it would really be a mistake to express this great mystery of the incarnation of God simply as the Infinite appearing in finite form. It is not a process of taking on something, like coming into the flesh of a man, but it is becoming something new and unique. It is God becoming man. Actually the best exegesis of this clause would be "and God became man." This is the message of Bethlehem. The *Logos* became fully man. Not simply "a" man, for He was not merely human. He was the only perfect man that ever existed, for before He became man He was God. And He never ceased to be that, even after He became man. Manhood or womanhood is not self-produced. Life is something that comes to us from without. But not in the case of the *Logos*. He became man. This could not be said of anyone else. He was unique, not only in His deity, but also in His humanity. For there is no other God like Him nor is there any man like Him. The Infinite can take on a finite form, but not imperfection, for that would invalidate His infinity. Therefore the infinite and eternal *Logos* became the finite and temporal Jesus of Nazareth without ever ceasing to be the eternal *Logos*. Certainly He could never have done what He did as a mere man.

This verb *egeneto,* then, must not be taken to mean that the eternal *Logos* took on human flesh, just as we put on a suit of clothes or a dress. There is creativity involved here. It was not simply a process of putting on something that He did not have before, but it was creating for Himself that which He was not before. And, indeed, in this verse we have His virgin birth implied. Jesus Christ was not the product of the union of a man with a woman. He was conceived of the Virgin Mary through the supernatural and infinite power of God. He became that which you and I are, but in a different manner and without sin. He was existent before He became flesh. He who created everything in the first creation could create for Himself a body like ours without sin. We, of ourselves, cannot even create a living cell.

A Christian was invited to admire a great skyscraper. After looking at its majestic height, he called his host's attention to a little flower that he had on his lapel, saying, "True, this building speaks of man's achievement, but this flower with its life speaks of God's creation. I can see God more clearly in the flower than in the skyscraper." How true. He who was infinite and eternal could very easily become man, flesh, through the instrumentality of the Virgin Mary. But He could not have done it if He had not been and continued to be what He was before He became flesh. And remember this fundamental principle, that when a finite person or thing becomes something else equally finite, it must in the nature of things cease to be what it was; but not so when the Infinite of His own volition and in His own strength chooses to become something in addition to what He was and is. It is entirely illogical to conclude that Infinity will create something finite in order to blot out Infinity. Only as we understand this concept shall we understand the co-existence of the divine and the natural in one and the same person, in Jesus Christ. He was the only One with one ego but two natures.

CHAPTER 14

JESUS CHRIST, PERFECT GOD AND PERFECT MAN

"And the Word became FLESH" (John 1:14a).

The 14th verse of the first chapter of the Gospel of John begins with the conjunction "and." Here "and" connects two thoughts. We don't believe, however, that this is meant to connect verse 13 with verse 14, but rather verse 1 with verse 14. Verse 1, as we saw, deals with the eternity of the *Logos,* or Jesus Christ, and verse 14 with the historicity of the Son of God as man. More specifically, this conjunction joins the first clause of the first verse with the first clause of verse 14. "In the beginning was the Word . . . and the Word became flesh." Between verses 1 and 14 we have a big parenthesis.

But why does John use the term "flesh" and not some other term? Why does he not say, "And the *Logos* became body," since the real concept that he is endeavoring to convey is that the spiritual became material, the invisible God became visible man?

First of all, we believe the reason the word *sarx,* "flesh," is used here by John is a specific one. What is the primary purpose for which Jesus Christ came into this world? We come into the world for the purpose of living. He really did not come for the same purpose. He came to die. And there was to be purpose in His death. It was to redeem mankind from sin. He came to seek and to save that which was lost. His life was merely a bridge to His death. By living supernaturally, He wanted to demonstrate that He was going to die supernaturally, of His own volition, even as He came into the world.

63

Hebrews 9:22 tells us that "without shedding of blood is no remission." In the purpose of God, it was the blood of Jesus Christ which would avail for the remission of the sins of the whole world. This had to be the blood of a perfect and sinless man, and Jesus Christ was the only one who could meet this requirement. That's why John in his first Epistle (1:7) asserts that "the blood of Jesus Christ his Son cleanseth us from all sin." But blood is in the flesh. I believe that John wanted to demonstrate from the very start the purpose for which Jesus Christ became man, to shed His blood for the remission of our sins. "The Son of man came . . . to give his life a ransom for many" (Matt. 20:28).

Many persons speak highly of the life that the Lord Jesus lived while here on earth, but they do not speak of His death and the blood He shed on Calvary's cross. Yet that is the very reason for which He came. We cannot possibly live the way He did unless we accept His death as the penalty for our sins and are saved by His blood. Then, and only then, will His life take on meaning for us, and can He become our example.

This word *sarx*, "flesh," must not be taken literally as merely the vehicle containing the blood, but also in its more general sense. *Sarx* or "flesh" in the Scriptures also denotes human nature in its bodily manifestation. It shows that Christ became fully man except for sin, for if He were a sinful man, He could not possibly atone for sin. What the term generally means is that Jesus Christ in His human manifestation had a true human body and a true human soul. Canon H. P. Liddon says with unparalleled scholarship in his lectures to the University of Oxford, recorded in his book, *The Divinity of our Lord and Saviour Jesus Christ:* "He, Jesus Christ, is conceived in the womb of a human Mother (Luke 1:1; Matt. 1:18). He is by her brought forth into the world (Matt. 1:25; Luke 2:7, 11; Gal. 4:4). He is fed at her breast during infancy (Luke 11:27). As an infant, He is made to undergo the painful rite of circumcision (Luke 2:21). He is a Babe in swaddling clothes lying in a manger (Luke 2:12). He is nursed in the arms of the aged

Simeon (Luke 2:28). His bodily growth is traced up to His attaining the age of twelve (Luke 2:40), and from that point to manhood (Luke 2:52). His presence at the marriage-feast in Cana (John 2:2), at the great entertainment in the house of Levi (Luke 5:29), and at the table of Simon the Pharisee (Luke 7:36); the supper which He shared at Bethany with the friend whom He had raised from the grave (John 12:2), the Paschal festival which He desired so earnestly to eat before He suffered (Luke 22:8, 15), the bread and fish of which He partook before the eyes of His disciples in the early dawn on the shore of the Lake of Galilee, even after His resurrection (John 21:12, 13),—are witnesses that He came, like one of ourselves, 'eating and drinking' (Luke 7:34). When He is recorded to have taken no food during the forty days of the Temptation, this implied the contrast presented by His ordinary habit (Luke 4:2). Indeed, He seemed to the men of His day much more dependent on the physical supports of life than the great ascetic who had preceded Him (Luke 7:34). These and a multitude of other attestations, such as His physical sufferings, His death, His burial, the wounds in His hands and feet and side after His resurrection, prove beyond a shade of a doubt that He fully participated in the material side of our common nature." (London, Longmans, Green, and Co. 1890, pp. 19-21).

The *Logos* as man, as flesh, also was possessed of a human soul, and this is amply evidenced by the human emotions which Jesus had while here on earth. He loved, He was angry, He cried tears, He was vehemently agitated, He was in agony of soul, which all indicate the emotions of a human soul. Thus we can truly say that the *Logos,* the eternal One, became fully man, became possessed of a material human body and a human soul.

We believe furthermore that this term *sarx,* "flesh," is used by John to show the depth of the humiliation of God in becoming man for our sakes so that we might become the sons of God. "Flesh" in Scripture is usually indicative of our sinfully conditioned human nature. It stands in contrast to the spirit of man. The flesh drags us

65

toward sin, and the spirit toward God. John uses it to show us how low the Lord Jesus had to reach in order to save us from sin. So low that no one would have the excuse that he could not be reached by the Saviour of the world.

This humiliation of Jesus is vividly portrayed by the Apostle Paul in his Philippian letter (2:6, 7): "Who, being in the form of God, thought it not robbery to be equal with God [Here He was equal with God His Father]: But made himself of no reputation [or 'emptied himself,' in the original Greek; not of His divine nature, of His deity, but of His form as the Infinite Spirit], and took upon him the form of a servant [He did it of His own volition and in His own power—it was nothing imposed on Him], becoming in the likeness of men [literal translation.]" This is indeed the greatest of mysteries— God voluntarily taking upon Himself the form, the shape, and the nature of men without sin. "And without controversy great is the mystery of godliness: God was manifest in the flesh" (I Tim. 3:16). And if it was a mystery for Paul, it cannot be any less of a mystery for us.

The verb *egeneto,* "became," in the phrase "and the Word became flesh," is in the second aorist tense, which indicates an historical event in the past. It points back to Bethlehem, when the Son of God was born among the lowest of creation, in a manger. And yet the amazing thing is that this historical event of the incarnation of the *Logos* was prophesied hundreds of years beforehand by the Prophet Micah, who said, "But thou, Bethlehem Ephratah, though thou be little among the thousands of Judah, yet out of thee shall he come forth unto me that is to be ruler in Israel; whose goings forth have been from of old, from everlasting" (5:2). And in the Greek Septuagint, that which is translated "of old" in the King James Version is *ap archees, archee,* the very word used in John 1:1a which is translated "beginning." Here, then, in the person of Jesus Christ, we have the eternal and infinite One entering the realm of the temporal and the finite in order to restore us human beings to fellowship with God the Father through His

66

shed blood on the cross.

We must say again, however, that He, the eternal *Logos*, even when He became flesh and walked the streets of this earth, continued at the same time to be God eternal. This is the inescapable conclusion we must reach as we read His life. His birth was contrary to the laws of life. His death was contrary to the laws of death. He had no cornfields or fisheries, but He could spread a table for five thousand and have bread and fish to spare. He walked on no beautiful carpets or velvet rugs, but He walked on the waters of the Sea of Galilee and they supported Him. Three years He preached His Gospel. He wrote no book, built no church house, had no monetary backing. But, after 2000 years, He is the one central character of human history, the pivot around which the events of the ages revolve, and the only Regenerator of the human race. Was it merely the Son of Joseph and Mary who crossed the world's horizon 2000 years ago? Was it merely human blood that was spilled at Calvary's hill for the redemption of sinners? What thinking man can keep from exclaiming, "My Lord and my God!"

CHAPTER 15

THE DISTINCTION OF PERSONALITIES IN THE GODHEAD

". . . and the Word was with God" (John 1:1b).

John in his Gospel has said that before the beginning of creation "was the word," the *Logos*, who is the Creator of the world, and that this eternal *Logos* became flesh. This is the declaration in the first clause of verse 1 and the first clause of verse 14.

Now we come to the second in this series of three parallels, made up of the second clause of verse 1 and the second clause of verse 14.

"And the Word was with God . . .
And dwelt among us."

Let us remember that the first verse refers to the eternity of Jesus Christ, while the 14th refers to the historicity of Jesus Christ. This we must bear in mind at all times as we examine this important portion of the Word of God. The subject of both verses is the *Logos*, the Word.

John is careful to point out to us that Jesus Christ, the eternal *Logos* of whom he spoke in the first clause of the first verse, is not the same person as God the Father. He declares that He is a distinct Person and ought not to be confused with the Father. In the 18th verse, John introduced this filial relationship that exists between the two persons of the Triune God, the Father and the Son. He told us that Jesus Christ is the *monogenees,* the only One of His kind, of the same nature as the Father, and who has always been in the bosom of the Father. The distinction, then, is between the eternal *Logos,* the eternal Word, and the Father—between the

Son and the Father—and not between one kind of God and another kind of God. They are both essentially the same; they are God of the same nature and substance.

John makes the distinction between the personalities of the *Logos*, Jesus Christ, and the Father, in this second clause of verse 1, "And the Word was with God." We are not to think, however, that this means that the Word was not God, since He was with God. The term "God" ought to be taken to signify "Father," the Father of whom John spoke in verse 18. Therefore John declares that this Father in verse 18 is God, and the God of the second clause of verse 1 ought to be taken to mean "Father." "And the Word was with the Father." There is no difference in nature and substance between the Word and the Father. The difference is only in their being two distinct personalities known throughout the New Testament as the Son and the Father. God chose to reveal this relationship to us so that we might understand what He does for us in and through the person of Jesus Christ. He makes us His children and He becomes our Heavenly Father. The greatest privilege that ensues from our acceptance of the Lord Jesus Christ as our Saviour is that we have God as our Father.

One sharp winter day, so runs a nursery tale, a poor woman stood at the window of a king's conservatory, looking at a cluster of grapes which she longed to have for her sick child. She went home to her spinning wheel, earned half-a-crown, and offered it to the gardener for the grapes. He waved his hand and ordered her away. She returned to her cottage, snatched the blanket from her bed, pawned it, and once more asked the gardener to sell her the grapes, offering him five shillings. He spoke furiously to her, and was about to turn her out, when the princess came in, heard the man's angry words, saw the woman's tears, and asked what was wrong. When the story was told, she said, "My dear woman, you have made a mistake. My father is not a merchant but a king; his business is not to sell but to give." So saying she plucked the cluster from the vine and dropped it into the woman's apron. To have a king for a father

69

is a great honor, but it is nothing in comparison with having Almighty God as a Father. We can certainly be glad that God does not deal with us as a merchant, but as a Father with his sons. That's the relationship that Jesus Christ came to establish between God and those who believe on Him.

The verb that is used in this second clause of the first verse is *een,* the same as that used in the first clause, which is the durative imperfect of the verb *eimi,* "to be." It invites us to look as far back as we can, as finite beings, and be convinced that there was never a time when the Word, Jesus Christ, the Son, the Second Person of the Trinity, was not with the Father. The *Logos* did not simply achieve a position of proximity to and close relationship with the Father, but He has always been with Him. There has never been a time when He wasn't with Him. That is the meaning of the verb *een* in the durative imperfect.

Two gentlemen were once disputing about the deity of Christ. One of them, who argued against it, said, "If it were true, it certainly would have been in more clear and unequivocal terms." "Well," said the other, "admitting that you believed it . . . how would you express the doctrine to make it indubitable?" "I would say," replied he, "that Jesus Christ is the true God." "You are very happy," rejoined the other, "in the choice of your words, for you have happened to hit upon the very words of inspiration. St. John, speaking of the Son, says, 'This is the true God, and eternal life' (I John 5:20)."

But it is not only in his First Epistle that John says that. He says in the very first verse of his Gospel. And it may be that the very reason the Holy Spirit chose the Greek language as the vehicle for the New Testament is that His revelation to us might be absolutely clear, final, and without any possible linguistic ambiguity. If the English language had been chosen in which to write the New Testament, the meaning of this verb *een* in the durative imperfect could not possibly have been expressed. The eternity of Jesus Christ, His ever-presence with the Father, is clearly expressed in the verb *een,* so inadequately translated in English as "was." A better rendering might be "And the Word has always been with God, or the Father."

The other word that needs examination in this second clause of the first verse is the preposition translated "with" in English. The Greek word is *pros,* which is to be distinguished from similar prepositions such as *en, para, sun, meta.* These ordinarily indicate a dormant position instead of motion and action, which is the usual but not the exclusive characteristic of the preposition *pros* used here by John. (For a very excellent examination of this preposition *pros* we refer our readers to A. T. Robertson's *A Grammar of the Greek New Testament in the Light of Historical Research,* Doran, Fourth Edition, pp. 624-6.) *Pros* could be translated as "toward" to express the idea of motion. It is as if the *Logos* and the Father were facing each other. There is no suggestion of the Son following the Father, for then the Son would not be co-equal with the Father. Although the *Logos* is called the Son, John wants us to understand that by no means is He dependent upon the Father in His eternity, His nature, and substance. Here we have two equal personalities, the *Logos* and the Father. They did not just happen to be together as we happen to be together with some of our fellow-human beings by virtue of circumstances, either at work, church, or in society. This is what would be expressed by any of the other Greek prepositions indicating mere togetherness without an independent voluntary interaction between the two parties. It is the distinction between the two personalities which John wants to make clear here, and yet he also wants to show that there is a living and constant relationship and fellowship between the Son and the Father. They are separate personalities and yet they are ever together. This is impossible for us to comprehend with our finite minds because it concerns the arithmetic of infinity. We have to praise God that it pleased Him to reveal it to us.

A gentleman passing a church with Daniel Webster asked him, "How can you reconcile the doctrine of the Trinity with reason?"

71

The statesman replied by asking, "Do you understand the arithmetic of heaven?"

We believe that in this preposition *pros* we have a most important and interesting explanation of why Jesus Christ, while sojourning on this earth, was constantly in communion by prayer with His Father, as the incarnate Son. Some who would like to repudiate the fact that He was fully God, even while He lived as man down here, find in this habit of the Lord Jesus a demonstration of His complete dependence upon the Father God which leads them to conclude that He could not have been truly God. But in this preposition we find Him constantly coming toward the Father, bringing us and our problems to Him. The whole 17th chapter of John is explained by this preposition. He prays to the Father on our behalf. He shows Himself to be the executive agent of the Godhead. He is not dormant but active, for He is down here in order to bring us close to the heart of the Father in heaven. Indeed, in this preposition we find the uniqueness of His work as the only Mediator between man and God.

CHAPTER 16

GOD PITCHES A TENT

". . . and dwelt among us" (John 1:14b).

———————

John has declared, not only that Jesus Christ as the *Logos* is eternal, the Creator of the world and therefore God, but also that He is to be distinguished from the Father as a separate personality, not in the Father but in constant fellowship and proximity with the Father.

What he has said in the second clause of the first verse corresponds beautifully with what he has said in the second clause of the 14th verse: "And the Word was with God . . . and dwelt among us." If Jesus Christ was not a personality distinct from the Father, He could not have come down to this earth to dwell among us. In these 18 verses of the first chapter of his Gospel, John presents these sublime truths of God's revelation to man in a most fascinating way. Jesus Christ, as a person distinct from the Father, could come down to our earth and dwell among us.

The most incomprehensible and mysterious thing that ever happened is that this eternal *Logos*, the infinite God in the person of God the Son, became incarnate and came to dwell among us. Why did He not come down simply as God? Why did He choose to come down in the form of man?

There is a beautiful story in ancient Greek poetry of a great warrior, the hero of Troy, clad in fierce armor, who stretches out his arms to embrace his child before he goes to the field of battle. The child is afraid of the dazzling helmet, nodding crest, and stern warlike aspect of his father, and shrinks back in terror and alarm. But there is a loving, tender heart beating within that panoply of steel. The father unbinds his glittering helmet, lays aside his fierce armor, and comes to his child with outstretched arms and tender words of love. And the child shrinks from him no longer but runs to his arms, pillows his head upon his bosom, and receives his parting embrace and kiss. Thus men were afraid in the Old Testament when God appeared in His majesty and terrible might. When people thought of God, they thought primarily of His omnipotence, His glory, the awfulness of His throne, the terrors of His justice, and shrank back from Him. But as the Greek father laid aside his fierce armor and came to his child in all the tenderness of paternal affection, so God veils His glory and splendor and awfulness, and reveals Himself to His children in the sweetest aspect of love.

This eternal *Logos* was to come to the earth for a limited and predetermined period of time. He was to come to accomplish a specific task, to save man from sin. To do that He had to become man without sin in order to sacrifice Himself on the cross and through His blood satisfy the justice of His Father, eliminate the cause of man's estrangement from God, and thus enable man once again to become a child of God. After this task was accomplished, Jesus Christ no longer needed to stay here on earth. Thus His sojourn among us was supposed to be temporary. In order that John might express the temporary aspect of the coming of the *Logos*, he used the Greek word *eskeenoosen*, which rightly translated is "tented, or pitched his tent."

The tent (*skeenee*) is something that is used for a temporary dwelling, either by nomads or soldiers. It was not the purpose of Jesus Christ to come down here and live as long as He could. He could have lived much longer than the short span of His 33 years. In this He also proved His deity while He was clothed with human flesh. Every one of us in our sound minds and bodies wishes to live as long as possible. We are inherently afraid of death, and yet here is One who came for the specific purpose of dying and who in His death would find the accomplishment of His life purpose.

Alfred Krupp of Prussia, the great cannon king, was literally a manufacturer of death. And yet he had such a fear of death that he never forgave anyone who spoke to him of it. Every employee throughout his vast works was strictly forbidden to refer to the subject of death in conversation. He fled from his own home when a relative of his wife suddenly died there, and, when Mrs. Krupp remonstrated, he became so enraged that a lifelong separation ensued. During his last illness he offered his physician a million dollars if he would prolong his life ten years. But no amount of money could buy an extension of his life. How different it was with Jesus Christ, because He was not only man but God at the same time. When He became man, He came down for a definite time and purpose. And actually you and I are here for a time, too. Many of us would walk differently, if we had the end of the way more in view. But unfortunately we act as if we could live forever down here, forgetting that this life is just a steppingstone to eternity, a preparation ground for things better or worse, according to the use that we have made of our lives while here on earth.

The word used here in one of its substantive forms, *skeenooma*, means "body," as in II Peter 1:13, 14: "Yea, I think it meet, as long as I am in this *tabernacle* [*skeenoomati*, in the dative case], to stir you up by putting you in remembrance; knowing that shortly I must put off this my tabernacle [the same Greek word], even as our Lord Jesus Christ hath shewed me." Thus, when John says that the *Logos* "tented" or *eskeenoosen* among us, he is actually declaring that although His sojourn among us was temporary, it was real. It was not a mere fantasy, something imaginary. Jesus Christ actually had a body, one like ours, but without sin.

The verb "tented" here is in the historic aorist tense, which would indicate that this appearing of the *Logos* in the form of a human body has been completed in an historical setting and is not to be repeated in the same manner and form and for the same purpose. When Jesus Christ rose from the tomb, He did not merely have a restoration or resuscitation of the old body; His old body was gloriously transformed. He thus took upon Himself a new resurrection body, which was unique and immortal. It was with this immortal, glorified resurrection body that He ascended into heaven, and it is in this that He will come back to the earth. Thus Jesus Christ came once and for all in the way that He did at Bethlehem. Never again will He come back in the body He had then, in the body of His humiliation, but in the body of His resurrection, in the body of His glorification. Thus the tenting of Jesus Christ among us was an historical event, never to be repeated in the history of the world. He will never come back to die for the sins of the world. He did that once and for all. He will come back no more as the meek and gentle Master of Galilee, but as the Judge of the earth. In this life only we have the unique and never-to-be-repeated opportunity of accepting Jesus Christ as our Saviour. If we fail to do it, we shall have to face Him one day as our Judge.

CHAPTER 17

GOD IN US AND AMONG US

". . . and dwelt among us, (and we beheld his glory . . .)"
(John 1:14).

———————

"And [the Word] dwelt among us." Infinity in the person of Jesus Christ comes down to the finite world. The Creator comes to dwell among His creatures.

The miracle of it all is the fact that He did this though the creatures were unfavorably disposed toward their Creator. They hated Him, and yet He came to dwell among His enemies. In that very thing we see the deity of Jesus Christ, for no human being seeks his enemies for his company. It takes God to come down and dwell among those who are opposed to Him. "When we were enemies, we were reconciled to God" (Rom. 5:10).

"I know men," said Napoleon in exile on the island of St. Helena, to Count Montholon, "I know men, and I tell you that Jesus is not a man! The religion of Christ is a mystery, which subsists by its own force, and proceeds from a mind which is not a human mind. We find in it a marked individuality, which originated a train of words and actions unknown before. Jesus is not a philosopher, for His proofs are miracles, and from the first His disciples adored Him. Alexander, Caesar, Charlemagne, and myself founded empires; but on what foundation did we rest the creation of our genius? Upon force. Jesus Christ founded an empire upon love; and at this hour millions of men would die for Him! I die before my time, and my body will be given back to the earth, to become food for worms. Such is the fate of him who has been called the great Napoleon. What an abyss between my deep misery and the eternal kingdom of Christ, which is proclaimed, loved, and adored, and is extending over the whole earth!" And turning to General Bertrand, the Emperor added, "If you do not perceive that Jesus Christ is God, I did wrong to appoint you general!"

Jesus Christ, the eternal *Logos*, came down among His creatures knowing that they were His enemies; yet He came without any earthly defenses, in the humility of unarmed flesh. Who ever heard of anyone setting out to conquer his enemies without arms? Christ conquered them with His love and His sacrifice on the cross of Calvary. He conquered His enemies by voluntarily dying for them. They could not have touched Him without His consent.

When the officers and soldiers came to the garden to arrest Jesus, He was unarmed. Had He been a mere man, He would have fled. But instead He approached them voluntarily. He asked them, "Whom seek ye?" "Jesus of Nazareth," was the reply. "I am he," was Jesus' ready response. Have you ever noticed what happened as soon as the Lord Jesus spoke these words? The armed soldiers "went backward, and fell to the ground." Jesus unarmed is far more powerful than His armed enemies (John 18:1-6). Why? Because He is God, the eternal *Logos*, confronting mere men.

Let us look at that small and very common Greek preposition *en*, translated "among" in this clause. "This preposition in itself merely states that the location is within the bounds marked by the word with which it occurs. It does not mean 'near,' but 'in,' that is 'inside.' " (A. T. Robertson, *A Grammar of the Greek New Testament in the Light of Historical Research*, Doran, Fourth Edition, p. 586.) The primary meaning, then, of this preposition is "in, inside." "With plural nouns *en* may have the resultant idea of 'among,' though of course, in itself it is still 'in,' 'within.' " (Ibid, p. 587.) "In," therefore, is the inherent meaning, while "among" is the resultant meaning.

It may well be that the Holy Spirit chose this preposition to show us that the main purpose for which Jesus Christ came into this world was to dwell "in" or "within" our hearts, and secondarily "among" us. Of course, His dwelling among us was a necessary corollary of His dwelling in us. But His dwelling among us was temporary, while His dwelling in us is more permanent. He is not here among us, but He surely is in the hearts of those who have accepted Him as their Saviour and Lord.

A teacher asked her class, "Where is God?" One boy replied, "In heaven," another, "Everywhere," and another, "God is here, in my heart." There is a tremendous difference between being just a neighbor and being a member of the household. A man may have a home close to the White House, but that does not make him a member of the President's household, a member of his family. What real profit would it have been for us if Jesus Christ had come merely to be among us, but not in us? It is recorded that those who found themselves in the presence of Christ, but who did not have Him in their hearts, felt uncomfortable and asked Him to depart from their borders. But those who received Christ in their hearts always greatly desired His company. The same thing is true today. A great many people feel most uncomfortable when they read the Bible or have to associate with people who know the Lord. This discomfort stems from the fact that Jesus Christ is not in them. We are glad to have Christ around us if we have Christ in us. And of course Christ is around us today in the form of His followers and their influence around us. His presence and the presence of Christians around us is a check on our conscience.

But how can we reconcile the fact that the verb *eskeenoosen*, "pitched his tent," expresses a temporary sojourn, and not a permanent one, with the fact that, when Christ comes into our hearts, He stays there forever? Does the verb refer to that which is temporary and transitory, and the preposition to that which is permanent? How long does Jesus Christ pitch His tent in us? As long as we are in this earthly life. He does not continue to indwell our earthly tent after the spirit leaves it and the body is committed to the earth from which it came. At the moment of death, He takes our soul or spirit to dwell with Him forever. Now we are in Him and He is in us; but then He will be with us and we shall be with Him. As the Apostle Paul expressed it when writing to the Philippians, "For to me to live is Christ, and to die is gain" (1:21). In life Christ is in us, and in death Christ is with us. "For I am in a strait betwixt two, having a desire to depart, and to be with Christ; which is far better" (1:23). That's why no one can do a Christian any real harm, for in this life he has Christ in him and in the life to come he has Christ with him. Martin Luther said, "If anyone knocks at the door of my breast and says, 'Who lives there?' my answer is, 'Jesus Christ lives here, not Martin Luther.' "

Thus we can readily see that, as the sojourn of Jesus Christ on this earth in His human body was temporary, so is His sojourn in our *skeenooma,* in our body. Doesn't Paul say in I Cor. 3:16, "Know ye not that ye are the temple of God, and that the Spirit of God dwelleth in you?" There is therefore full agreement between the verb *eskeenoosen,* "pitched his tent," which refers both to the temporary stay of Christ on this earth and to the human body, and the preposition *en* in its twofold meaning both as "in" and "among." When we accept Jesus Christ as our Saviour, He dwells in our bodies as long as the bodies in their present form and make-up last; and since the bodies themselves are temporary, His sojourn in us is also temporary.

There is one thing further which we would like to mention concerning the tense of the verb *eskeenoosen,* "pitched his tent." It is in the aorist tense, which indicates that there is a particular moment when Jesus Christ comes into the human life, and from then on life in Christ begins and Christ begins His life in us. It isn't just a feeling but a revolutionary event. And once Jesus Christ comes in, He is there to stay. No one can prevail against Him. He fights our battles and wins our victories.

Somebody was asked if he knew that he was converted. "Why, bless your heart," was the answer, "I was there when it happened!" When Jesus Christ comes into our hearts, we know it, and others will, too.

80

CHAPTER 18

MAN'S WONDER AT THE GLORY
OF THE INCARNATE GOD

". . . and dwelt among us, (and we beheld his glory . . .)"
(John 1:14).

When John wrote "And [the Word] dwelt among us," whom
did he mean by the personal pronoun "us"?

First of all, he must have included himself as a personal witness
of the incarnate Christ. John allowed Jesus Christ to take up His
abode in his heart, after which he desired always to be with Him in
a physical sense. He was one of the inner-circle disciples. What he
says about Jesus Christ comes out of his own personal experience
of Christ and as a result of his intimate knowledge of Him. He has
every right to speak, and we ought to heed his testimony, for it is
valid. It is first hand; it is not hearsay.

But John was not the only witness of the appearance of the
incarnate God on this earth. There were others, so that the
testimony might be undeniable. "In the mouth of two or three
witnesses shall every word be established" (II Cor. 13:1). Jesus
Christ will condescend to dwell within any heart, and His desire is
to dwell in every heart, including yours and mine. God is no
respecter of persons (see Rom. 2:11). He will dwell in the heart of
the rich as well as of the poor, of the king as well as of the common
citizen, of the educated as well as of the uneducated. The only
condition is personal faith in Him and opening the door of one's
heart. "Behold, I stand at the door, and knock: if *any man* hear my
voice, and open the door, I will come in to him, and will sup with

him, and he with me" (Rev. 3:20).

Charles H. Spurgeon made a penetrating observation when he said that there were many rooms in the ark but only one door. Similarly, there is only one door in the ark of our salvation, and that is Christ. There are not a multiplicity of Christs preached, one in one place and another in another. The same Christ indwells a variety of people. There is a unity in the midst of diversity as the same Christ dwells in the hearts of many believers. Christ gives new birth to all who accept Him, but He does not make them all uniform. It is good to remember that, when we get provoked because other Christians aren't exactly like us. We all have the same element of human life, and yet our bodies do not all look the same. Wouldn't it be quite boring if everybody looked alike? Remember that the Word came down to this earth to dwell, not in you and me exclusively, but in all those who believe on Him, even if they are somewhat different from you and me. In the 16th verse of this same chapter, John adds with great emphasis "And of his fulness have all we received, and grace for grace." That is the very purpose for which He came, to dwell in human hearts. If any will receive Him, He will come in, no matter what the condition of the heart, no matter how sinful it may be.

To this second clause of John 1:14 a parenthetical statement is added which is of paramount importance: "And we beheld his glory, the glory as of the only begotten of the Father."

Again John does not say, "I beheld," but "we beheld." He includes every believer who saw the Lord Jesus Christ in the flesh and everyone who on the basis of their testimony now sees Him by faith. In the incidents of the life of Christ which he relates in the body of the Gospel, from John 1:19 on, he presents a whole array of such believers who beheld the glory of Christ and who could be counted in this "we." This is why it is most probable that John wrote this so-called prologue of John 1:1-18 after he wrote the incidents from John 1:19 to the end. Thus, this portion which we are examining should rather be called the epilogue and not the

82

prologue. It is the doctrinal summarization of the biography of the Lord Jesus Christ as the incarnate God.

The verb John uses here, *etheasametha,* translated "beheld," is quite intriguing. This verb (*theasthai* in the infinitive) is used twenty-two times in the New Testament, but never of spiritual vision. (See John 1:32, 38; 4:35; 6:5; 11:45; I John 1:1; 4:12, 14.) When John uses this verb, he does not refer to a supersensory perception of God or Jesus Christ as Spirit, but rather to the actual viewing by the physical eyes of something tangible outside the viewer. The Holy Spirit led John to use this Greek word in order to dispel any misapprehension about the reality of the body, of the physical appearance, of the Lord Jesus on this earth. In the early church a heresy arose called *docetism,* which taught that Christ had no real material body and human nature but only an apparent body, a phantasm of humanity. This heresy taught also that Christ's acceptance of the ordinary laws that govern our life, His eating, drinking, birth, and death, were so many illusions. We cannot but think that the Holy Spirit, the real Author of the Bible, knew that such a heresy would arise and inspired the use of this word which unmistakably refers to the physical view of a physical object. The body of Jesus Christ was real and could be seen by many during His earthly life.

But a further distinction needs to be made regarding the peculiar meaning of this Greek verb (*theaomai* in the first person indicative) translated "beheld." It does not mean simply "to see with the physical eyes" but to see "in such a way that a supernatural impression is gained." (Arndt and Gingrich, *A Greek-English Lexicon of the New Testament and Other Early Christian Literature,* University of Chicago, p. 353.) Let us look at the account of the baptism of the Lord Jesus, and we shall see how this particular meaning of the word is made clear. In John 1:32, John the Baptist speaks and says, "I saw [*tetheamai* — the same Greek word] the Spirit descending from heaven like a dove, and it abode upon him." This was not just a simple viewing with

83

John's physical eyes, but a viewing that left upon him a supernatural impression, because it was a supernatural event. John saw the dove and also became aware that it was the Holy Spirit. Thus we conclude that this verb *theaomai*, "to behold," actually refers to the physical sight of a physical object, but that the perception, the understanding of the nature and substance of that which is seen, is wholly supersensory. John the Baptist saw the dove; he actually did see it with his physical eyes; but the understanding of what that dove represented — the Holy Spirit — was something that his physical senses could not comprehend. He needed something beyond these to understand the mystery of the Godhead; he needed the Spirit of God Himself. "And without controversy great is the mystery of godliness: God was manifest in the flesh, justified in the Spirit, seen of angels, preached unto the Gentiles, believed on in the world, received up into glory" (I Tim. 3:16).

To come back to the particular meaning of this verb in our verse, "And we beheld his glory, the glory as of the only begotten of the Father," John actually declares that Jesus Christ in human form was seen physically by himself and others. And yet in that human form he could supersensorily perceive, not a mere man, but God incarnate. This supersensory perception could only be vouchsafed him as a result of the operation of the Spirit of God in his heart. Only as the Spirit of God revealed it to Him and he was willing to accept that revelation that is above and beyond our sensory perceptive powers, that this person called Jesus Christ who walked the streets of Palestine doing good and healing the sick and raising the dead was God incarnate, could he really behold Him as such.

Furthermore, this verb *theaomai*, "to behold," means "to look on, gaze at, view, mostly with a sense of wondering, of amazement." One cannot but be amazed when he looks at Christ. As St. Chrysostom says: "When thou hearest of Christ, do not think Him God only, or man only, but both together. For I know Christ was hungry, and I know that with five loaves He fed five thousand men,

84

besides women and children. I know Christ was thirsty, and I know Christ turned water into wine. I know Christ was carried in a ship, and I know Christ walked on the waters. I know Christ died, and I know Christ raised the dead. I know Christ was set before Pilate, and I know Christ sits with the Father. I know Christ was worshipped by the angels, and I know Christ was stoned by the Jews. And truly, some of these I ascribe to the human, others to the divine nature, for by reason of this He is said to be both together."

Skeptics ask, "Why did not Jesus by reasoning prove His deity?" But amid the blaze of His miracles, this would be like placing a label on the sun. Does the sun need a label? Of course not. Nor did the Lord Jesus Christ, for John and others knew that He was God incarnate. They as well as we, if we have physical eyes to see and spiritual supersensory perception to understand, cannot but behold Him with wonder and amazement and say, "He is indeed God, who became man without ceasing to be God in order to make us the children of His Father God."

CHAPTER 19

CAN GLORY BE SEEN?

"And the Word was made flesh, and dwelt among us, (and we beheld his glory, the glory as of the only begotten of the Father,) full of grace and truth" (John 1:14).

————

The problem which immediately arises for any thinking mind is, how can physical eyes see something that is immaterial? *Etheasametha*, "we beheld," refers to physical observation. But at the same time the word *doxa*, "glory," is something that cannot be seen with our physical eyes. No man ever saw glory walking the streets of his town, did he? Is there an inconsistency here in terminology? No, there can be no inconsistency in the Scriptures. Often we are just too human to understand divine truth and revelation. The important thing for John and the other believers to see in Jesus Christ was not His physical complexion and appearance, but rather what was behind that form. If they saw in Him only a man, without perceiving His eternal nature and deity, He would have held no attraction for them, no amazement, and no salvation. That which they could perceive supersensorily was far more important than that which they could see with their physical eyes, and since it was the realization of the deity of Christ which produced amazement in the disciples, that was the more important of the two. Therefore it is the supersensory perception in the verb *etheasametha*, "we beheld," which makes it agree with the word *doxa*, "glory." It is as if the disciples had exclaimed, "This man, talking to us, is not only what He appears to be, a real man, but He is God. And as God we cannot but admire Him, worship Him."

86

This, of course, is fully explained and qualified by the next phrase, "glory as of the only begotten of the Father." That's the glory that the disciples beheld. It was not an ordinary glory, the glory that may belong to a creature, but the unique glory of the Creator. Glory, however, is a demonstration of the fact that greatness resides within. We speak of the glory of the sun, of the mountains, and of nature. We call them glorious when their greatness baffles us, makes us realize our own insignificance. Glory is splendor, radiance. Everything in heaven is said to have this radiance (I Cor. 15:40), especially God Himself (Exod. 24:17; 40:34; Num. 14:10), and there is certainly a difference between heavenly and earthly glory.

This glory of the *Logos,* or the Word, Jesus Christ, is designated to point out to .nan all the divine attributes, Christ's absolute love, wisdom, grace, holiness, knowledge, and all that pertains to Infinity. When man, finite man, stands before Infinity incarnate, he cannot but stand aghast, amazed, baffled. That was the case with all those who beheld Jesus Christ in the flesh. They saw Him, not only as a man in history, but in His pre-existent state in eternity. The glory that they saw was that of the only begotten of the Father.

There is no definite article before the adjectival noun *monogenous,* "only begotten," and the noun *patros,* "of the Father." But the absence of the definite article could not render them indefinite, and therefore this phrase could not be translated "glory as of *an* only begotten of *a* father." Nouns which speak of persons or objects of which only one exists need no article. In Greek this is the opposite of the English usage. To emphasize the uniqueness of a person or object in English, we have to use the definite article, but not in Greek. Also these two nouns have qualitative force. They indicate what kind of glory John is speaking about and what kind of only begotten Son, or God, Jesus Christ was, and what kind of Father His Father was. (A. T. Robertson, *A Grammar of the New Testament in the Light of Historical*

Research, Doran, Fourth Edition, p. 794).

The disciples perceived this glory to be that of the only begotten from the Father. The force of the "as" in the phrase here does not have the force of comparison, because there is nothing with which to compare this glory. They knew by reading the Old Testament Scriptures what should characterize this Messiah, God incarnate; and as soon as they saw Him appear in the flesh, they could see all the Old Testament prophecies fulfilled in His person. Therefore they exclaimed, "This is the only begotten of the Father!"

We have dealt extensively with the adjectival noun *monogenees* (here *monogenous* in the genitive), commonly translated "of the only begotten," and we saw that, when referring to the person of Jesus Christ, it refers to His being of the same nature and race and family as the Father — God of very God. Therefore what is declared by this statement, "glory as of the only begotten of the Father," is that the incarnate Jesus was clothed with and possessed no less glory than His Father as God. The quality of the glory of the Son was the same as of the glory of the Father. When Jesus Christ came to this earth, He did not cease to be that which He was in His preincarnate existence. It was God walking the streets of Palestine, the Creator within His creation. How could the creatures, the thinking creatures, help but be awed by the sight of such an event as Infinity making His appearance in and among them?

A minister was once called into the room of a dear saint of God who had suffered much in the body. He had often visited her and, in spite of pain, found her greatly rejoicing. This time, however, he was told that she was in trouble and wished to see the minister urgently. Wondering what the trouble could be and how the devil might be tempting her, the minister rushed to her bedside. She said, "I cannot pray any more. As soon as I begin, my prayers are all turned into hallelujahs. I would have esteemed it a privilege if God had permitted me to spend my remaining days in supplications for my friends; but as soon as I open my mouth, it is all glory, glory, glory!" The minister could not but congratulate her on being

88

drafted into the employment of the celestial choir before her time. She lived for two weeks in a gust of praise, and so she died. At the very end of her earthly life, she could see the face of Jesus, and it was the face of glory, the glory as of the only One who brought heaven to earth for us to share. What a privilege to behold the glory of God in the face and person of the Lord Jesus! Before anyone can do so, however, he must allow Christ to indwell his heart by faith and yieldedness to Him.

CHAPTER 20

DID JESUS CHRIST HAVE ALL HIS GLORY ON EARTH?

"And the Word was made flesh, and dwelt among us, (and we beheld his glory, the glory as of the only begotten of the Father,) full of grace and truth" (John 1:14).

———

Some commentators and theologians have tried to teach that when Jesus Christ came to this earth from His preexistent state in eternity He laid aside His deity. They believe that He was God before He became man, but that, while He was here on earth as man, He was not God. And then, when He left this earth after His resurrection and His ascension, He regained His deity which He had laid aside. This is what is commonly known as the kenotic theory, which is primarily based on a misunderstanding of Philippians 2:6, 7, which says, "Who, being in the form of God, thought it not robbery to be equal with God: but made himself of no reputation, and took upon him the form of a servant, and was made in the likeness of men." Where the English says, He "made himself of no reputation," the Greek actually says, "And he emptied himself." Those people who do not believe that Jesus Christ was God, while here on earth, take this to mean that He emptied Himself of His deity. We shall see, however, that this is a completely unwarranted assumption. F. B. Meyer pointed out that the kenosis, or self-emptying of our Lord Jesus Christ at the time of His incarnation, was "like keeping my right hand, by a voluntary act of my will, behind my back, doing all my work with my left hand. Nevertheless the right hand was there. The prerogative and ability to use it was His, in spite of the fact that sometimes He chose not to."

Throughout the New Testament we become aware of the fact that Jesus Christ humbled Himself in coming to this earth. He was not humiliated but He voluntarily humbled Himself, for He as the Creator came down to live for a while with His creatures. If it is humbling for a king to leave his palace and live among his common subjects, how much more for God to dwell among His enemies? Even in this text of Philippians 2:7, it is more than apparent that it is not His deity that is spoken of, but His voluntary humiliation. The thing that He left behind Him was the glory which He had with the Father in all eternity, in His preincarnate state. This glory, however, does not involve either His nature as deity or His attributes as God. If Jesus Christ was not God while here, He could not have done the supernatural things He did.

But what did His glory involve, then? In His high-priestly prayer, just before He was about to leave this earth physically, He said, "And now, O Father, glorify thou me with thine own self with the glory which I had with thee before the world was" (John 17:5). It is therefore apparent, from this Scripture and others, that Jesus Christ had with the Father in His preincarnate state some kind of glory which He did not have while here with us on earth, and which on leaving us He would regain. The difficult problem is to ascertain what that glory was.

In order that we may arrive at the right conclusion, we must study the etymology of the word *doxa,* which is the Greek word for "glory." This noun is derived from the verb *dokein,* which in its intransitive form means (1) seeming as against truth, appearance as against reality and (2) reputation, renown, always in an honorable sense, unless an adjective changes the force. In the New Testament, the word is used as in profane Greek, to denote the recognition or status which anyone finds or which belongs to him. What, for instance, does that very familiar verse, Romans 3:23, mean? "For all have sinned, and come short of the glory of God."

What does it mean to "come short of the glory of God"? So often we repeat these verses over and over without stopping to think of the real meaning. "Glory" here means simply "the recognition" of God. What the verse actually declares is that a sinner lacks recognition on the part of God. It will help our understanding of Scripture if we examine the particular meaning of a word in a specific context. "Glory," of course, in some instances may refer to an attribute of God or merely to splendor, but let us not forget that it also means "recognition."

When Jesus Christ came from His eternity to our temporal world, He missed one thing, the glory that He had with the Father, that is, the recognition that He enjoyed with the Father, the honor that He had with the Father. It was impossible for man, even redeemed man, to give Him the same recognition, the same honor, the same renown that He had enjoyed with the Father in His preincarnate state. That in no sense meant that He left behind any part, or the whole, of His deity, or any or all of His divine attributes, but simply that by coming down here on earth He did not have the same recognition among men, among His creatures, even His redeemed ones, as He had with the co-eternal and co-equal Father. To recognize all that lies within another person, you must possess as much or more. A layman cannot possibly appreciate all the qualities and recognize all the abilities of a medical doctor. It takes a medical doctor of equal stature to recognize them. That is why, before a person is permitted to practice medicine, he is submitted to a professional state examination. In a similar way, only God the Father could recognize and appreciate all that was in God the Son. Jesus Christ could not find that recognition while here on earth among men. That is why He yearned for it and looked forward to having it again on His ascension from this earth.

In the 14th verse of the first chapter of his Gospel, John states that the disciples of Christ, those who believed, recognized two things in Him as they saw Him with their physical eyes. They supersensorily perceived with the eyes of faith (1) that He was of the same nature, of the same family, as the Father; He was *monogenees;* and (2) that He still had the glory that He had with the Father. While He was down here on earth, the Father still recognized Him as very God of very God, co-equal and co-eternal with Him, although this recognition was not given Him by all men. Don't forget that John 1:14 deals with the incarnate state of Jesus Christ. Neither His nature nor His power had changed at any time.

We note that the preposition used in John 1:14 and also in John 17:5 is the same, the Greek word *para.* This preposition holds the key to the understanding of the whole concept brought out here. *Para* actually means "beside, alongside." It is to be distinguished from two other Greek prepositions, *apo,* which fundamentally means "the starting point of something," and the preposition *ek* which generally means "out of" "from within." John uses the first preposition in 1:14 and 17:5, where he speaks of the glory of Jesus Christ which He had in His preincarnate state.

Now why is this preposition important? Because it shows us that Jesus Christ did not derive His glory from the Father. He did not take out of the Father a certain amount of glory which He had before He came to this earth, which was retained by the Father while He was here on earth, and which was going to be restored to Him after He left this earth. Nothing of the kind. John is merely speaking of the recognition which the Son has always had alongside the Father, beside the Father. The Father recognized the glory of the Son, and the Son recognized the glory of the Father.

When Jesus Christ came to this earth in human form, those among whom He moved recognized Him to be of the same nature as God and recognized the recognition that He had with or alongside His Father. That is the real meaning of the phrase "and we beheld his glory, the glory as of the only begotten of the Father." Actually, it could be paraphrased, "And we saw Jesus Christ with our physical eyes; we admired Him, for in Him we perceived supersensorily that He is of the same nature and family as God and therefore Infinity and Eternity, and our recognition was the same

93

as that which He had when He was alongside the Father. The recognition which the Father gave Him, we give Him, too, since we see Him as God incarnate."

It takes faith, the supernatural activity of the Holy Spirit in one's heart, to recognize all that Jesus Christ is. Not all who saw Jesus Christ accepted Him as God. Only those who received Him were given full understanding of Him. Only as God dwells within us can we have a true comprehension of God. Infinity must dwell within us in order that we may recognize its glory.

It is only those who accept Jesus Christ who can see Him in all His glory. They know that He is God and that He never ceased to be God. It is eternal suicide not to accept Jesus Christ.

CHAPTER 21

WAS JESUS CHRIST "A GOD" OR GOD?

". . . and the Word was God" (John 1:1c).

Thus far in our study of John's Gospel we have seen that the Word, Jesus Christ, "was" before the beginning of the world, was eternal. But since the only eternal One is God, the First Cause of all things, Jesus Christ must be God. However, His personality is to be distinguished from that of God the Father, and that distinction is made clear in the second part of the first verse, which literally translated reads, "And the Word had been toward God." Here John speaks of two personalities in the Godhead, co-equal, co-eternal, but not dependent on each other. (In this particular passage, of course, John is not speaking of the third personality of the Triune God, the Holy Spirit, of whom other parts of his Gospel speak more specifically, as for instance John 1:32; 14:26; 15:26; 16:13, etc.)

However, lest someone might misunderstand the distinction he makes between the two personalities — the *Logos,* Jesus Christ the Son, and God the Father — John goes on to make as clear a declaration as possible concerning the deity of the Word, or Jesus Christ. He says, "And God had been the Word."

This brings us to the third couplet, made up of the last part of the first verse and the last part of the 14th verse of John 1.

"And the Word was God . . .

Full of grace and truth."

The King James Version of John 1:1c reads, "And the Word was God," but in the original Greek, the word "God" comes immediately after the conjunction "and," rather than at the end of the clause. This was done deliberately in the Greek in order to emphasize what this Word really was.

In the three statements of the first verse of John 1, we have the answers to the three following questions:

1. Since when "was" the Word, Jesus Christ?

(Answer: from eternity, since before there was a beginning. "Before the beginning the Word had been.")

2. Who was this Word?

(Answer: He was a personality independent from the Father but in eternal fellowship and relationship with Him. "And the Word had been toward God.")

3. What was this Word?

(Answer: This Word, although independent of the Father God, was no less God than the Father. "And God had been the Word.")

Now it is true that there is no definite article before the word "God." This has induced those who want to make Jesus Christ an inferior personality to the Father, a created being instead of the eternal Creator, to translate this word as "a God" instead of "God." Are they justified in doing so from the linguistic point of view?

In this clause, "And God had been the Word," we have a verb, a subject, and a predicate. It is most essential in this case to find out which is the subject and which is the predicate — the verb, of course, clearly being "had been," or "was," as we have it in the King James translation.

In the previous two clauses, the subject has been "the Word," preceded in each instance by the definite article. It would be only natural to conclude that in this third clause the subject has not changed, that it is still "the Word." This is not only the subject of the three clauses of the first verse, but also of the 14th verse. "And the Word became flesh." And it is certainly understood as the subject of the next clause, "And the Word pitched his tent in us or among us." John speaks primarily about the Second Person of the

Trinity and not about the entire Godhead — the Father, the Son, and the Holy Spirit — in this particular doctrinal treatise. It is therefore highly unlikely that the subject of the clause, "And God had been the Word," is God. It is quite obviously "the Word."

"As a rule the predicate is without the article even when the subject uses it." So says one of the greatest Greek New Testament grammarians, A. T. Robertson, in his *Grammar of the Greek New Testament* (Doran, Fourth Edition, p. 767). Here we have the subject with the definite article, and the predicate without it. It is "the Word" and "God." "And God had been the Word." It is therefore not necessary for the definite article to precede the predicate "God" in order that the name God may have its full import. The order in which the words appear in this clause does not in any way influence us in determining which is the subject and which is the predicate.

Although the general practice is the one followed by John in not placing the definite article before "God," he could have placed it there. This, however, would have altered the linguistic structure so that the meaning would not be definite and specific. The two words under discussion in this clause, "God" and "the Word," would be interchangeable. We could say, for instance, "And the God had been the Word." Then "the Word" would become the predicate and "God" would become the subject. The words "God" and "the Word" are not convertible terms, even as the words "God" and "love" are not in I John 4:16, "God is love." In Greek it is "The God is love." The definite article "the" (*ho*) is used before God but not before "love." Why? Because "God" is the subject and "love" is the predicate. If the definite article also occurred before "love," then the two nouns would be interchangeable. We could also say, "Love is God," just as correctly as we could say, "God is love." But the Holy Spirit chose the Greek language in which to give us the New Testament revelation, and the Greek language is so specific and definite that only those who are ignorant of the language, or those who misconstrue it, can arrive at pernicious anti-Scriptural and unsound doctrines. If the Greek language allowed us to say "Love is God" just as readily as we say "God is love," then the God of the Bible would not be a person but simply an abstract quality. Correctly, then, A. T. Robertson notes, "When the article occurs with subject (or the subject is a personal pronoun or proper name) and predicate, both are definite, treated as identical, one and the same, and interchangeable." (Ibid, p. 768.)

If we were to translate the third clause of John 1:1 as "And the Word was 'a' God," then we should do the same in every other instance where the Greek word *Theos,* "God," is used without the definite article. John 1:18 would then have to be translated, "No man hath seen 'a' God at any time." How ridiculous that would be. How many gods do we have, anyway?

Let us not forget that in the first verse John deals, not with the historical Christ, but with the eternal One, the eternal *Logos,* who "was" before there was anything. The reason John leaves out the definite article before "God" in the first verse as he does in the 18th verse is that he may show us two things:

1. Christ's general character. Here Jelf's statement bears repeating: "The effect of the omission of the article is frequently that the absence of any particular definition or limitation of the notion brings forward its general character." (*A Grammar of the Greek Language,* by William Edward Jelf, John Henry, and James Parker, 1859, p. 124.) John wants to tell us here that the general character of the *Logos,* the Word of whom he is speaking, is God — God in His nature and all His attributes — and has always been that. There was no time when He was not God.

2. Christ's deity in general. Again we like what Jelf has to say: "Some words [and he refers, of course, to Greek words] are found both with and without the article, and seemingly with but little difference; but without the article they signify the general notion conceived of abstractedly, and not as in actual existence; with the article the objective existence is brought forward, as *Theos* (God), the Divinity; *Ho Theos* (the God), the God we worship." (Ibid,

p.124.) Thus we see that John in this first verse was referring, not to the Christ of history as He appeared on occasions in the Old Testament or at His incarnation, but to Christ in His eternal state. He wants to emphasize that His nature, His substance, is the same as that of God the Father. It is not His separate personality that is stressed here in the third clause, but His nature; not *who* He is, but *what* He is. He is God. His separate personality was stressed in the second clause of the first verse, and that is why in that clause the definite article appears before the word "God," "And the Word had been toward the God." "The God" in clause two refers to the personality of the Father; while "God" in the third clause refers to the nature of the Word as God.

That great English preacher, Joseph Parker, once said, "The divinity of the Son of God is not proved merely in proportions. I think that he who believes in the divinity of Christ has all history, etymology, and philosophy on his side. My dependence is not founded upon the construction of a phrase, or the mood and tense of a verb, and yet we have nothing to fear from that side. I rely upon his moral reach and spiritual compass. When he touched my soul into life, I did not call for a Greek grammar, or Hebrew lexicon, or volumes of encyclopedias, to find how the thing stood. I believe because 'once I was blind, and now I see.' The heart is sometimes a better interpreter than the understanding. What better proof do I want? 'He has redeemed my life from destruction.' "

Christ could not have redeemed and saved anybody if He were merely "a God." But He did save multitudes as the God of heaven who came down to this earth for the explicit purpose of redeeming mankind.

CHAPTER 22

WAS JESUS CHRIST MERELY DIVINE OR WAS HE GOD?

". . . and the Word was God" (John 1:1c).

———

There has probably been more controversy over the translation of the first verse of the Gospel of John than of any other verse in the New Testament. The third clause, especially, has given rise to much speculation. There are some, for instance, who would translate it "And the Word was divine." Among those who translate it thus is Moffat. Is he correct? How important is it whether the original Greek text states that Jesus Christ was "God" or was "divine"?

Many people conceive of Jesus Christ as a man who was so good, who lived such an exceptional life, and who performed such miracles that He achieved greater stature than anyone else. One of my philosophy professors once listed the great religious leaders of history, among whom he named Jesus Christ. His intent was to show us that all had the same beginning but that Jesus Christ outdid them all in His accomplishments. This is absolutely wrong. Jesus Christ did not begin His life here on earth like all the others, but He came down from heaven, from eternity. He did not originate down here and then go up, but He gave origin to all things and then came down to the world He had made. Jesus Christ could never have done what He did, if He were not what He was.

And He was not merely "divine," but "God" in all His fullness and essence. There are two Greek words that are quite similar but which must be distinguished, not only in their meaning, but also in their origin. One is the adjective *theios,* "divine," and the other the noun *Theos,* "God." There is a difference between the two. The terms are not interchangeable. What is divine is not necessarily God, but God is always divine.

Correspondingly we have two substantives which are derived from these words. From the adjective *theios,* "divine," we have *theiotees,* "divinity," and from the noun *Theos,* "God," we have *theotees,* "deity." It is definitely wrong to translate them both by the English term "Godhead," as was done in the New Testament in two instances (see Rom. 1:20 and Col. 2:9). In the first chapter of Romans the Apostle Paul is talking about the unregenerate man groping after God. Man tries to discern God in His creation. Is this possible? Can man really find God, the personality of God, in nature? Hardly. True, God does reveal Himself after a fashion in nature, but not fully. The full revelation of God was made in His Son, the Lord Jesus Christ. Nature reveals power and majesty behind it. And this power must exist in the One who made this world. If God in His fullness and essence could be known by man through nature and nature alone, His revelation through His Son would have been superfluous. Man can know so much of God through nature and no more.

Let us consider Romans 1:20, "For the invisible things of him from the creation of the world are clearly seen, being understood by the things that are made, even his eternal power and Godhead; so that they are without excuse." Now that word translated "Godhead" in the original Greek is *theiotees,* "divinity," coming from the adjective *theios,* "divine," and it does not mean "Godhead" at all but simply "divinity." It refers to the majesty and glory of God in His creation but not to the essence of His personality. Many people recognize the power of God in nature but fail to see Him with the eye of faith and appropriate Him. They know He is powerful and majestic, but they have not experienced Him as a Person in their hearts and lives. There is a great difference between these two states of being. Not all who recognize the power and majesty of

101

God possess God. Man can conceive of many divinities, but for God to become known to man He had to reveal Himself in the person of His Son.

The Apostle John, in his declaration in the third clause of the first verse of his Gospel, does not speak merely of some of the visible attributes of Jesus Christ which would indicate that He is divine, that He attained divinity, but declares that He is God, that He is deity who became humanity without ceasing to be deity. Man by accepting God through Jesus Christ becomes divine, but He does not become God. He has within him divine nature, but he has not become God.

The word *theotees,* "deity," occurs in Col. 2:9, "For in him [Jesus Christ] dwelleth all the fulness of the Godhead bodily." The word translated "Godhead" here is *theotees,* "deity," and not "divinity." It refers, not to the manifestation of Christ in His external acts, but to His essential nature.

It would, therefore, be totally wrong to translate the statement which John makes in John 1:1 as "and the Word was divine." The word which is used in the original Greek is *theos* "God," not *theios,* "divine." Jesus Christ did not merely have divine attributes, but He was God in His essence and nature. He was not a man who attained divinity, but God who humbled Himself to take upon Himself human nature in addition to His deity.

It was Napoleon who said, "Everything in Christ astonishes me. His spirit overawes me, and His will confounds me. His ideas and His sentiments, the truth which He announces, His manner of convincing, are not explained either by human observation, or the nature of things. His birth, and the history of His life; the profundity of His doctrine, which grapples the mightiest difficulties, and which is of those difficulties the most admirable solution; His Gospel; His apparition; His empire; His march across the ages and the realms, — every thing is for me a prodigy, a mystery insoluble, which plunges me into a reverie from which I cannot escape — a mystery which is there before my eyes, a mystery which I can neither deny nor explain. Here I see nothing human. The nearer I approach, the more carefully I examine. Everything is above me. Everything remains grand, — of a grandeur which overpowers. His religion is a revelation from an Intelligence which certainly is not that of man."

Napoleon certainly caught the meaning of the statement which John gave us, "And the word was God." This Intelligence which is responsible for the creation of the whole world is not human intelligence, nor is it intelligence that has some divine attributes, but it is deity, it is God. And only as such, as God, can Jesus Christ save anyone.

CHAPTER 23

THE INCARNATE CHRIST, THE REVELATION OF GOD'S GRACE

". . . full of grace and truth" (John 1:14c).

In our consideration of the first 18 verses of the first chapter of John's Gospel, it is most essential that we distinguish between two verbs that are used repeatedly. One refers to the eternity of Jesus Christ as God before becoming man, and the other to the historicity of Jesus Christ since His incarnation.

The verb *een,* which is the durative imperfect of the verb *eimi,* "to be," is purposely used in some verses and not in others. We find it in verse 1: "In the beginning was the Word, and the Word was with God, and the Word was God." Here reference is made to the continuous existence of Jesus Christ as God. The declaration is that Jesus Christ, as the Word, has always been.

Also in verse 2: "The same was in the beginning with God." Here again reference is made to the co-eternity of Jesus Christ with the Father. He "was" before there was a beginning.

But in verse 3 we have the use of an entirely different verb, *egeneto,* "were made." "All things were made by him; and without him was not any thing made that was made." Here reference is made to the creation of the world. That is an historical fact. The world had a beginning, and that is why the verb *gignomai,* "to become," is used in its various forms. The world is not eternal in its nature (i.e., it has not always been in existence), but only the One who made it.

Then in the 4th verse John reverts to the use of the verb *een,* which we might better translate "had been." "In him was life; and the life was the light of men." Jesus Christ did not acquire life at the time of His appearance on earth. He always had it, for He is the originator of all life.

And then, in the 6th verse, reference is made to the coming to this earthly scene of John the Baptist as a witness to and a forerunner of Jesus Christ. "There was a man sent from God, whose name was John." This should rather be translated "There *came* a man sent from God." John the Baptist was not eternal, and that is why the verb *een,* "was" or "had been," is not used of him.

In the 8th verse the writer of the Gospel wants to make sure that we do not attribute to the forerunner of Christ anything that does not belong to him, and that is why he says, "He was not that Light, but was sent to bear witness of the Light." Here the verb *een* is used. John had not been that Light eternally. He came to be the reflecting light. He is not the Eternal Light, as Jesus Christ was.

In verse 9 attention again is called to the person of Jesus Christ: "That was the true Light, which lighteth every man that cometh into the world." Christ did not begin to be the Light from the time of His appearance on earth. He had always been the Light of the World.

In verse 10 we have both verbs used. "He was [*een*] in the world, and the world was made [*egeneto*] by him, and the world knew him not." Jesus Christ had been before the beginning of the existence of the world. He had to be, in order to be the cause of the world, in order to make the world. He is eternal, while the world is temporal.

Then, in the 14th verse, we find the declaration that the eternal Word became the incarnate Christ. "And the Word became [*egeneto,* not 'was made' as the King James Version has it] flesh." He was not eternally in the flesh, but only from the time of His incarnation.

In the 15the verse, John the Baptist declares, "This was [*een*]

105

he of whom I spake, He that cometh after me is preferred before me: for he was [*een*] before me." John says that Jesus Christ was in existence before him, despite the fact that Jesus Christ was born about six month later. Physically, then, Jesus Christ was not before John the Baptist, but as the eternal *Logos*, the Word, He had been.

It is essential for us to remember the distinction between these two verbs in this context, *een*, referring to eternity, and *egeneto*, referring to an historical fact and setting. Jesus Christ *een*, always "had been," while John the Baptist and the world and everything in the world *egeneto*, "became," came into being by Him who always was.

The last clause of the first verse corresponds with the last clause of verse 14. "And the Word was God . . . full of grace and truth." The verb translated "was" is the Greek *een*. Jesus Christ in His preincarnate state had been God. And the reason He came down to earth was to manifest to us His nature as God. It is not easy for God to manifest to us human beings the fullness of His nature. He is infinite; we are finite. He had to use finite language to make clear to us infinite truth. The best that man could do in understanding the nature of God in Jesus Christ was to observe some of His main attributes and characteristics. By noting how Jesus Christ fed the hungry, healed the sick, comforted the afflicted, we come to the conclusion that He was the personification of compassion. His acts of love demonstrated to us that He was love.

Thus the two attributes of Jesus Christ that stand out as He becomes man are grace and truth. As a mere human being He could not have shown these to us. Only as God could He be full of grace and truth. And because of this he can be called grace, He can be called truth. If Jesus Christ manifested only human grace and human truth, they would not only be imperfect but of little value to other human beings. There is a reason for the inspired writer of this Gospel using the word "full" in this statement, and there is also a reason for our connecting it with the last statement of verse 1. Only as God could Jesus Christ be *full* of grace and truth. Man can perform acts of grace and acts of truth, but no man in his natural state is either full of grace or full of truth in the sense that God is.

What John really declares is that, when Jesus Christ came down here to earth, He came primarily to show us that as God His nature was that of grace and truth. In order to enable human beings to understand that, He had to come and live among us and in us. Without that, we would have had no real sense or understanding of God's grace and truth.

CHAPTER 24

WHY GRACE BEFORE TRUTH?

". . . full of grace and truth" (John 1:14c).

God has many attributes. He is goodness and at the same time He is truth. He is omniscient, and in His omniscience He knows who will accept Him and who will reject Him. He is also all-merciful. In His mercy and grace He extends salvation to all. The interplay of these attributes of God constitutes one of the greatest of mysteries to the human mind. We are unable fully to comprehend them. It is the old problem of man's finite understanding trying to grasp the workings and the nature of the Infinite. It is just impossible. And yet the Scriptures do reveal to us in a goodly measure the interplay of some of God's attributes.

Only in the Gospel of John do we find two of God's attributes spoken of in combination. They are "grace" and "truth," which are mentioned in John 1:14 and 17: "And the Word became flesh, and dwelt among us, (and we beheld his glory, the glory as of the only begotten of the Father,) full of *grace and truth* . . . For the law was given by Moses, but *grace and truth* came by Jesus Christ." Nowhere else in the New Testament are grace and truth spoken of together in this manner and order. And they refer to the person of Jesus Christ as the incarnate God, and not to His preincarnate and eternal state. This is not coincidental; there is a definite purpose in it. John wants to show us that in the person of Jesus Christ we can see God as grace and truth.

What was the primary purpose of Christ's coming to this earth? He has answered this Himself. In His conversation with Nicodemus

He said, "For God sent not his Son into the world to condemn the world; but that the world through him might be saved" (John 3:17). The truth of the matter is that the world in its sinful state deserved condemnation. Why does a court exist? To punish the guilty, of course, but, before punishment is imposed by the judge, every effort is made to discover the truth about a situation or the act or acts of a person accused. Condemnation presupposes the discovery of truth. The two are interwoven. This is the sense in which John uses the term "truth" here in relation to grace. When Jesus Christ came into the world, He found it worthy of divine condemnation and punishment. He knew that fact before He came, of course, since He was absolute Truth, One who knew without the necessity of hearing human evidence. In fact, that is why He came into the world, because the world was guilty and merited condemnation.

Truth involves justice. When a person is found guilty of an offense, the court proceeds to apply justice, to impose a righteous punishment. We know that "the wages of sin is death" (Rom. 6:23). Guilty humanity cannot escape divine punishment. But must all mankind die eternally? Could no one pay the penalty for the race? Such a person would have to be sinless and in this sense different from other human beings for his death to be able to atone for the sins and the guilt of all humanity. No man from this earth would suffice in this respect. It would have to be someone sent from above. And that One was Jesus Christ, the eternal Word.

Thus the primary purpose for which Christ came to earth, as is so clearly and unmistakably declared in John 1:14, was to die, that the blood in His flesh shed on Calvary's cross might become the propitiation for the sins of the world. God is a just and true God. He cannot bypass sin nor the punishment for sin. Nor did He, for out of love He brought it to bear upon His own Son, the Lord Jesus Christ. And because of the forgiveness offered to all as a result of Christ's death, it could be said that God in Christ was "full of grace and truth" and not "truth and grace."

The reason "grace" is put before "truth" in this verse is not to

109

indicate to us in any way that one attribute of God is greater than another and supersedes the other. The attributes of God run in parallel lines, if we may conceive of them in this inadequate human fashion. When and why they meet is beyond us, but the results are definitely in our favor. During the dispensation of grace, which is commonly known as the time since Jesus came to earth and in which we are now living, grace is offered to all, because Jesus Christ suffered the punishment for the sins of all. Now is our opportunity to appropriate this grace offered us by Jesus Christ and because of Him. The time will come when there will be no more "grace and truth" for those who have rejected the opportunities of the day of grace. The day will come, after this dispensation is over, when it will be all "truth" and no grace. The suffering of Christ will no more avail for our sins, and man will have to suffer for his own sin. Yes, Jesus Christ came to introduce God as "full of grace and truth." He manifested that fully in His person.

Many of us try to hide the truth because it would discredit us in the eyes of others. But, in the person of Jesus Christ, the truth about man's sinfulness was fully unveiled yet gloriously atoned for. You need not hide your sinfulness from God. Bare it before Him, for He is full of grace and truth. "Grace," or *charis,* actually denotes "God's grace and favor towards mankind or to any individual, which, as a free act, excludes merit, and is not hindered by guilt, but forgives sin; it thus stands out in contrast with (*erga*) works, (*nomos*) law, (*hamartia*) sin." (Hermann Cremer, *Biblico Theological Lexicon of New Testament Greek,* T. & T. Clark, Edinburgh, 1954, p. 573.) It seems that, the more we lay bare our hearts before God, the more we experience the fullness of His grace. However sinful you may be, remember that in Jesus Christ it is always "grace and truth." It is no use trying to hide the truth, for He knows it anyway, and the reason He came to earth "full of grace and truth" was that He knew the whole truth about you.

This is true, not only before our individual salvation, but after it as well. We must not think that after a person is saved he ceases to

110

need the grace of God above all else. Dr. W. P. Mackay, in his book *Grace and Truth under Twelve Aspects* (Edinburgh, John H. Bell, 1903), gives the following illuminating illustration:

Let us suppose, he says, that a convict, who has just finished his term of penal servitude, wishes to lead an honest life. He comes to a man who has a large jewelry establishment and who requires a night watchman. He is engaged to watch this building through the quiet hours of the night when he has everything under his care and every opportunity to rob his employer. On the first evening, he meets one of his old companions, who questions him, "What are you doing here?"

"I'm the night watchman."

"Over this jeweler's shop?"

"Yes."

"Does he know what you are?"

"No, no, be silent; if he knew, I should be dismissed."

"Suppose I let it out that you are a returned convict!"

"Oh, I pray don't; it would be my last day here, and I wish to be honest."

"Well, you have to give me some money to keep quiet."

"Very well, but don't let anyone know."

Thus the poor man would be in sad fear and trembling, lest it should come to the ears of his employer what his previous character had been.

Let us suppose, however, that instead of the employer's engaging the man in ignorance of his character, he went to the convict's cell and said, "Now I know you — what you are, what you've done, every robbery you've committed, and that you are worse than you believe yourself to be. I am about to give you a chance of becoming honest. I'll trust you as my night watchman over my valuable goods." The man is faithful at his post. He meets old companion after old companion, who threaten to inform upon him. He asks, "What will you tell about me?"

"That you were the ringleader of housebreakers."

111

"Yes, but my master knows all that better than you do; he knows me better than I know myself."

Of course, this silences them forever. This employer, then, would be full of grace and truth. But there could hardly be a human master of this kind. Jesus Christ is the only Master who is "full of grace and truth." Jesus Christ is gracious to you and me because He knows the truth about us, that we deserve nothing but hell. But through His grace heaven can be our share, if we personally and by faith appropriate His grace.

CHAPTER 25

THE GRACE OF THE GLORY OF CHRIST

". . . full of grace and truth" (John 1:14c).

A piece of jewelry was once submitted to the most expert appraiser in New York City. He applied his tests for weight, cut, color, and the like, to the emeralds, balanced the gold against the little brass weights on his scales, considered a minute, and then wrote upon the sheet a valuation which was so small a fraction of the expected figure that the eager customer uttered a cry of dismay.

"They are not first-rate stones, you see," he explained.

"Not first-rate?" cried the owner. "How can that be? They were a royal gift."

"Ah," cried the gray-haired connoisseur, "I have handled many royal gifts and long ago learned that kings keep their best for themselves."

How true. There is one King, however, who had the greatest glory that could ever be imagined. His glory was far greater than any human glory. It was the glory as of the only begotten of the Father. It was no less than the glory of God, for He was God Himself. And this was Jesus Christ.

The 14th verse of John 1 reads, "And the Word became flesh, and dwelt among us, (and we beheld his glory, the glory as of the only begotten of the Father,) full of grace and truth." We have to determine who or what was full of grace and truth.

Unlike English adjectives, the Greek adjectives have genders and can be declined. This is because the nouns also have genders. For instance, the word "glory," *doxa,* in Greek is feminine, and

113

here in this verse the word "glory" is in the accusative case (*doxan*). If, therefore, the adjective "full" agrees in gender with the word "glory," it, too, has to be in the accusative, which would be *pleeree*. One of the Greek manuscripts of the New Testament does have this adjective as *pleeree*, which grammatically would correspond with the word "glory." And to this most of the Greek Fathers agree, such as Irenaeus, Athanasius, Chrysostom, and others. There is a great lesson in this reading of the adjective "full." It is as if John wanted to qualify the glory of the Lord Jesus Christ as He appeared in human form.

The glory of Christ in His preincarnate state was unsurpassable. It was the glory of God, the Creator. But the greatest glory of His glory, insofar as we human beings are concerned, was manifested when He came to this earth to die for us and through His death to bestow upon us the glory of becoming the children of God, a glory which is greater than that which we lost when we sinned in Adam. In other words, the greatest glory of God was Jesus Christ, and the greatest glory of Jesus Christ was His humiliation for our sakes. Here was a King who did not keep the best for Himself, but gave even Himself for us. His glory was full of grace and truth.

It was the grace of Christ which made the glory of God accessible to man. Man hardly appreciates greatness, majesty, and glory in another that does not bring him any personal benefit. A king who does not seek through his greatness to serve his people is sooner or later dethroned. Greatness that is selfish is not real greatness. The glory of God became the light of men in the person of Jesus Christ and the grace that He manifested on earth. "Greatness," wrote Beecher, "lies not in being strong, but in the right using of strength; and strength is not used rightly when it only serves to carry a man above his fellows for his own solitary glory. He is greatest whose strength carries up the most hearts by the attraction of his own."

It is related that, when the story of West India slavery was told to the Moravians, and it was said that it was impossible to reach the slave population because they were so separated from the ruling classes, two Moravian missionaries offered themselves and said, "We will go and be slaves on the plantations, and work and toil, if need be under the lash, to get right beside the poor slaves and instruct them." And they left their homes, went to the West Indies, went to work on the plantations as slaves and by the side of slaves, to get close to the hearts of slaves; and the slaves heard them, and their hearts were touched, because they had humbled themselves to their condition. That was grand; it was glorious; and yet Christ's example was more glorious, for He stepped down from heaven to earth to get close to our side; He laid Himself down beside us that we might feel throbbings of His bosom, be encircled in the embrace of His loving arms, be drawn right up beside Him, and hear Him whisper in our ears, "God is full of grace and truth."

What would be the meaning, however, of this declaration of John if the adjective "full" were taken as *pleerees?* It would refer to the Word, which has been the subject right along. Origen favors this reading. And, indeed, there is hardly any difference in the exegesis of the passage. Whether "full" refers to the glory of Christ or to His person makes no real difference. The first would declare how great His humiliation was contrasted to His greatness, and the second would point out that in His nature Jesus Christ is "full of grace and truth." John declares that in the Jesus Christ of history we saw Him physically, gazed at Him and perceived His glory; we recognized that He was God incarnate, and furthermore we perceived His grace and truth. Three things characterized Jesus Christ in human form — His glory, His grace, His truth.

We must be careful lest we think that Jesus Christ became gracious by engaging in acts of grace and truth. The miracles and the benefactions of Christ were the natural and voluntary outcome of His inner Being. Grace ensues in acts of graciousness, and truth results in truthfulness. The most amazing thing was that Jesus Christ came to show His grace, not toward friends, but toward enemies. Herein was His glory made more glorious. You remember the great argument which Jesus Christ had in the temple with the Jews of His day concerning the matter of His claim that he was the eternal God manifest in the flesh. His enemies took up stones to throw at Him. In John 8:59 we read these amazing words, "Then took they up stones to cast at him: but Jesus hid himself, and went out of the temple, going through the midst of them, and so passed by." He could have had every one of them slain just by the word of His mouth, for it was He who had created the world. And yet His greatness and glory were manifested in His grace toward His enemies, so that they might know that He is Truth, whom to know is life eternal.

The only way in which you can participate in the glory of Christ is in believing in Him and allowing His truth so to possess you that you will recognize that you are nothing and that in His grace you can possess everything, for you can possess Him.

CHAPTER 26

WAS CHRIST DEPENDENT ON THE FATHER?

"The same was in the beginning with God" (John 1:2).

———

A great deal of controversy concerning the person of Jesus Christ has been carried on throughout the centuries. The first two verses of the Gospel of John serve as a corrective for three misapprehensions about the person of Christ. First, that of the Arians — who regard Christ as a being inferior to God — and their successors, such as the so-called Russellites or Jehovah's Witnesses. Second, that of the Sabellians, who deny any distinction of persons in the Trinity and say that God sometimes manifested Himself as Father, sometimes as Son, and sometimes as Spirit, and that the Father and the Spirit suffered on the cross. Third, that of the Socinians and Unitarians, who say that Jesus Christ was not God but man, a most holy and perfect man, but only a man. Unfortunately, many persons within the various denominations reject the deity of Jesus Christ; yet this is the basis of the true Christian faith. No wonder most of our modern Christianity is so sadly impotent. Jesus Christ as a mere man cannot save anyone, but as God He can save all who come to Him.

John the Evangelist does not want to leave the least doubt concerning the eternity and the independent co-existence of Jesus Christ with the Father, so after his threefold declaration in verse 1 he summarizes and reemphasizes the matter by saying in verse 2, "The same was in the beginning with God." This declaration comes immediately after the definite and unmistakable assertion that "the Word was God." Again John is afraid that someone might think that, because of his statement that "the Word was God," Jesus Christ has no existence independent from that of the Father. "The Word was God" and yet a different personality from that of God the Father. Truly this is beyond our understanding, because we are dealing here with facts of eternity and infinity which, though plainly revealed to us, are difficult of comprehension by our finite minds.

No one could possibly unfold the fullness of Christ. Though something of Christ is unfolded in one age and something in another, eternity itself cannot fully unfold Him. "I see something," said Luther, "which blessed Augustine saw not; and those that come after me will see that which I see not." It is in the studying of Christ, as in the planting of a newly discovered country; at first men sit down by the seaside, upon the skirts and borders of the land, and there they dwell; but by degrees they search further and further into the heart of the country. The best of us are yet but upon the borders of this vast thing called eternity, infinity.

The word with which this second verse begins is *houtos*, in Greek. Literally translated it means "this one, this person," referring to the Word of whom John spoke in verse 1. He places emphasis upon this demonstrative pronoun. It is as if he were saying "I am not speaking about a different person. It's the same One." *Houtos* is in the masculine singular, indicating the stress that John wants to place on the fact that this Word he spoke about is not merely an idea, intelligence, but that it is a person — Intelligence personified.

Then again, the verb that is used here is the one which was consistently used in the first verse. It is the verb *een*, which is the durative imperfect of the verb *eimi*, "to be." We could translate it more correctly in this instance as "had been." This Person, the Word, Jesus Christ, "had been" before there was a beginning. The expression "in the beginning" is exactly the same here as in verse 1, which we fully discussed in our booklet, *God Becomes Man.* John is saying that this Word was in existence before the beginning

118

of the created world. Therefore He was eternal. But by sheer logical deduction we know that only God is eternal. There cannot be two first causes. There is only One. And since Jesus Christ, the Word, is the One, He must be God. Jesus Christ "was" before there was anything else at all. His eternity is an argument for His oneness with the Father.

Jesus Christ, by His constant designation as the Son, must not be considered as belonging within time and space. Take as an illustration the sun and its rays. Does the radiance of the sun proceed from the substance of the sun itself or from some other source? We all know that it proceeds from the substance itself. Yet, though the radiance proceeds from the sun itself, we cannot say that it is later in point of time than the existence of that body, since the sun has never appeared without its rays. It is for this reason, says Chrysostom, that Paul calls Christ "brightness" (Heb. 1:3), setting forth thereby His being from God and His eternity. The fact that Jesus Christ, as the Word, is presented as a separate personality from God the Father does not mean that He is less eternal, less infinite, and therefore less God and less responsible for the creation of the world, than God the Father.

The distinction between the Word and God the Father is further made clear by the expression "with God." Unfortunately, this is not the correct translation of the original Greek, *pros ton theon,* which should rather be translated "toward God." It is the same phrase as in the second clause of the first verse. It does not mean "with," for that would indicate a dormant and dependent relationship of the Son with the Father. This preposition *pros* indicates an active and equal relationship between the two parties. It is not as if the one is a stronger magnet than the other, attracting it to himself. There was no creation of the one by the other, nor is there any dependence for sustenance. It is a fellowship in eternity. And exactly because it concerns the fellowship of the infinite personalities of the Godhead in eternity, we finite beings within time and space cannot understand it. If we could do so, why was it then necessary for Jesus Christ to come to this earth to become the full revelation of God to us, to become God's expression and speech to us?

The last phrase of our verse places the definite article before the word "God," which is missing in the last clause of verse 1. As we saw in our studies of verses 18 and 1, the definite article is omitted before the word "God" because the stress is on the general character of the invisibility, infinity, and eternity of God. We are told in the third clause of verse 1 that the substance of the Word is exactly the same as that of God, that Jesus Christ is deity. Here in the 2nd verse it says literally, "This person had been toward the God." Why the article? Simply because John wants to make it clear that he is definitely referring, not to the Godhead in its triunity, but to God the Father. Otherwise, if there was no need for individualization, there would be no necessity of using the article. (W. E. Jelf, *A Grammar of the Greek Language,* Vol. II — Syntax, Third Edition, John Henry and James Parker, 1859, p. 123.) In verse 18, the distinction between the two personalities is made clear by the explicit mention of the Father, "God [no article] no one has seen at any time; [the] only-begotten God [the one fully God], the one who has always been *in the bosom of the Father,* he hath exegeted him." Here in verse 2, instead of using the specific word "Father," John uses the definite article before "God" to indicate the individual personality of the Father. Thus, if we were to give an exegesis of this 2nd verse of John 1, we would put it this way: "This person had been before the beginning of the creation toward God the Father." Thus the distinction between the personalities of God the Word (i.e., God the Son) and God the Father is made crystal clear. And it is very important that we make it plain that we are not worshiping many Gods but one God in three persons, although John here deals with only two, the third One being the Writer, through John, of this inspired record.

CHAPTER 27

THE MYSTERY OF THE UNIVERSE SOLVED

"ALL THINGS were made by him" (John 1:3a).

The first two verses of the Gospel of John contain four important statements concerning the eternity and nature of the person of Jesus Christ called the Word, the *Logos.*

1. "In the beginning was the Word"—Before there was anything, the Word had been.

2. "And the Word was with God"—a declaration of the eternal independent fellowship of the Word with God the Father.

3. "And the Word was God"—i.e., God the Word. Although Jesus Christ was independent of the Father in personality, in substance He was very God of very God.

4. "The same was in the beginning with God."—Here there is a distinction between the eternal personalities, although they are co-equal and co-eternal.

Having made these declarations concerning the person and nature of Jesus Christ in His eternal state, John moves on in the 3rd verse to the work of the *Logos,* the Word, the Christ. Jesus Christ as God is never to be conceived of as inactive. He existed before the visible creation, and this creation is the result of His work. The 3rd verse, then, deals with the first work of Jesus Christ. "All things were made by him; and without him was not any thing made that was made." The truth is first stated positively and then negatively. Everything was made by Him and there is nothing that was not made by Him.

Why does John speak of the work of the Word in addition to what he has already said about His person and nature? And why in this particular order? We usually invite people to look at the magnificence of God's creation in order to point out to them the necessity of a Creator. But John starts with the Creator and the description of His personality. Why? It is because Jesus Christ could not have done what He did without being what He was. How nonsensical of people to tell us to pay attention to what Jesus Christ did and not to be concerned with what Jesus Christ was. It takes an architect to rear a cathedral; it takes a sculptor to cut forms of symmetry and grace from marble; it takes a painter to depict life on his canvas; it takes a machinist to construct engines that can serve humanity. And it took God to create the world. The recognition of God as eternal, omnipotent, omniscient, and omnipresent constitutes the solution of the riddle of the universe.

A recent newspaper item stated that a young French physical scientist has perfected Einstein's Ecumenical Equation, which he believed would provide the solution to the mystery of creation and the explanation of the laws of nature. Man always wishes to find the solution of the mysteries of nature within nature, as if he were inescapably a slave of nature. If you start with God, as John did, then nature is not a riddle. If, however, you begin with a natural God, a merely human Jesus and not a supernatural One, then not only will the universe constitute a riddle to you, but Jesus Christ will also be a riddle, for you cannot explain the supernatural things He did. It is therefore logical and natural for John to start with "the God," to tell us what He is and since when He has existed, before he tells us of what He did.

But John has another reason for starting with the deity of Christ before going on to tell us of His work of creation. He follows what we call the deductive method of reasoning. We accept an axiom, a principle, as true, and from that we derive many other truths. We accept Jesus Christ's deity. We accept Him as God and therefore omnipotent and eternal. Therefore there is nothing that He cannot do, and there is nothing or nobody who was before He was. When we accept God as omnipotent and existing before everything and

122

everybody, we shall naturally see on all nature, as it were, the stamp, "Made by God." In the inductive process of reasoning, we begin with the created world and, recognizing that things could not just create themselves, we are forced to stamp them in our minds "Made by an Unknown." Starting with the creation, we arrive at the idea of the necessity of a Creator, but even this idea will be finite, for the finite mind of man can only produce finite ideas. The idea of infinity has to come from outside ourselves; it has to be revealed truth. In other words, we cannot get to God, the real God of the Bible, the revealed God, unless we start with God, and that is exactly what John does here. He starts with God, and it must logically follow that there is nothing that does not bear the mark of God's workmanship upon it.

Many people challenge God to do certain things in their lives or in nature as a condition for their believing in Him. The Lord Jesus performed innumerable miracles when He was down here on earth, but not all who viewed these miracles believed on Him and accepted Him as God eternal and omnipotent. The faith of those who had accepted Him was strengthened, as we read in the account of the miracle of making water into wine at Cana of Galilee. "This beginning of miracles did Jesus in Cana of Galilee, and manifested forth his glory; *and his disciples believed on him*" (John 2:11). They were already His disciples, but they had their faith confirmed, strengthened. But many unbelievers, after seeing His miracles, hated Him and opposed Him all the more. If you start with yourself, you will come up with innumerable questions to which you will not find many satisfactory answers. You are likely to go around in circles; but if you start with God, you will find no more riddles, nor will you be as naive as our French atomic scientist who thinks he has found the formula of the mystery of creation and the laws of nature. Start with God if you want to get to God. Start with God if you want to be the master of nature and not its slave.

The Greek word with which our verse starts is *panta*, translated "all things" in the King James Version. In the Greek, the definite article is omitted before this adjective in order to make the meaning more absolute. John wants to speak of more than what we can see here and now. He wants to encompass the totality of things at all times—those that we have discovered about the past, those that we now have, and everything appertaining to the future. In other words, he leaves nothing to man to claim as his own creation. All man does with his great achievements and explorations is to discover things already existing. There may be stars and systems in this universe of ours of which we are not aware. These are all included in the *panta*, in the "all," of our verse. Whether we know about them or not, they are all there as part of God's creation.

The word *panta* used by the Apostle here is the plural nominative of the neuter *pan*. He uses this to stress, not only the absolute totality of things, but also their individuality within that totality. The word as used here also means "all kinds of things." (Liddell and Scott, *A Greek English Lexicon*, Oxford, 1958, p. 1345.) God created each thing qualitatively, as the Old Testament says, "after its kind." In Genesis 1:21, for instance, we read, "And God created great whales, and every living creature that moveth, which the waters brought forth abundantly, *after their kind*, and every winged fowl *after his kind*: and saw that it was good." In other words, God created monkeys to remain monkeys and never to change into human beings. If they did change, how did some manage to achieve it and others not? There may be a development in the species but not a change of the species. That is what is implied by the word *panta*, "all," here.

CHAPTER 28

HOW CAN CHRIST BE BOTH THE CAUSE AND THE AGENT OF CREATION?

"All things were made BY him" (John 1:3a).

Many years ago, the council of ministers which examined me for ordination put before me some very difficult theological questions, as such councils usually like to do. One of them was "Who created the world exclusively and specifically, God the Father, God the Son, or God the Holy Spirit?" This question pricked not only my ears, but also the ears of everyone present. Considered superficially, this question might not seem too difficult on first hearing. Yet it seems to be a question to which there can hardly be a conclusive answer.

The three persons in the Godhead are distinct, and yet in each dwells the fullness of the Godhead. This is a truth that we must always remember as we think of the various activities and particular ministries of each person of the Godhead. In each activity there is the fullness of God, for the particular work of each One could not be accomplished if each One was not fully God. For instance, Jesus Christ in becoming man could not convict anyone of his sinfulness unless He was fully God. But now what about the creation of the universe?

John 1:3 says, "All things were made by him; and without him was not any thing made that was made." Reference, of course, is made here to Jesus Christ. In our previous study we saw that the adjective *panta,* translated "all things," in its absolute sense means the totality of everything animate and inanimate, known or

125

unknown, in the past, present, and future. After the word *panta*, "all," comes the preposition *dia*, translated "by" in the King James Version. "All things were made by him." In the English language, however, the preposition "by" is so vast in its meaning, and encompasses so many things, that it is not at all a fair translation of the Greek preposition *dia*. A better translation would be "through," making Jesus Christ the medium, the agent of creation.

If we carefully study the history of the word *dia*, we shall find that it is kin to *duo* ("two") or *dis* ("twice"), with the resultant idea of "between, in two." In its basic meaning, the preposition *dia* indicates the intermediary between two things, two persons, or the cause and the end result. This preposition is found in many compound words such as "diagram." What is a diagram? It is something that stands between the conception of something and its actual construction. The diagram of an architect is his sketch. And what is that? It is that which stands between his thought, his conception of the building, and the actual building. Another word is "diaphragm." What is a diaphragm? It is something that shuts off the contact between two things or two elements.

Here John tells us that "All things were made through him," through Jesus Christ, through the eternal *Logos*. It is as though he were telling us that Jesus Christ stands between the Creator and the creature, as the cause of the latter. He becomes, in other words, the executive agent of the Godhead without for one moment ceasing to be God. There is a marvelous and mysterious working co-operation among the persons of the Trinity. Thus we can say that God created the world through the Word, through Jesus Christ. Who created the world exclusively and specifically? God through Jesus Christ. But since in God there are all three persons of the Godhead—the Father, the Son, and the Holy Spirit—then all three participated in the creation of the universe. Specifically, Jesus Christ became the medium, the agent of creation. But since in Him dwelt all the fullness of the Godhead (Col. 1:19; 2:9), there is a way

126

in which we could say that all three persons of the Trinity were in Christ when the world was created. Let us remind ourselves again, however, that we as men find it impossible to comprehend the working relationships of the infinite God in three persons. This is as much as we have had revealed to us. If our minds could take in more, God would have revealed more. The truth about what is beyond us must be so majestic and so much higher than our present condition and state that we are just incapable of comprehending it. The same is true of life after death. It must be so much above what we have here and now that it would be impossible for us to understand it even if God did reveal it to us.

Thus we find Jesus Christ standing between God and the creation, fully responsible for it as the agent who brought it into being. We have the same working relationship between the persons of the Triune God when it comes to the redemption of the created world. Since Christ as the *Logos,* the Word, was the agent through whom the world was created, He became also the agent through whom the world was redeemed. He, the eternal Word, then became the agent of creation and the agent of redemption. That is why it is claimed throughout the Scriptures that it is through Christ and Christ alone that we, the fallen creation of God, are saved. May we not only enjoy the creation of God, but by faith appropriate the redemption of God through Jesus Christ. Thus Jesus Christ becomes not only the mediator of creation but also of redemption. "For there is one God, and one mediator between God and men, the man Christ Jesus" (I Tim. 2:5).

Not for one moment, however, should we conceive of Jesus Christ as being in any way inferior in essence to God the Father, or any less than God because He became the agent of creation and redemption. He can be both the cause—the origin—and the medium. And only as God eternal could He be that. Only as God could He be two things at one time, and in two places at once. You and I could never do it. The fact that, as God, Jesus Christ could be both the origin and the medium of creation is indicated in Romans

11:36, "For of [ex] him, and through [dia] him, and to [eis] him, are all things." I Cor. 8:6 is also a pertinent verse, "But to us there is but one God, the Father, of [ex] whom are all things, and we in him; and one Lord Jesus Christ, by [dia] whom are all things, and we by [dia] him."

And then we read in Genesis 1:26, "And God said, Let *us* make man in *our* image, after *our* likeness." God created man and everything else through His Word, and yet in one sense all three persons of the Trinity participated in the work of creation, even as all three participate in the work of redemption and salvation of man.

The verb used here is *egeneto,* "became or came into existence." All things came into existence through Him, through Jesus Christ. This verb is entirely different from the verbs used thus far concerning the person of Jesus Christ in eternity. The only thing that the Word, the *Logos,* "became" was flesh, when He became man in order to save man. But He never "became" Word; He always "was" the Word.

This verb in the aorist, *egeneto,* "came into existence," takes us back to the seven days of the creation of the world. This happened at a certain given time in history, indicating that there was a "time" when there was neither time nor space nor the things in them. This verb definitely precludes the belief in the eternity of creation, that all things were from the beginning. Only the Creator, the Word, was in the beginning. Everything else came into being at a certain time in history.

CHAPTER 29

WHO CREATED EVIL?

". . . AND WITHOUT HIM was not any thing made that was made" (John 1:3b).

———

Many times for the sake of emphasis it is first necessary to state something positively and then negatively. For instance, someone may say, "This is the only place I have visited today; I did not go anywhere else." Such a statement is the one about creation and the agent of creation which we find in John 1:3. "All things were made by him; and without him was not any thing made that was made." In this study we shall deal with the negative part of the statement. "And without him was not any thing made that was made." What is the real point of this negative repetition?

"And without him." There is no doubt that reference is made here to the Word, the *Logos,* who is the subject of these opening verses of John. The Greek for "without" is *chooris,* which as a preposition means "without or apart from." Here, of course, since reference is made to the Word, to Jesus Christ in His eternal state, it means that nothing exists which was made apart from the activity of Jesus Christ.

The first thing that we learn from this is that our created world is not eternal. There was a time when this world did not exist. Of course, time did not exist before that, either. Likewise a time will come when the created world in its present form will cease to exist and will be replaced by a new heaven and a new earth. The Apostle Peter clearly states all this in his Second Epistle, chapter 3, verse 10-13. "But the day of the Lord will come as a thief in the night; in the which the heavens shall pass away with a great noise, and the

129

elements shall melt with fervent heat, the earth also and the works that are therein shall be burned up. Seeing then that all these things shall be dissolved, what manner of persons ought ye to be in all holy conversation and godliness, looking for and hasting unto the coming of the day of God, wherein the heavens being on fire shall be dissolved, and the elements shall melt with fervent heat? Nevertheless we, according to his promise, look for new heavens and a new earth, wherein dwelleth righteousness." Therefore we come to the conclusion that what exists apart from God Himself is not eternal. In its present form it had a beginning and it will have an end.

The second important lesson that this preposition *chooris,* "without," teaches us is that the created world in its present form and status lacks self-creativity. Things and people did not become what they are of their own volition and in their own strength. They could not be what they are without God's directive or permissive will. Observe that we said "directive or permissive will." As you look around you or within, you will see that in our present world both evil and good exist together. Did God—or even more accurately did Jesus Christ, since He is spoken of here—actually create the evil things as they exist today? No, we do not believe that He did, for God is good and He can only have created that which is good. Evil results only from man's original disobedience to God. And this applies not only to the evils that personally beset man but also nature, for the whole of nature has been corrupted by man's sin. God is holy, and, since He is holy, when man disobeyed Him, He could not but allow him to suffer the consequences of his choice and disobedience, and that must be the opposite of the consequence of obedience to the Creator. Man desired his separation from God through his disobedience to His law, and in that separation lay the beginning of all evil. God actually created all things in their original form good and holy, separated unto Himself. But at the same time He gave man, the center of His creation, the privilege of choosing to preserve that relationship with his Creator.

130

Man chose not to, and therefore in his estrangement from his Creator he has turned himself and the world around him into a miserable state, so miserable that it took the coming of God into the world in the person of Jesus Christ to redeem man and to re-establish his relationship with the Creator. Thus things in their present form could not be what they are without God's permissive will, but God's permissive will does not render God responsible for man's direct choice.

As an illustration we may consider the case of a murderer. If God had not imparted life to that man, he would not exist today. But he has turned out to be a murderer. Should a jury pronounce judgment upon God as the responsible agent of the murder? Of course not. The man did not have to murder; he chose to do so. God could not be blamed for creating the mere possibility of evil choice, even as the parent cannot be blamed for bringing a child into the world simply because there is a chance that the child may become a murderer one day. Without the possibility of evil, good could not exist either, since good exists only as the result of man's deliberate rejection of evil when confronted with a choice.

We have to distinguish very definitely in this matter of the creation between the First Cause and the second causes. God created the elements in this universe. Man has been able to discover some. No one knows how many there are that have not yet fallen within the cognizance of man. God made the atom. There is no atom that God did not create. Yet God did not create the atom bomb. Man made that. But man could not have done it without the atom. The final form of God's first creation is to a great extent man's responsibility. But even man's ability to produce in a secondary manner must be originally ascribed to the First Cause of all creation. God gave man dominion over His creation. Had man obeyed God, the result of his second cause would have been good, but unfortunately they are in many instances evil. Let us never reproach God for that for which He is not to be blamed. Let us take our rightful blame and thus seek nothing but the mercy of God upon us.

131

The expression, "and without him was not any thing made that was made," means that whatever exists could not have created itself from nothing. And yet the evils that exist cannot be ascribed to the First Cause of the creation but to the second causes. Furthermore, there would be no second causes without the First Cause. But we cannot blame the First Cause for the results of the second causes when these results are evil.

The verb that is used in the expression, "and without him was not any thing made that was made," is the same verb *egeneto* that was used in the positive part of our verse. Literally translated, it should read "came into being." "And without him not a thing came into being." Man cannot ever take the credit for having created anything, for having brought anything into existence. What man actually does is to give form and shape to what God has originally made. Here is a table. God is the indirect First Cause of this table, but man is the direct manufacturer of it. God created and creates, but man simply manufactures something out of what God made. There is not a thing that man has actually brought into existence. Creation is the work of God. He only can create. The architect can rear a cathedral, the sculptor can cut forms of symmetry and grace from marble, the painter can depict life on his canvas, the machinist can construct engines that will serve the nations; but not one of them can create. They work with materials already in existence. They bring existing things into new combinations. A man would have to wait forever for his dessert course at dinner if his wife were to enter a kitchen that had no flour, no water, nothing in it, and expect to create a cake.

The declaration which John makes, therefore, is that there isn't anything, no matter what its present form and moral status, which was not originally made by Jesus Christ, in spite of the fact that its original shape may have been different from its present one, and that it was once good but now may be evil.

CHAPTER 30

CAN JESUS CHRIST BE BOTH CREATURE AND CREATOR AT THE SAME TIME?

". . . and without him was NOT ANYTHING made that was made" (John 1:3b).

Whatever is not made is God, and whatever is made is not God. That is what the Apostle John is endeavoring to prove in the first three verses of his Gospel. He states that before there was a creation, God existed as Creator. He was not made. He was self-existent and therefore God. He made the world. The world did not make itself. It has neither eternity nor self-creativity; therefore the world is not God. It is a definite mistake to refer to nature as God. God is entirely distinct from His creation.

The second part of verse 3 states, "And without him was not any thing made that was made." Apart from Him, nothing could have created itself. That is the real meaning of John's statement. When Napoleon was returning to France from the expedition to Egypt, a group of French officers one evening entered into a discussion concerning the existence of God. They were on the deck of the vessel that bore them over the Mediterranean Sea. Thoroughly imbued with the infidel and atheistical spirit of the times, they were unanimous in their denial of this truth. It was at length proposed to ask the opinion of Napoleon on the subject, who was standing alone, wrapt in silent thought. On hearing the question, "Is there a God?" he raised his hand and, pointing to the starry firmament, simply responded, "Gentlemen, who made all that?" The answer the Apostle John would have given is "They could not have made themselves."

133

"And without him, or apart from him, was not any thing made that was made." Here certainly reference is made to Jesus Christ, to the Word, who has been the subject of these first three verses of the Gospel of John. The Apostle has been trying to present Jesus Christ as God, as deity. As proof of His deity, John presents Him as the Creator of all things. And since He is the Creator of all things, He must be God. No reference has been made yet to the personality of God the Father. John is limiting his discussion to God the Son, to the Word.

Now there are those who teach that Jesus Christ is the first creature of God the Father and also the Creator of the world. But this teaching contains both a logical and Scriptural inconsistency. One cannot be both a creature and the Creator. The second part of John 1:3 excludes the possibility that Jesus Christ was both a creature and a creator in His pre-incarnate state. After stating that "all things through him came into being," John goes on to say, "and without him was not any thing made that was made." The "him" refers to Jesus Christ. The "all" of the first part of the verse and the "not any thing" of the second part are all-inclusive, i.e., they cover the entire creation and have no exception anywhere in the created universe.

The expression "not any thing" in Greek is "not even one thing or one item." There isn't anything in the created world which does not have its origin in Jesus Christ. If He Himself is considered by anyone to be part of the created world, then, since the entire created world, including Himself, is due to Him, it is logically deduced that He is self-existent and that He owes His existence to none other than Himself. The same is true with God the Father. Therefore the two, God the Son and God the Father, are co-equal and co-eternal. What is spoken of One is also spoken of the Other in their eternity. If Jesus Christ is the Creator of all things, and without Him there is not even one thing that was created, He cannot be the creature of anyone else. Since, therefore, He is the Creator of all things, He must be God, and as God He is self-existent. One cannot be both a creator and a creature. If Jesus Christ was a creature, it could never have been said of Him, "All things were made by him; and without him was not any thing made that was made." Within the realm of finiteness and time there has never been anyone who is known to have created himself. Self-creation involves infinity and timelessness, and John has already stated that Christ possesses these. Therefore He is self-existent. If Jesus Christ is robbed of His deity and His absolute creatorship, then He is a finite being, and a finite being can never create anything by himself. The Apostle Paul affirms the statements made by John when he writes to the Colossians in chapter 1, verse 16, "For by him [Jesus Christ] were all things created, that are in heaven, and that are in earth, visible and invisible, whether they be thrones, or dominions, or principalities, or powers: all things were created by him, and for him." How could anyone give us a clearer statement?

In this second part of John 1:3, the verb "was made" appears twice. "And without him *was* not any thing *made* that *was made.*" In the Greek, although these two verbs are the same, they are in different tenses. The first is *egeneto,* which is the second aorist middle indicative of the verb *ginomai* ("to become or to come into existence"), and it is exactly the same tense as the verb in the first part of the verse. But the second is *gegonen,* which is in the second perfect active indicative. The exact translation of this second verb is "that which has been made." And the resultant meaning, of course, is "that which now exists." The perfect tense refers to an act of the past with its results felt at the present time. John indicates, then, that all that we see around us and all that we are is due to the creative power of Jesus Christ. Let us not think ourselves so advanced and so creative that we lose sight of our Creator, Jesus Christ.

One of the main reasons why this second verb is in the perfect tense is, no doubt, that we may realize the connection which exists between God's creative power and His sustaining grace. Without the sustaining grace of Jesus Christ, we could not live a single moment, nothing could continue to exist. "But by the grace of God I am what I am," Paul declared (I Cor. 15:10). And he was right. There is a close relationship between the creatorship and the providence of God, and we shall do well to recognize it. His providence is also a proof of His deity and the fact that He is not a creature. Sometimes we sinful human beings tend not only to doubt the creatorship of the Lord, but also His providence.

We are reminded of the Ladies' Aid Society, the members of which had all been complaining that the dry season would ruin the crops. But there was one lady who was not complaining. They asked her if the drought had not hurt her fruit or garden. She said, "Yes, but I'll tell you what cured me of worrying. I used to fret over everything, and one spring when I sat down to have a good cry because an untimely frost during peach-blossoming threatened to ruin our splendid prospect for fruit, my Aunt Martha came in and reminded me that she had lived eighty years, and the world's crop of provisions had never failed yet. 'If we don't have peaches, we'll have punkins,' said she. And I have noticed since then that, in spite of all the frosts and droughts, I've never suffered for food, and I don't believe you have, either." They all smiled rather sheepishly, and the president said thoughtfully, "That's true. 'Peaches or punkins.' I'll try to remember that." We, too, should try to remember that everything continues to exist because of Jesus Christ and in spite of us and our sinfulness.

CHAPTER 31

WHO ORIGINATED LIFE?

"In him was life . . ." (John 1:4a).

_____

What is life, anyway? We can describe those persons and things which possess it, but we find it difficult to describe life itself. They tell us that a person immediately after death weighs exactly the same as before. But one moment he had life and the next he did not. What happened to that which made the difference between a living, responsive being, and a body in a casket unable to respond to external stimuli? Man with all his technological advances has not yet been able adequately to explain this mystery of life. But it would be irrational to deny its existence simply because of our inability to explain it. Life, even in its lowest forms, as it exists in a worm or a fly, is a mystery to us. We can describe its manifestations, but that is about all the wisest of men can do. And the mystery grows as we rise from simple animal life to the life of intellect, to the life of human affection, and to spiritual life.

We should make a distinction between life in Christ or in God and life as we know it, i.e., created life. They are not one and the same. The one is self-existent and uncreated, fully incomprehensible by man apart from revelation. The other—natural life—is created by God and fully depends for its continuance upon Him.

God, knowing our limitation in understanding both the beginning of inanimate things and the life that makes physical bodies think, love, speak, hear, and move, has given us His revelation in His Word so that we may not be completely in the dark. After telling us that all things were made by Jesus Christ and that not even one thing that exists was not made by Him, He goes on to tell us something of the origin of this mysterious element called "life." He says through John, "In him was life." Reference here, of course, is made to the Lord Jesus Christ in His pre-incarnate eternal state as He is presented in the first three verses of John's Gospel. The Word, Jesus Christ, is the answer to the riddle of life.

The first word of this verse is one of the commonest Greek prepositions, *en,* the basic meaning of which is "in." "In him was life." The particular distinctive meaning of this preposition can be discerned only as we take it in conjunction with the meaning of the verb used here. This is *een,* the durative imperfect of the verb *eimi,* "to be." In English we have no such exact tense; hence the necessity of translating it as "was," although in this context "had been" would have been preferable. This is the same form of the verb as was used in the first two verses by John when speaking of the eternity of the Word. John told us that before there was a beginning the Word "had been." He traced back to the beginning of things and found that the Word must have been before there was anything else.

How can we account for life, this intangible, mysterious element? Was it something that man created? No. "In him life had been." It does not say, "With him life had been," as if life were something self-created, co-existent and co-eternal with Christ, something that could exist independently of Him. Life was not eternally existent independent of the Word. It was something fully dependent on Him from the very beginning of its existence.

The second thing we deduce from the preposition "in" and the verb *een,* "had been," is that this life originally did not join itself to the Word, giving Him life, but that life was always inherent in Him. There has never been a time when the Word did not have life—as we finite beings begin to possess life at conception or birth and lose it at death. Life is something that you and I possess, but He actually *was* life. His life was not "conceived." Did He not say, "I am. . .the life" (John 14:6)? On the other hand, speaking to human beings, He said, "Ye have no life in you" (John 6:53). Life for the Lord

138

Jesus Christ is not an external endowment, as it is with us, but an inherent part of His personality.

What John actually says, then, amounts to: "From eternity He has been life. Life owes its existence to Him. He is its originator. Nobody else made it, or can make it, or will make it." Man can make rockets, but he cannot make a living hair, or a living cell of any kind. "In him life had been eternally." We must be very careful not to equate created life with the Lord and to say therefore that life is God. The Word is life, but life is not the Word. God is a self-existent personality, and life as we know it and are experiencing it has been generated by Him; but that which He generated cannot be said to have become equal with Himself. That which He gives to us who call ourselves living creatures He has always had in Himself, without having received it from anywhere or anyone.

Now let us examine the meaning of the word "life." In Greek it is *zooee*, from which we derive our English word "zoology." Zoology is the study of animals, which are living things. Primarily this word refers to physical life as opposed to death. It is that which we have when we are not dead. This element of physical life has always been in Christ. You and I possess life, but let us remember that it is the gift of God in Christ.

A secondary meaning of the word *zooee*, "life" is "the means of sustenance." This means of the sustenance of our physical lives has always been in Christ. He gives us life and then gives what is necessary for the sustenance of our lives. We could not remain living beings without His keeping us so. Neither life nor the maintenance of life is any achievement of our own. Let us not take pride, then, in what we can do for ourselves; for that which we can do is under the supernatural providence of the Lord Jesus Christ. To think that the Creator of all life is concerned for each one of us individually is indeed beyond the imagination of man.

Once a great king visited a town to lay the foundation stone of a new hospital. Thousands of school children greeted him and sang for him. Soon after the king had passed a group of children, a teacher saw a little girl crying. She asked, "Why are you crying? Did you not see the king?" The little girl sobbed out, "Yes, teacher, but the king did not see me." How different the Lord Jesus Christ is from earthly kings. Not only does He give life to each one, but He is also personally interested in and personally maintains each life.

In the writings of John in particular, however, the word *zooee*, "life," is also used in a spiritual sense, in the same way that the word "death" is used to connote the sinful condition of man and the result of his sin. Life is spoken of in the the New Testament as the highest and noblest possession of the saints of God. It is the opposite of spiritual death. On the one hand, then, we have sin and death, and on the other we have holiness and life. The Lord Jesus Christ is never said to have been either sin or death. Man brought these upon himself. Both physical and spiritual death are the natural consequences of man's voluntary sin. But holiness and life have always been the attributes of the Lord Jesus Christ. And those who accept His redemptive work on the cross of Calvary become recipients of these spiritual elements of holiness and life.

This spiritual life, then, speaks of the absolute blessedness and happiness of God which were always inherently in Jesus Christ. And since they are in Him, if we accept Him, they become ours also. That is why, when a person accepts the Lord Jesus Christ as his personal Saviour, he undergoes such a radical transformation in his entire spiritual make-up and attitude. He is a new creature, for he has new spiritual life, the life of Christ.

"Oh, dear!" said one girl to another. "Don't you wish you never had to do anything you didn't like?" The other thought a moment. "I don't know," she replied. "I think I'd rather like everything that I have to do." But that can only be possible as the transforming life of Christ enters the human heart.

140

CHAPTER 32

THE LIFE OF THE ETERNAL CHRIST BECOMES OURS

"In him was life; and THE life was the light of men" (John 1:4).

————————

The mystery of life is solved in the person of the Lord Jesus Christ. As we consider this "life" which John mentions in verse 4, we notice that no definite article appears before "life" in the first clause of the verse, although it does appear in the second clause. Why is this? John speaks of "life" and "the life." The word for "life" here in the original Greek text is *zooee,* which as we said in our previous study means primarily the physical element of life as opposed to death, as well as the means of sustenance of that life. But it also means spiritual life and the means of sustenance of that life.

In the Greek language, however, there are certain things that we must look for when we see the omission or inclusion of the definite article. Why is the article omitted from the first clause? William Edward Jelf, the great Greek grammarian, tells us, "The effect of the omission of the article is frequently that the absence of any particular definition or limitation of the notion brings forward its general character." *(A Grammar of the Greek Language,* Vol. II, p. 124.) Then he goes on to say, "Some words are found both with and without the article, and seemingly with but little difference; but without the article they signify the general notion conceived of abstractedly, and not as in actual existence, with the article the objective existence is brought forward." What does all that mean in relation to our verse?

In the first clause John tells us that life was the general

141

character of the Word, of Christ in His eternal state. Here he is not speaking of the Word as we know Him, as He revealed Himself to us in the flesh, but as He had always been before He came into the realm of history. Eternally Jesus Christ was not only God, as brought out in the first two verses of John's Gospel, but as such He was also life. It is as if John wants to point out that life is a quality of the eternal. He also wants to point out that there has never been a time when Jesus Christ, the eternal *Logos,* was dead. Every other creature, every other person who is not God, has had a beginning as far as his life is concerned, but not the Lord Jesus Christ. He *is* life and in Him there is no death, nor could death long prevail over Him even when man crucified Him. Another proof, then, of His deity is that there was no beginning to His life as there is with yours and mine.

Here, we believe, John wants to stress the inherent quality of Jesus Christ as contrasted with the inherent quality of man. In Christ was life. In man there is death. Man is born physically alive, but actually he is spiritually dead. This spiritual death is the consequence of man's sin. It is this sin which brought utter misery to man. This was never the intent of Jesus Christ, that man should be miserable through his disobedience and sin. Paul, speaking of the misery of the heathen, writes in Ephesians 4:18, "Having the understanding darkened, being alienated from the life of God through the ignorance that is in them, because of the blindness of their heart." In Christ there has always been life, which is absence of sin and misery.

But what interests man is the manifestation of that life. Therefore, the general quality of life, which from our viewpoint we can only conceive of in the abstract, must project itself from its subjective existence in God to an objective effectiveness in us. The life of God must be brought out of God and in touch with man. To demonstrate this quality of Christ's life, its reaching out to man, John prefaces the word "life" with the definite article. He reduces abstract and general life to the tangible and particular as far as man is concerned. What good is life if it is so remote from us that it cannot affect us? All of this has more of an application to the spiritual life that is made available by God to man. What John declares, then, is that this life of Christ which has within it divine happiness and blessedness can become yours and mine. Life moves from the Infinite to the finite.

John at the very outset is not so much concerned with the why and how of our depraved state of spiritual death as he is with our deliverance from it. A traveler passing by, and seeing a man fallen into a deep pit, began to wonder aloud how he fell in. The poor man in his utter misery shouted, "If you are a friend, stop questioning how I fell in and start helping me out!" The Lord Jesus Christ is not satisfied with being alive, happy, and blessed in Himself. He wants to share that life with us. We may in our foolishness want a full explanation from Him as to why He permitted us to fall in the first place, but John tells us that the most important and urgent thing is our salvation from sin and death. Before everything else, we need life, His life. Life, the general and abstract life of Jesus Christ, becomes *the* life—the particular, tangible life that you and I need so desperately. We need it because the natural man is a spiritual monster. His heart is where his feet should be, fixed upon earth; his heels are lifted up against heaven, which his heart should be set on. His face is toward hell, his back toward heaven. He loves what he should hate, and hates what he should love; joys in what he ought to mourn for, and mourns for what he ought to rejoice in; glories in his shame, and is ashamed of his glory; abhors what he should desire, and desires what he should abhor.

Has *life* become *the* life you need? If not, there is nothing that hinders you from having it. You can appropriate it by faith in Jesus Christ. The Lord Jesus Christ said, "I am come that they might have life, and that they might have it more abundantly" (John 10:10b). What is the means of appropriating this life? The Lord tells us Himself in John 6:47, "Verily, verily, I say unto you, He that believeth on me hath everlasting life."

A famous atheist once said, "I can stand all the arguing of Christian apologists, but I have a little servant who is a disciple of Jesus Christ, and her good, pure, honest, truthful life staggers me sometimes." The one irresistible argument for the Gospel's power is a regenerated, consecrated life which is a demonstration of the life of Christ. The world may miss seeing the life of God in nature, but they cannot miss seeing it in the lives of those men and women who have the life of Christ. What a wonderful thought, to know that we as human beings can become the carriers of the life of God and our lives can become the reflectors of His life.

CHAPTER 33

A PARTIAL BIOGRAPHY OF A PERFECT LIFE

". . . and the life was the light of men" **(John 1:4b).**

We now come to the second clause of this important verse. Again we notice that the verb *een* — the durative imperfect of *eimi*, "to be" — is used here. It indicates that this life of God has always been available to produce life in man. There has never been a time in man's history, nor in fact from all eternity to all eternity, that the life of God in Jesus Christ was not the source of life in man. We must bear in mind the great significance of this as it sets forth the work of the Lord Jesus Christ. In the entire Bible we are told that there is only one Saviour and that is our Lord Jesus Christ. He it is who was the Saviour of all the Old Testament saints, in spite of the fact that His name was veiled in prophetic terms.

The first declaration of this Saviour is given in Genesis 3:15, when the Lord said to the serpent who tempted Adam and Eve, "And I will put enmity between thee and the woman, and between thy seed and her seed; it shall bruise thy head, and thou shalt bruise his heel." Here is a prediction of the long struggle between Satan and mankind. The seed of the woman was the Messiah, the eternal Christ who became incarnate at Bethlehem. Satan bruised the heel of Jesus Christ in His human form, but Christ bruised Satan's head, where his poison is concealed. And thus it is in Christ that liberation and redemption were to be found from the very beginning, ever since the fall of man.

That is exactly what John also declares when he says, "In him was life, and the life was the light of men." That verb "was" should rather be translated in this context "had always been." No one in the past was able to find life save in the person of Jesus Christ, even before His incarnation. No one now can find life except in Jesus Christ. And no one will ever find life except in Him. The people who lived in the Old Testament economy were looking forward to the sacrifice of Jesus Christ on Calvary's cross, while we look backward on an accomplished fact.

There are two Greek words which are commonly translated by just one English word, "life." These are *zooee,* from which we derive our English word "zoology," and *bios,* from which we have the English words "biology, biography," etc. In John 1:4 it is *zooee* that is used. The primary distinction between these two words is that *bios* generally refers, not to life as the breath of life, not that intangible and invisible principle which animates matter, but rather to the extent of life, the period of one's life, the means by which life is sustained, and the way that life is lived. "Biography," as we understand it in English, incorporates the true meaning of *bios,* for it deals with the duration of a man's life, what he did, and how he did it. Biography has nothing to say about how a person received the breath of life. Unfortunately, the English word "biology" is somewhat misleading, for it does not really represent the true meaning of *bios,* the manner of life, but relates to life itself; it examines the living organisms themselves and not merely their behavior.

Why do we go into so much detail about this? Simply because we want to make it clear that John does not speak here of what the Lord Jesus Christ did, but of what He was. He wants to point out that what he is going to say in his biographical sketch of the Lord Jesus could not have been so unless He was what He was. It is not so much His biography that should arrest our attention as His "life" — His life before He came to this earth, His life while He was here, and His life after He left this world. It is true that we are saved both by what Christ was and what He did, but if He was not who He was, He could not have done what He did, and even if He could have done it, it would not have availed for our salvation.

John wants to emphasize right at the outset that it is not performances that comprise life, but life rather that produces performances. Life, then, does not refer primarily here to the words Christ spoke, or the splendor of His works during His short public ministry, but to life as it essentially was in Him. It was not first of all the outward expression of life, but the inward element of life. Jesus Christ did not base His kingdom on events, but in and upon Himself. Take as an illustration the Sermon on the Mount. Never was a greater discourse heard. But the multitudes did not seem to be so much moved by the sermon taken by itself, as by the One who proclaimed it. There was something about Him that arrested and riveted their attention. Why? Because "in him was life; and the life was the light of men." In another instance we see that His enemies were afraid to arrest Him. They came back without Him, in spite of their weapons. He did not hinder them from attacking and arresting Him. But they were automatically hindered just by looking at Him who was Life. There emanated from His eyes a resistless sovereignty which no human words could describe.

As George Matheson said, "Christ has illuminated the world, not by what He did, but by what He was: His life is the Light of Men. We speak of a man's life-work; the work of Jesus was His life itself. . . . It is good to be told that the pure in heart shall see God, but the vision of heaven in a pure man's face outweighs it all. They tell us that the Easter morning has revealed His glory; rather would I say that His glory has revealed the Easter morning. It is not resurrection that has made Christ; it is Christ that has made resurrection. To those who have seen His beauty, even Olivet can add no certainty; the light of immortality is as bright on His Cross as on His Crown. 'I am the resurrection' are His own words about Himself — not 'I teach,' not 'I cause,' not 'I predict,' but 'I am.' " (*Searchings in the Silence,* Hodder and Stoughton, pp. 137, 138.)

The Lord Jesus Christ did not become great in the sense that you and I speak of men becoming great and mighty. We do not

147

follow Christ primarily for what He did and said, as people usually follow human leaders. We follow Christ for what He was. His biography in the four Gospels is just a small indication of what He was, but it cannot be taken as a complete picture of Him. God did not intend that it should be so. There are things that are not said of Him that may have greater splendor than the things that are related. Only those things that we finite human beings can comprehend have been spoken of Him. The four evangelists faithfully followed the direct inspiration of the Holy Spirit to present to us some aspects of Christ's life — those aspects that we needed to know for our salvation. But all of their descriptions, plus all that is outside the realm of our comprehension and therefore unrecorded, have been summarized by John's statement that "In him was life; and the life was the light of men." His glory and life exceed our fondest imagination! Only as we partake of His life through faith, both in what He was and what He did, can we really see who and what He was.

CHAPTER 34

CHRIST'S LIFE OUR LIGHT

". . . and the life was the light of men" (John 1:4b).

The word used in the second clause of this verse is again *zooee,* "the principle of life," and not *bios,* "the duration, the means, and the manner of life." Why? Speaking, of course, from the spiritual viewpoint and applying the spiritual meaning of *zooee,* we observe that when the Lord Jesus Christ becomes our new life, something very radical takes place within us. The Christian life is not just a change of certain actions or the performance of certain external acts, but a radical revolution of life which involves a complete reorientation of the individual. It is the entrance into our being of an entirely new principle of life. The Christian life is not basically a code or a set of rules to be kept. It is the penetration and possession of our beings by Jesus Christ and His life. When we receive Jesus Christ as our Saviour, we do not simply begin a new biography, but we are initiated into a new life element. What we do in the outside world then becomes the result of that which has happened within us, the indwelling of Jesus Christ.

There is a story of a simple-minded man who came to a watchmaker and gave him the hands of a clock, saying, "I want you to fix these hands. They haven't kept correct time for me now for six months." "Where is the clock?" asked the watchmaker. "It's out at the house." "But I must have the clock." "But I told you that there is nothing wrong with the clock except the hands, and that's why I brought them to you. You just want the clock so that you can tinker with it and charge me a big price. Give me back those hands." And he went away to find a more reasonable watchmaker.

Equally foolish are those who try to regulate their lives without being made right on the inside. And their reasoning is very similar to that of the simple-minded man of our story. They say, "We only wish to avoid this or that habit." But the Master Watchmaker says, "I cannot regulate the hands unless I have the heart." The purpose of Jesus Christ is not primarily to change certain of our bad habits or to make us philanthropists. That is all a by-product of giving us His life. And when we have His life, the things that please Him will be done naturally and spontaneously, without any undue effort. It will not be a question of trying to do good any more, but of being good, since we are saved. When the fountain is clean, clean water must come out.

"Socialism," declared a street orator, "can put a new coat on a man!" "Jesus Christ," cried a voice in the crowd, "can put a new man in the coat—and that is better still!" Jesus Christ can give us life which we can fully enjoy in the midst of a world where spiritual death abounds. Our inner life does not have to be conditioned by the circumstances around us or by the walking dead among whom we live. We have the eternal life of Christ within us. It will help us as Christians to realize that our situation is comparable to living in a cemetery—among the spiritually dead. To try to make the dead ethical is nonsensical. What the world needs is life, the life of Christ to become their life.

This life of Christ as men have observed it among themselves and within themselves, John declares, has always been the light of men. What does he really mean by that? What is the relationship between life and light? In order to understand that, we must first determine the meaning of the word "light." In Greek it is *phoos*, from which come our English words "phosphoric, photograph," etc. No one has been able to give an adequate and exact definition of light in the physical sense. Light as we derive it from the sun and as we manufacture it through electricity is a very real thing, but it is

150

nevertheless inexplicable.

In Genesis 1:3 we read, "And God said, Let there be light: and there was light." Physical light in the physical world was one of the first elements in the creative work of God. Light in its physical, objective existence must be ultimately ascribed to God, and apart from revelation it presents a mystery to man. Subjectively, however, light may be defined as the sense-impression formed by the eye. A blind man, judging subjectively, could very understandably arrive at the conclusion that there is no light. The same thing applies in a spiritual sense to the spiritually blind, who vehemently deny the existence of spiritual light. Yet they are just as wrong as the physically blind who deny the objective existence of physical light. The distinction between the objective and subjective realities of things is an important one in theological and Biblical discussions. Light exists as an objective reality. But we recognize it subjectively. We shall do well to remember that this parallel must also be drawn in the spiritual realm between objective and subjective spiritual light. It does not benefit a blind man to be in a sunlit world in the same sense as it does the sighted person. Nor does the light of God in Jesus Christ benefit one steeped in blind unbelief. A sensory perception of the light in man, through faith, is essential for the objective reality to become a subjective appropriation.

Now does John refer here to physical or spiritual light — to the objective or subjective light in Christ? The Greek word *phoos* could very reasonably be taken to refer first of all to the source of physical light. We humans in our finite world have to look at the sun to find the source of our light. But John wants us to look far beyond that and to see that the sun could not exist without the eternal Word. He, ultimately, is the source of light, shed abroad in this present world as we know it through the sun. We must not forget that John deals with the ultimates, with infinity in its relation to finiteness. He speaks here of the source of physical light apart from any subjective perception we may have of it. God must be the Author of that.

151

As life, the eternal life of Christ, becomes our life, both in a physical and a spiritual sense, so does His light, the objective light, become our light subjectively. But as in partaking of the life of God our bodies do not become physically immortal, nor do we ourselves spiritually become gods, so it is with our participation in His light. We do not become eternal lights, but lights in a relative sense only.

Life and light are presented here primarily in a spiritual sense and they are shown to be inseparable. A dead person cannot see. A man must have life in order to have the ability to receive light. What John actually stresses here is that in order for man to be able to sense the light of God, the eternal light of Jesus Christ, he must first of all have His life. Without His life, man will always be in utter darkness. The only way anyone can see the beauty of Jesus Christ is by making His eternal life his eternal possession.

Note that the definite article appears before the word *phoos,* "light," implying—in addition to the life of Jesus Christ—the accessibility of His light. The primary purpose for which Jesus Christ is light is for our benefit. What would be the use of a sun whose rays could not reach us? It is the same with God.

CHAPTER 35

JESUS CHRIST THE ONLY LIGHT OF MEN

". . . and the life was THE light of men" (John 1:4b).

———————

John does not say that the life of Jesus Christ was just one of many lights that have shone in the world, but that it is the only light of men. The definite article is used before the word *phoos,* "light," and this gives exclusiveness to it. There is an absoluteness, a uniqueness in Jesus Christ. There have been many marvelous teachers, but Jesus Christ is more than a great teacher— He is *the Light.*

Phoos is most commonly used to mean the light of the sun or of the day, while the word *phengos* is generally used for the light of the moon or other luminaries of the night (Matt. 24:29; Mark 13:24). There is an absoluteness in *phoos,* which shows us that there is an absoluteness in Jesus Christ. He is not like the moon, which gives only borrowed light, but He is the origin of light—of spiritual, regenerating light.

It is said that Tennyson was walking one day in a beautiful flower garden when a friend said to him, "Mr. Tennyson, you speak so often of Jesus Christ. Will you tell me what Christ really means to your life?" Tennyson stooped and pointing to a beautiful yellow flower said, "What the sun is to the flower, Jesus Christ is to my soul."

There is no doubt that John speaks primarily of the spiritual light of Jesus Christ in His eternal nature. When God created man, he gave him the ability to see. More especially, He made man's heart the residence of His light. And that is why John says that "The light was always the light of men, ever since man was created." Man was the special creation of God, made in His image. This was not so with the animals and other creations of God. That is why no living creature, other than man, has a spirit with which to know God and communicate with Him. There is no salvation for dogs and cats. The souls of these animals have mere physical life, which may be conceived of as no more than the animation of matter; but they have no spiritual souls or spirits which look upward. The souls of animals look around them, but the spirit of man looks upward. That ability was given to man by God, even as the sun gives the recipients of its light the ability to see it in all its majesty. God cannot be seen apart from Christ, even as the sun cannot be seen apart from the rays which it sends forth. God's light, therefore, is directed especially toward man; but we must also bear in mind that the light that man receives is purely a gift of God. Man has no light of his own. Whatever he has is all as a result of God's initiative and action. Rejecting His light deprives us of the privilege of seeing the origin of light, God. And everything outside of Christ is darkness.

Originally God's light in its fullness was made available and accessible to all men. But man fell from the favor of God by choosing to disobey Him, thus plunging himself into utter spiritual darkness. The Apostle Paul says, "As by one man sin entered into the world, and death by sin; and so death passed upon all men, for that all have sinned" (Rom. 5:12). Ever since his fall, man has been groping in darkness as a result of rejecting the eternal light of God.

We must not think that this verse, John 1:4, teaches universal salvation, that the life of Jesus Christ is now actually the light of men, that all men have this light in them and are therefore saved. This is not so. Objectively, Jesus Christ is indeed the light of all men. No one has ever been able to see God outside of Jesus Christ. No one can be saved without the activity of Jesus Christ. But in this economy of grace, since the fall of Adam and consequently the fall of all mankind, Jesus Christ is not the actual possession of all, but the potential and possible possession of all who will receive Him.

That is why Jesus Christ came to the world and died for our sins, so that we might have the opportunity of having anew His life and His light. But this second time, the light of the Gospel is appropriated by us voluntarily by faith. A little later in this chapter, John states it very clearly: "But as many as received him, to them gave he power to become the sons of God, even to them that believe on his name" (1:12). True, the light originates with Jesus Christ, but in order that man may have it now he must appropriate it by faith in Jesus Christ, through the supernatural energy of the Holy Spirit.

An unbeliever once ridiculed the power of the Gospel of Jesus Christ by saying, "If Jesus Christ is able to save to the uttermost, why is it that there are so many unbelievers?" The Christian to whom he was speaking stopped a very dirty little boy who was passing by and turning to the unbeliever said, "Can you blame soap and water for the filth of this boy?" It was available but he hadn't used it. The power of the Gospel is available to all, but only those who accept it experience its regenerating power.

This is made clear in the very next verse, "And the light shineth in darkness" (1:5). The Greek verb here is *phainei,* which is used intransitively — that is to say, its action is not necessarily transferred upon the object. Man is not forced to see and appropriate that light. It simply shines like the beacon light in the harbor, which it is the captain's duty to watch for that he may direct his ship safely to harbor. The light of Jesus Christ shines constantly. Through the Holy Spirit man is permitted to see it and be guided by it. The fact that the verb is in the present indicative means that it never goes out, it is ever shining. No one can ever blame God that the shipwreck of his life is due to darkness caused by God.

155

CHAPTER 36

MAN'S DARKNESS AND GOD'S LIGHT

"And the light shineth in darkness . . ." (John 1:5a).

———

Reference is made here to the spiritual light for God's special creation, man. God in His eternal omniscience saw that man would choose darkness rather than light. Man did so in Adam. "And this is the condemnation, that light is come into the world, and men loved darkness rather than light, because their deeds were evil" (John 3:19). Since God knew what the choice of man — the first man — would be, He made provision in eternity for the redemption of man after his fall. This we see clearly in the tense of the verb *phainee*, "shineth," which is the durative present indicative of the verb *phainoo*, "to shine." This indicates that the light of Christ did not begin to shine at his incarnation, but shone from all eternity. There had never been any other light than that of Christ to light the path of man. That is why it is wrong to say that, before the physical coming of Jesus Christ into the world, people were saved through the law, or their consciences, or in any other way than through Christ. It has always been through Christ and the various means that it has pleased him to utilize for the illumination of men's hearts.

In a very real sense, however, the light of Jesus Christ shines in a special way after the fall of man, and in a still more real and comprehensible way after His incarnation. No doubt that is why the durative present of the verb is used here instead of the durative imperfect, which has been used heretofore to demonstrate the eternity of the person of Jesus Christ. Special emphasis is laid upon

156

the present availability and accessibility of the light of Jesus Christ. Nevertheless, in our eagerness to see the emphasis placed on the present, let us not make the mistake of restricting this light to the New Testament period. John still speaks of the eternal *Logos* (Word) in His eternal essence and His eternal work. The light of Christ has shown in the past for everyone, but its pragmatic value is for the here and now.

John through this verb *phainee,* "shines," shows us God's part in the illumination of mankind. *Phainee* declares that the light of Christ shines forth, without assuming that there are any who behold it. It shines irrespective of the attitude of those for whose benefit it shines. The acceptance or rejection of the light of Christ does not affect its availability or the intensity with which it shines. God makes it available to all, without being affected by the attitude of those who behold it or who refuse to behold it.

Here is a simple but admittedly inadequate illustration. It is difficult to illustrate the eternal counsel of God by adducing physical phenomena. Let us say that the sun is shining. This fact is not conditioned by our acceptance or rejection of it. The sun is there and it shines no matter what we do about its light. God, who made the sun to give light, also gave us eyes to apprehend the light. But some people may choose to close their eyes and then foolishly claim that they cannot see. God is not to be blamed for their inability to see. God has given both the light and the ability to apprehend it. But He has also given eyelids and the ability to close them, thus bringing darkness over our eyes. Yet even when we close our eyes, the light continues to shine. Therefore our being in darkness is our fault entirely, in Adam and as individuals. God will always shine. He has given us eyes to see. But He cannot, by virtue of His nature, take away our eyelids, i.e., our ability to let His light become ours or to shut it off from our view. Only a blind man can claim that the sun is not shining; but, if he has any intelligence at all, he will accept the testimony of many who have seen the light and come to the conclusion that the inability lies within himself.

No one switches on a flashlight in an area flooded by direct sunlight. We put on the light in order to dispel darkness. It is the darkness that makes the light necessary. God from eternity knew that men would choose darkness rather than light and therefore He had to bring His light in Jesus Christ to shine in the midst of darkness. In the original Greek text, the definite article is used before the word "darkness." Thus this clause literally translated would read, "And the light shineth in *the* darkness." Here John speaks about a unique, specific light shining in a specific darkness. He is speaking about the darkness brought into this world as a result of sin and death.

Of the two Greek words denoting darkness, *skotos* and *skotia*, the latter is especially used by John. The figurative meaning of *skotia* is not "sin," as is usually the meaning of the word *skotos*, but "the consequences of sin." (Cremer, *Biblico-Theological Lexicon of New Testament Greek*, T. & T. Clark, 1954, pp. 866, 867.) Let us look at I John 2:10, 11, where this is most apparent. "He that loveth his brother abideth in the light, and there is none occasion of stumbling in him. But he that hateth his brother is in darkness [*skotia* with the definite article], and knoweth not whither he goeth, because that darkness [*hee skotia*, 'the darkness'] hath blinded his eyes." Here we have the vertical relationship of man toward God and his consequent horizontal relationship toward his fellow man. Man is sinful, not because he mistreats his fellow men, but because he disobeyed God, and the consequence of that disobedience is the hatred he has toward his fellow men. On the other hand, the consequence of the right relationship with God is love toward our fellow men. *Skotia*, therefore, stands mostly for the consequences of sin, while *skotos* stands for sin itself.

Consider also the last two clauses of I John 1:5, which read, "God is light, and in him is no darkness at all." The word used for darkness in the original Greek is *skotia*, which is of the feminine gender and with which the pronoun *oudemia*, "not a single one," agrees. God is light and in Him there is not a single darkness. What

158

does that mean? It means "not a single consequence of sin."

Thus in our verse, "And the light shineth in the darkness," the light shines because of the darkness that has been brought about as a result of sin. Man is reaping the consequences of his sin. His misery, his unhappiness, his corruption are all the consequences of his sin toward God. There can be no peace among men, because there is no peace between man and God. Man is in a pitiful condition as he reaps the consequences of his sin. He cannot find his way about without the light of Jesus Christ.

Unfortunately, one of the consequences of sin is self-deception. Man is in utter darkness, but he is deceived into believing that he can see, that he has the spark of life and light. And as long as man thinks he has enough light generated by himself to bring happiness upon himself, he will never find the happiness of God, the salvation of Jesus Christ.

An Indian and a white man were brought under deep conviction of sin by the same sermon. The Indian was immediately led to rejoice in pardoning mercy. The white man was for a long time in distress, almost to despair. But at last he was brought to a joyous sense of sins forgiven. Some time after, meeting his Indian brother, he said to him, "How is it that I should be so long under conviction, when you found peace at once?" "Oh brother," replied the Indian, "I will tell you. There comes along a rich prince. He proposes to give you a new coat; you look at your coat and say, 'I don't know; my coat looks pretty good; it will do a little longer.' He then offers me a new coat. I look at my old blanket; I say, this is good for nothing, and accept the beautiful new garment. Just so, brother, you try to keep your own righteousness, you won't give it up; but I, poor Indian, had none, so I was glad at once to receive the righteousness of God — the Lord Jesus Christ."

As long as you think that you have light of your own, that you are good, the light of Jesus Christ will not benefit you at all. Jesus Christ shines only where there is recognition of the consequences of sin toward God. Jesus Christ cannot save self-deceived, good people. His light shines in the darkness.

CHAPTER 37

CAN DARKNESS CO-EXIST WITH LIGHT?

". . . and the darkness comprehended it not" (John 1:5b).

———————

John has reference here to the eternal Christ as the Light which shines in the world, especially among men. The light of Jesus Christ, not only in history but from eternity, has been a necessity because of the darkness that man brought upon himself. The "darkness" here, *skotia*, is actually the consequence of man's sin against God; it is the misery, unhappiness, and corruption of his present state. It is death, both physical and eternal — death, of course, meaning the separation of man from God.

However, God was not the direct cause of this darkness, no more than He is directly responsible for the evil that exists in and among men. He did not create darkness so that His light might shine forth in it. He did not make man sinful so that He could save him. In God there is no sin, nor can sin in others be attributed to Him. But what about Isaiah 45:7, which reads, "I form the light, and create darkness: I make peace, and create evil: I the Lord do all these things"? The Hebrew word for "evil" here is *ra*, which primarily means "sorrow, wretchedness, adversity, afflictions, calamities." The Septuagint has *kaka*, meaning adversities such as we have mentioned. It is not stated that God created sin. Sin (in Greek *hamartia*) is failing to reach the mark, the goal. God had no goal to reach. It was man's responsibility to reach the goal. The goal was to obey God and believe all that He said. Man's will had to be exercised in the achievement or failure to achieve that goal. The possibility of failure would not bring upon God the moral responsibility of man's failure. So that when we are told in Isaiah that God created darkness, reference is actually made to the consequences of sin and not to sin itself.

To illustrate: God created certain laws to govern the natural world, among them the law of gravity. Objects are attracted toward the center of the earth. A man may choose to disagree with this law and believe it is not so. It is his privilege to do so. He decides to test this law. He throws himself out an upper window of a tall building, claiming that he will not go downward, but up. Even so, Adam and Eve came to believe the consequence of their disobedience to God would not be death, but omniscience and omnipotence. Our skeptical man throws himself from the top floor of the building and is killed. Who is morally responsible for his death? Is God who made the law of gravity, or the man because he disobeyed that law? Of course, the man is responsible. God gave man the privilege of choosing, but He determined the consequences for both right and wrong choices. The consequences of obedience could only exist if there were also consequences of disobedience. Thus we can say that God is the Creator only of the consequences of sin, but not of sin itself. The important thing is that God is Himself the originator of the conditions under which the misuse of the power He delegates is possible.

Since John uses the word *skotia* primarily to refer to "the consequences of sin," what does he mean by "and the darkness comprehended it not?" The consequences of sin — unhappiness, misery, corruption — are primarily experienced by man. The light of God in Christ Jesus shines among men, but because men chose sin they are now in the process of experiencing the consequences of their choice. Who can deny that man is inwardly unhappy? Therefore, when John says that "the darkness comprehended not the light," he refers to the men who are experiencing the consequences of their sinful choice. "Darkness" here refers to the men in whom darkness dwells and not to darkness as an abstract quality.

What does the Greek verb *katelaben*, translated "comprehended,"

161

really mean? There are two distinct meanings of this verb *katalambanoo* (in the present indicative), both of which are common even in Modern Greek. The first is "to seize, to capture, to pounce upon something for the purpose of making it your own." The second is "to understand, to capture with the mind." We believe that both meanings could apply perfectly well in this context. The men who are reaping the consequences of their sins did not understand the light of the Gospel of Jesus Christ in the first place. And that has been true right along. Paul stated it clearly when he said, "For the preaching of the cross is to them that perish foolishness; but unto us which are saved it is the power of God. For it is written, I will destroy the wisdom of the wise, and will bring to nothing the understanding of the prudent . . . hath not God made foolish the wisdom of this world? For after that in the wisdom of God the world by wisdom knew not God, it pleased God by the foolishness of preaching to save them that believe" (I Cor. 1:18-21). And again Paul says, "But the natural man receiveth not the things of the Spirit of God: for they are foolishness unto him: neither can he know them, because they are spiritually discerned" (I Cor. 2:14). One of the consequences of man's sinful choice is his inability to understand the light of the Gospel of Jesus Christ.

A little boy who had been born blind at last underwent an operation to restore his sight. The light was let in slowly. Then one day his mother led him out of doors and uncovered his eyes, and for the first time he saw the sky and earth. "O Mother!" he cried. "Why didn't you tell me it was so beautiful?" She burst into tears and said, 'I tried to tell you, dear, but you could not understand me." Sinful man is also blind to the splendor and the glory of the light of the Gospel. The only way he can comprehend it is to let the light in, through the enabling of the Holy Spirit.

Man not only failed to understand the light of the Gospel, but he definitely misunderstood its beneficent purposes. Light reveals that which darkness may cover up. We have often seen stores still lighted inside after closing hours. Darkness would be conducive to thefts. A thief hardly dare carry on his robbery under the lights. Light, therefore, is considered the enemy of darkness for it brings into the open the works and deeds of darkness. Thus we find a hostility on the part of darkness for light. Sinful man not only fails to understand the wonderfulness of the Gospel but goes a step further — he hates it and tries his utmost to extinguish that light. This is another of the consequences of sin, hatred toward the light that reveals it. Misunderstandings produce hatred. Sometimes a man hates his brother or fellow man simply because he does not understand him. Understanding makes for friendship. It is the same with the Gospel. The revelation of God in Jesus Christ is not given to shame us but to save us. The remedy for our illness can only be applied as the diagnosis is made and the diseased part exposed to the light.

This brings us to the application of the second meaning of the verb *katalambanoo* "to seize, to overcome, to take." The darkness did not overtake, did not seize, did not captivate the light. Many attempts have been made to extinguish the light of Jesus Christ, but they have utterly failed. The verb here is in the aorist, which indicates that all attempts of the past to put out the light of the Gospel have failed. It is as if John wants to tell us that, as the attacks failed in the past, they cannot but fail in the future. The light continues to shine in spite of all the attacks that have been made upon it.

A minister was once dining in a hotel with some commercial travelers who made jokes about him. He did not move a single muscle of his face to show that he was aware of their remarks. After dinner one of them approached him, saying, "How can you sit quietly and hear all that has been said about you without uttering a rebuke?" "My dear sir," replied the minister, "I am chaplain of a lunatic asylum."

The light is fully aware of the aggressive war being waged against it by the darkness of sinful men. But it still shines. As long as He continues to shine, Christ will have enemies fighting Him.

163

And that is also true of those who have the light of Christ in their hearts and lives. If the darkness of this world does not fight against us, we may well question whether what we thought was light in us may not after all be darkness. There can be no peaceful co-existence between darkness and light.

CHAPTER 38

CAN MAN BE AND DO WHAT CHRIST WAS AND DID?

"There was a MAN sent from God, whose name was John" (John 1:6).

———

In the first two verses of his Gospel, John speaks of the eternity of the Word, of the distinct personality of the Word, and of the deity of the Word. This is the affirmation of his own belief about Jesus Christ. In verse 3 he presents the Word as the Creator of all that exists. In verse 4 he declares Him to be the Originator of all life and light. And in verse 5 he speaks of the purpose and work of Jesus Christ and His character as Light of the world.

Then John stops for a moment to think. What if someone should conclude that he is speaking about another person than Jesus—about John the Baptist, for example, the earthly cousin of the Lord Jesus, who was so greatly admired by many? "It is not about him that I have been speaking," John says in effect. "He is not the Word; he is not the Light of the world. He was a great man, but he was not God."Thus, in the interest of clarity, he interrupts his declarations about Jesus Christ to tell us that he recognizes the greatness and ministry of John the Baptist as the forerunner of Jesus Christ as He appears on the human scene for His public ministry. This parenthesis is given in verses 6 to 8.

John the Baptist is often called the forerunner of the Lord Jesus Christ as the Messiah. He is the prophet of God standing between the Old and New Testaments, between law and grace, between hope and fulfillment. For about 400 years after the last prophet of

165

the Old Testament, Malachi, there was no prophetic voice of God upon earth recorded in the Scriptures. After such a long time, John the Baptist appeared, breaking the silence of the past and initiating a new era. It was natural that attention should be focused on him, and that some people might even believe him to be the promised Messiah, since Malachi had so graphically described the great reforms that were needed in preparation for the coming Messiah.

Because the primary purpose of the Gospel of John is to show forth Jesus Christ as God, the writer of this Gospel takes special care to point out that even such an exceptional man as John the Baptist was not the equal of Jesus Christ. He was concerned lest a mere man receive the glory and adoration that belong to the Son of God. The Apostle John felt it important to clarify right at the outset who is man and who is God, since man cannot save.

In studying all the Scripture references to John the Baptist, we conclude that he never presumed to be what he was not. He was a humble man yet a truly exceptional one, who attracted popular attention. That is why all the references in the Gospel of John pertaining to John the Baptist tend to depreciate the importance of his person and work in comparison with the Lord Jesus Christ. Why does the Evangelist treat him in this way? There is an historical reason for it.

At the time when John was writing his Gospel, in the latter years of the first century in Ephesus, the sect emerged whose followers called themselves *Hemerobaptists*, a Greek word meaning "daily bathers" or those who were baptized daily. Between the time when Paul preached the gospel in Ephesus and the time of the writing of John's Gospel, the person of John the Baptist, who had died the death of a martyr for the faith, had assumed proportions which threatened the supremacy of Jesus Christ. Some people believed that he was not merely the forerunner of the Messiah, but that he himself was the Messiah. As J. B. Lightfoot says, "His baptism was no more a single rite, once performed and initiating an amendment of life; it was a daily recurrence atoning for sin and sanctifying the person." (*St. Paul's Epistles to the Colossians and to Philemon*, Grand Rapids: Zondervan, p. 403). And then he goes on to say, "In the latter half of the first century, it would seem, there was a great movement among large numbers of the Jews in favor of frequent baptism, as the one purificatory rite essential to salvation" (p. 404).

This is a danger that confronts all of us, the tendency to deify man. Let us remember, however, that such a tendency inevitably leads to a corresponding depreciation of Jesus Christ. Carnal presumption about ourselves or others is a weed that grows in the puddled mire of our own hearts. It is sinful not only to presume ourselves greater than we are, but also to presume others more exalted than they are, especially when we compare them with the person and work of Jesus Christ. "Presumption is a fire-work made up of pride and foolhardiness. It is indeed like a heavy house built upon slender crutches. Like dust, which men throw against the wind, it flies back in their faces, and makes them blind." (Author unknown).

We have our John the Baptists even today. We choose a saint or some esteemed person to take the place of Jesus Christ. No doubt, if such a saint of God could rise from the dead, he would vehemently object to what we were saying about him and the worship we accorded him. Jane, a deeply religious woman, presumed that the Virgin Mary, the mother of the Lord Jesus, could do the work of her Son just as effectively as He. And of course, being a woman, she was more attracted to a woman. She was discussing her religious beliefs with a friend, who on the other hand believed that no one could be what Jesus Christ was and is, and that no one else could effect the work of salvation in the human heart. But nothing could persuade Jane. The friend who believed in the exclusiveness of Jesus Christ to save was employed as a maid in a doctor's home. One day Jane became seriously ill and called for the doctor, her friend's employer. The friend answered the phone and said, "I am sorry, but the doctor is not in." And then this Christian woman, who had put all her trust in Jesus Christ, thought of all the theological discussions that she had had with her friend and added, "But, Jane, you know the doctor's mother is in. Maybe she can help you." "Is she a doctor?" "No, but she is the doctor's mother. She will do, won't she?" Immediately Jane could see what her friend was driving at. She wanted to show her in this vivid way that a mother, although she is to be highly respected and honored, cannot be what her son is or do the work of her son. This is true of the Virgin Mary or of anyone else. They cannot be what Jesus Christ is or do what He does, for they are temporal, but Christ is eternal; they are men, but He is God. This is the message which John the Evangelist wants us to get from chapter one, verses 6 to 8.

He begins the contrast between Jesus Christ, the eternal Word, and John the Baptist with a most significant statement. In English it is translated, "There was a man," but the original Greek statement is different. It contains only two words, *egeneto anthroopos.* The verb *egeneto* is better translated "there arose, there came." It is different from the verb *een* (the durative imperfect of *eimi,* "to be"), which John has been using all along to indicate the eternity of Jesus Christ. The verb used with reference to the appearance of John the Baptist is in the second aorist tense, and refers to a definite historical fact. When John the Baptist was born into the world, that was the beginning of his existence, but it was not so with Jesus Christ. He "was" before He "appeared," being God Himself.

No definite article appears before the generic noun *anthroopos,* "man." "There came a man," says verse 6. What the Evangelist wants to emphasize is the nature of this person, this historical person called John the Baptist. He was "man" in comparison to Jesus Christ who was God. To make the meaning clearer, we could paraphrase it thus: "This person of whom I am going to speak now [in the next three verses] was man." He was not God the Word, but just man—in his origin, his make-up, and his work. This statement is in contrast to the third statement in John 1:1, "And the Word was God." Here the Evangelist states the contrast: "And John was man." So is everybody else except Jesus Christ, who, in spite of the fact that He appeared in human form on this earth, was not simply man but the God-man. Many human beings, unfortunately, have been and are being worshiped as gods. If they could, we believe they would cry out from their graves to tell us that they were but men, and that for salvation and life we should go to Jesus Christ.

CHAPTER 39

WHAT DOES IT TAKE TO BE AN APOSTLE?

"There was a man SENT FROM GOD" (John 1:6a).

Certain people today think that there is something mystical about being an apostle. They have the idea that the only apostles were those whom Jesus Christ chose while here on earth. Some go even further and claim that the successors of the original apostles are definitely known, and no one else can claim to be one.

There is one apostle in the New Testament, however, who was not chosen by Jesus Christ during His earthly ministry, but who pointed to the coming of the Messiah. That one is John the Baptist. But someone may say, "Where in the New Testament is he called an apostle?"

In John 1:6 we read, "There was a man sent from God." In the first place, the writer of the Fourth Gospel states that John the Baptist was merely a man. This is of paramount importance. The Evangelist wants us to remember that whatever else this person became, he was primarily a man. God's greatest concern is man. He came to save man. He sends men to warn men of impending doom if they fail to repent. When the rich man was tormented in Hades and was concerned about his five brothers still on earth, he asked Abraham to send Lazarus to warn them. But Abraham answered, "They have Moses and the prophets; let them hear them" (Luke 16:29). These were all men. God is interested in men and uses men. This, of course, includes anyone belonging to the human race, male or female.

This man, John, was sent from God. The word translated

170

"sent" in Greek is *apestalmenos*, which comes from the same root verb *apostelloo* as the word "apostle." As a verb it means "to send away for some mission or service." The declaration here, in a broad sense, then, is that John the Baptist was an apostle.

But what does it mean to be an apostle? In secular Greek, the word *presbus*, "ambassador," was commonly used. The word "apostle" is distinctively a New Testament appellation. It is a compound word made up of the preposition *apo*, meaning "from or away," and the verb *stelloo,* meaning "to send." There are three distinctives in this word which will repay careful study.

An apostle is one who has been sent by somebody else. He does not go as his own representative. As an individual he is not of much account, but as a representative he is worth a great deal. Behind the individual is recognized the country, or the king, or the president who sent the ambassador. An ambassador who seeks to promote himself, instead of the one he represents, will soon be removed. John the Baptist is said to have been an apostle who came from God. He was sent by God. And he proved truly faithful to the One who sent him. Dr. J. H. Jowett, speaking of the time when he was in Northfield, says, "I went out early one morning to conduct a camp meeting away off in the woods. The camp dwellers were two or three hundred men from the Water Street Mission in New York. At the beginning of the service prayer was offered for me, and the supplication opened with these inspired words: 'O Lord, we thank Thee for our brother. Now blot him out.' Then the prayer continued: 'Reveal Thy glory to us in such blazing splendor that he shall be forgotten.' "

That was John's attitude, to glorify Jesus Christ as God and to call attention to Him rather than to himself. He realized he was sent from God and that his ministry was of heavenly origin. Hear him speak: "He that sent me to baptize with water, the same said unto me, Upon whom thou shalt see the Spirit descending, and remaining on him, the same is he which baptizeth with the Holy Ghost" (John 1:33). "Ye yourselves bear me witness, that I said, I

171

am not the Christ, but that I am sent [*apestalmenos*, the same Greek word] before him" (John 3:28).

John the Baptist was sent from God in a very special way. His coming was predicted some 400 years before by the Prophet Malachi. "Behold, I will send my messenger, and he shall prepare the way before me: and the Lord, whom ye seek, shall suddenly come to his temple, even the messenger of the covenant, whom ye delight in: behold, he shall come, saith the Lord of hosts" (3:1). In one sense, of course, John was unique, even as the very special apostles of Christ who saw the Lord personally. And yet, in spite of the fact that the forerunner of Christ was made the subject of prophecy so long ago, the Evangelist still insists that John the Baptist was a mere man, and what counted was not what he had in himself but his faithfulness to the One who sent him, God. Let us not forget that every human spirit is the creation of God. It comes into the world from Him. That is the Christian doctrine of man. Let us realize that, since we are sent here by God, our lives are of some value. Alone as you are, one of millions, if God sent you, you are surely worth something. He must have sent you for some reason. He cannot have made you without any purpose. And if you were made for a purpose, not only is it your first duty to fulfill that purpose, but the way for you to fulfill it is by being yourself. There may be a million Johns, but there are no two alike. If you so closely resemble another person in face, in stature, and in form that even your friends mistake him in the street for you, the resemblance is merely superficial. He is not really like you. He does not have your moral attributes or your mental endowments in the same blend and proportions. Many of your moral characteristics may be alike. In many tastes and aptitudes you may resemble each other. But you two are really as distinct as the North Pole is from the South. God made him as well as you, but He had another purpose for you or He would not have made you. So, as those sent by God, let us make the best of life. Let us not waste its golden days and its priceless gifts. Let us not pine over the past. Let us rejoice in the light that has

172

come to us. Each day will bring to us an opportunity of blessing. Difficulties and hardships will not rob life of its fulfillment. No self-imposed changes would really better your life. You are sent by God. It is yours to fulfill the end for which you are sent. It is His to arrange the circumstances in which you work.

John the Baptist was sent by God Himself. His commission came, not from any human personality or organization, but from God directly. If anyone made that claim today, in our well-organized religious society, he would probably be classified as "beside himself." We live in a world of human recognitions but of few divine commissions. An examining committee of ministers once met to determine the qualifications of Billy Sunday for ordination as a gospel minister. Among other questions fired at the world-famous baseball player was a request that he identify a well-known Church Father and define some of his writings. Billy was stumped. After fumbling around for a moment, he looked up with a twinkle in his eye and said, "I never heard of him. He was never on my team!" The learned theologians deliberated together but found it hard to make a decision. Finally one of them moved that Billy Sunday be recommended for ordination, adding, "He has already won more souls for Christ than the whole shebang of us put together!" The secret—he was sent by God.

How sad that apostleship has degenerated to a humanly appointed office. To be an apostle means to have the authority of the one who sends you. The whole United States stands behind our ambassador to the Soviet Union. If it were not so, he would be of little account. But who dares touch him? Touching him means touching the entire United States with all its might. So it is with those of us who are spiritual ambassadors of God. We represent an authority in the world, and the world cannot touch us or harm us without touching the very God who sent us. This relationship between the commissioner and the commissioned is reciprocal. If the apostle is faithful to God who sends him, then God will back the apostle with all the weight of His authority and power. But if he

173

goes around representing himself, then he has no power but his own and at best that is nothing.

John the Baptist was a real apostle. The faithfulness of his life and the fervency and efficiency of his testimony proved it. He was not hired by any man, so he did not seek to please man, but God who sent him. Can it be said of us that we have been sent of God? Do we manifest His authority? A brilliant liberal preacher, who had pleased his congregation with flowery phrases as he discoursed glibly of the importance of breadth of view and the danger of bigoted opinions, was bidding farewell to them as he was about to leave for a new parish. A young man approached him and said, "Pastor, I am sorry we are losing you. Before you came, I did not care for God, man, or the devil, but through your delightful sermons I have learned to love them all!" Unfortunately, that is the kind of messengers many churches have. No wonder the world is in such a low spiritual state today. Men who claim to be apostles of God lead others to think kindly of the devil! How desperately we need men sent from God, like John the Baptist.

CHAPTER 40

WHAT WE ARE VERSUS WHAT WE SAY

". . . whose name was John. The same came for a witness, to bear witness . . ." (John 1:6b, 7a,b).

———

John the Baptist was an exceptional man, yet a common one. There was a very special way in which it could be said of him that he was sent by God. He was born, not of a virgin, but of one who had long passed the age when childbirth was possible. He came of a priestly race through both parents. His father, Zacharias, was a priest of the course of Abia, or Abijah (I Chron. 24:10), who was offering incense at the very time when a son was promised to him. Elisabeth, his mother, was of the daughters of Aaron (Luke 1:5).

The birth of John was the long-awaited fulfillment of prophecy. It was an angel from heaven who proclaimed the wonderful character and mission of the son for whom this saintly couple had prayed so long. They had about given up hope, which was why they found it difficult to believe the words of the angel. Often the end of life's way has hidden in it the fulfillment of all our dreams and aspirations. It is not wise to conclude prematurely that God does not keep His promises.

Elisabeth, probably embarrassed that at this advanced age she was found with child, retired into the hill country for greater privacy. She was soon followed by her cousin Mary, who later became the mother of the Lord Jesus. Three months after this, while Mary was still with her, Elisabeth was delivered of a son. The birth of John preceded the birth of our Lord by six months. On the eighth day, in conformity to the law of Moses (Lev. 12:3), the child of promise was brought to the priest for circumcision, and as the performance of this rite was the accustomed time for naming the child, the friends of the family proposed to call him Zacharias after his father. The mother, however, insisted that he be called John, a decision which Zacharias—still speechless because of the judgment of God upon him for his lack of faith—confirmed by writing on a tablet. At once his speech was restored to him. God's wonderful interposition in the birth of John impressed the minds of many with a certain solemn awe and expectation (Luke 3:15).

John the Evangelist, unlike Luke, speaks only of the Baptist's character and ministry, telling nothing of his childhood and growth. He satisfies himself with telling us that John the Baptist was a man and not God, in spite of his extraordinary conception; that he was sent by God, and that his name was John.

Luke 1:80 tells us all that we know of John's history during the thirty years between his birth and the beginning of his public ministry. "The child grew, and waxed strong in spirit, and was in the deserts till the day of his shewing unto Israel." John was ordained a Nazarite from birth (Luke 1:15). Dwelling by himself in the wild and thinly peopled region west of the Dead Sea, he prepared himself by self-discipline and constant communion with God for the wonderful office to which he had been called. His dress was that of the prophets of old—a garment of camel's hair (II Kings 1:8) secured by a leather girdle. His food was such as the desert afforded—locusts (Lev. 11:22) and wild honey (Ps. 81:16).

After having told us that the Baptist was a man in spite of his extraordinary birth, that his coming and his mission had long been prophesied, and that he was an apostle sent by God, John the Evangelist then gives us his name, as if in that was contained his character and what God believed him to be. After all, this name was not given to him by his parents, as is usually the case with newborn children, but was given directly by God. "But the angel said unto him, Fear not, Zacharias: for thy prayer is heard; and thy wife Elisabeth shall bear thee a son, and thou shalt call his name

John "(Luke 1:13). There must have been some significance in this particular name. In those days parents usually gave their children names which revealed their secret hopes and aspirations for them. Here, in the name given this child, we have the purpose of God revealed for his life. John meant "God's gracious gift," or "to whom Jehovah is gracious." That's what John was to his parents and to the world. How wonderful if we were all to recognize this when we have children—that they are not really our own but are God's gracious gifts to us, to be treated as such, and that we are constantly to praise God for them.

John was taught early in life by his parents just who he was and why he was here. A Sunday school teacher once asked her class how soon a child should give her heart to God. One little girl said "When she is thirteen years old," another "ten," another "six." Then the last child in the class spoke up and said, "Just as soon as we know who God is." No doubt that is exactly how it was with John. He was introduced to God by his parents, who told him that God was the One who gave him to them. And he never ceased to be His all through his life.

What was the purpose for which John the Baptist was given to the world? To accomplish miracles? No, because it is recorded in John 10:41, "John did no miracle." He did no miracle and yet he was the one chosen of God to point men to the Messiah, Jesus Christ. We need not be able to perform miracles in order to point men and women to Jesus Christ. The Evangelist tells us what John's mission was. "The same came for a witness, to bear witness of the Light, that all men through him might believe" (John 1:7). Is this merely repetition: He "came for a witness" and then "to bear witness"? Do these two statements refer to the same thing or to different things? We believe they refer to two distinct parts of human witnessing to divine truth and revelation.

The first part of verse 7 could be aptly paraphrased, "This one came to be a witness." This speaks of the quality of the witness as a man—his character, his composure, his spiritual and moral

177

standing before the world. It speaks of the person of the witness and of his trustworthiness. In court a witness has to state who he is, and that statement has to be supported by the evidence of his behavior. If he has a police record, his words will not carry much weight. It is the character of a person that renders his testimony acceptable or dubious. This is what the Evangelist is declaring about John the Baptist—that his life and conduct were such as to make the testimony of his mouth acceptable. We have to speak in accord with our nature, and only as we do this will our words be of any value.

A fountain pen salesman persuaded a merchant to order five hundred pens. He was writing the order in his notebook when suddenly the merchant exclaimed, "Hold on! I'm canceling that order!" and turned to wait on a customer. The salesman left the store in angry perplexity. Later, the merchant's bookkeeper asked, "Why did you cancel that fountain pen order?" "Why?" responded the man. "Because he talked fountain pen to me for a half-hour, using a number of forcible arguments, and then booked my order with a lead pencil. His practice did not agree with his profession." The first thing that the Evangelist wants to tell us about John the Baptist is that his practice agreed with his profession. Can that be said of us?

CHAPTER 41

THE COST OF WITNESSING

"The same came for a witness, to bear witness of the Light..."
(John 1:7a, b).

If someone were to ask us who was the greatest man born of woman, what would our answer be? Perhaps we would think of a great conqueror like Alexander the Great or Napoleon, or the father of philosophy, Socrates, or some personal hero of ours. Many would undoubtedly speak of Jesus Christ. But it would not be accurate to classify Him as a mere man born of woman. He was in existence before He was born of the Virgin Mary.

The Lord Jesus Christ gives a surprising testimony as to whom He considered the greatest among men. "Verily I say unto you, Among them that are born of women there hath not risen a greater than John the Baptist" (Matt. 11:11). Yet in what did his greatness consist? In the uprightness of his life and the faithfulness of his testimony. He came to be a witness and to give his witness. The trustworthiness of his message depended upon the righteousness of his life.

The whole purpose of John's coming into the world is succinctly put in John 1:7, "The same came for a witness, to bear witness of the Light, that all men through him might believe." We have seen that the thought is much clearer if we translate the first part of this verse, "This one came to be a witness [literally 'unto witnessing or testimony' or 'unto a witness']." John's whole life proved to be a witness for Jesus Christ. That is the first thing that is recorded of John and that was the basis of his greatness in the sight of God.

179

A group of teen-age girls was discussing a new leader for their Bible class. Their frank comments on the woman in question were enlightening and amusing. One girl said, "If you kids pick Mrs. L— to be our teacher, I'm quitting." "Why, what's wrong with her?" asked several of the group. "Plenty," was the reply. "Remember how I used to go to help her with her housework on Saturdays? Well, she still owes me money and she won't pay. Also, she talks a lot about being a good Christian, and boy, you should hear her say nasty things about some of her neighbors. Honest, kids, I know I shouldn't talk about her, but, please, let's wait until we find a teacher who lives what she teaches us on Sunday." Is this just an isolated case, or is it not rather the rule with many who stand up to witness for Jesus Christ? Their mouths may speak of Christ— but their years, months, days, hours, and moments are not saturated with the Spirit and Life of Christ. John was a Christ-honoring witness. The very purpose for which he came into the world and went about his daily round was to live out Christ among his fellow men. Would to God this might be the purpose of every Christian's life.

But the testimony of our life is not enough. There must also be the testimony of our mouth. It is the mouth that can explain our reasons for being what we are and doing what we do. As soon as John the Baptist began to preach the message of repentance in the wilderness, he introduced himself as "The voice of one crying in the wilderness" (Matt. 3:3), borrowing the term from the Prophet Isaiah (40:3). He was a life; he was a voice.

John came that he might witness with his mouth. The second clause of our verse is one of purpose introduced by the Greek word *hina,* meaning "in order to." This is followed by the verb *martureesee,* which is in the aorist tense. This, coupled with our factual knowledge of the shortness of John's ministry, leads us to see this suggested in the tense. The length of his testimony was not the important thing, but rather its quality. It isn't how much we say for Christ, but what we say, that counts. John the Baptist was a young

180

man in his early thirties when he suffered a martyr's death, nevertheless, he bore in full the testimony for which he came. Rather than ask, "Lord give us long years to serve Thee well," let us pray, "Lord, help us to pack the years or months of our life with meaningful and effectual testimony for Thee." We should feel no disappointment over a short life as long as that life has accomplished its purpose in testifying for Christ.

What did John witness about? He bore witness of the Light. Undoubtedly reference is made here to the eternal Christ who was to appear in human form. The word "Light" (*phoos)* is used here in the absolute sense, just as it was in verse 4. In this passage Jesus Christ in His eternity is called the Word, the Life, the Light. These words, used in their absolute sense, are names of the Lord Jesus Christ, which names, however, stand for the manifestation of some special characteristic of the Lord. Here, in connection with the testimony of the Baptist, the word Light is used in order to show the purpose of this testimony. John spoke of Christ as Light.

But does light need someone to point to it? Isn't light self-revealing? Do we need to stand out in the street and shout to those who pass by, "That's the sun," as we point to it in all its brightness? The sun is self-revealing in the same sense that Jesus Christ was and is as the Light of the world. The fact that John the Baptist came to give his witness about the Light did not in any way steal from it the power to reveal itself. The necessity for the human testimony of the Baptist is a clear indication of the complete depravity of man, his inability to comprehend that which is spiritual. His mind and heart have been so darkened by sin that, seeing the Light, he does not recognize it as the Light. We must also remember that what men and women actually saw down here on earth was a human Jesus. Their darkened vision could not see anything superhuman in Him. It was necessary for someone like John the Baptist to tell them that this One who walked with them, who ate with them, and who was even buffeted and spat upon by them, was the Light.

Man's total darkness and depravity, then, are the reason for the necessity of witnessing for Christ. The Light shines, but people do not comprehend it; they do not understand the nature of it. That is why we who know Him must tell others who Christ is and what He can do.

A witness speaks from experience. Otherwise his testimony is worth nothing in a court of justice. The first thing a judge asks a witness is what he personally knows, what he has personally seen of a situation about which the truth is sought. Secondhand or hearsay testimony is not accepted. So it is with those who witness for Jesus Christ. They must first be exposed to the Light of Jesus Christ themselves and then speak about it. Only the man who knows Christ can tell others about Him. The tragedy of the hour is that so many of those who pose as spiritual Christian leaders have never become acquainted with Jesus Christ as the Light and the Life of their lives. Today we have a superabundance of preachers, but not enough witnesses. Anyone can preach, but it takes one who is really a Christian, and who has sacrificed something for his faith, to witness to the truth he has found.

It is most interesting to note that in Greek the word *martus*, which has always meant "witness," later came to mean "martyr" also. This additional meaning of the word was the result of so many Christians being persecuted and killed because of their faithful witness. A martyr came to mean one who pays with his life for his belief and faith. And that is what John the Baptist was. He was a witness, but the faithfulness of his witness brought about his martyrdom. John was not afraid to bear witness to Christ, even before the king. He rebuked sin no matter where it was found or what the consequences to himself. When Herod committed a grievous offense against purity and the sanctity of marriage, it was John the Baptist who met him with a denunciation of his sin. He knew full well it might cost him his life, but that did not hinder him from rebuking sin. Because of this he lost his head, but he won the crown of heaven. Such was the witness of John the Baptist, courageous and uncompromising. Would to God we had more such witnesses!

CHAPTER 42

THE PURPOSE OF WITNESSING

". . . that all men through him might believe. He was not that Light, but was sent to bear witness of that Light" (John 1:7c, 8).

———————

Why should Christians witness to the saving light of the Gospel of Jesus Christ? Not because He cannot reveal Himself directly to man and save him. Since God is omnipotent, there is nothing He cannot do in connection with the salvation of the individual soul. However, he has ordained the means by which those who come in contact with us should believe. A most amazing thing in God's plan of salvation is that He does not really need us and yet He chooses to use us. What a privilege and honor this is, for us to be workers together with God!

The purpose of witnessing should always be practical. It should lead others to say, "I believe on the Lord Jesus Christ." And when they say this, the work of the witness has come to a successful completion. John, in speaking of the witness of the Baptist, expresses it this way, "in order that all may believe through him" (literal translation). What does this mean?

First, we have here the expression of will and desire on the part of the witnessing one, though not necessarily a conclusive response from the one witnessed to. This declaration does not say that all those to whom we witness will necessarily be saved. Would to God it were so, but it is not. The Lord Himself spoke to thousands, but only a few believed on Him. As we witness, we must always have the salvation of the person we speak to in mind, but that does not

183

mean that he or she will necessarily believe. Conviction is entirely a work of the Holy Spirit.

There are many hungry people in the world today. We may bring them food to eat and as a result rightfully expect to see happy faces that are the expression of contented stomachs. But we cannot force food down their throats. In this whole business of witnessing for Christ, the full operation of the Holy Spirit has to be taken into account. We cannot make converts ourselves. Our part is to witness, not to convert. The two are related but not activated by the same person. We witness and God saves through the Holy Spirit. He may save without our witnessing, but, since He chooses to want our witnessing, it would be unthinkable for us not to have a share in His work. However, we must know where we stop and He begins exclusively. A strong desire on the part of the witness does not necessarily bring about conviction on the part of the hearer.

Mr. Spurgeon once preached what in his judgment was one of his poorest sermons. He stammered and floundered and felt that his message was a complete failure. He was greatly humiliated and, when he got home, he fell on his knees and said, "Lord God, Thou canst do something with nothing. Bless that poor sermon." All through the week he uttered that prayer. He woke up in the night and prayed about it. He determined that the next Sunday he would redeem himself by preaching a great sermon. Sure enough, the sermon next Sunday went off beautifully. At the close, the people crowded about him and covered him with praise. Spurgeon went home pleased with himself and that night he slept like a baby. But he said to himself, "I'll watch the results of those two sermons." What were they? From the one that had seemed a failure he was able to trace forty-one conversions. And from that magnificent sermon he was unable to discover that a single soul had been saved. Spurgeon's explanation was that the Spirit of God used the one and did not use the other. The motive of witnessing is most important in our Christian walk.

But someone may object, "Doesn't John say 'in order that all may believe through him'? What does 'all' mean?" The Greek word used here is *pantes.* We must remember that belief in the Scriptures is an individual matter and not a collective achievement. When a pastor preaches the Gospel to his congregation, he doesn't actually urge the group as a whole to believe, but the individuals within the whole. And of course his desire is that every individual within the whole may believe. The witnessing may be either to a single individual or to many individuals within a group. But the response in believing is always individual. Each person believes for himself. No one can believe for someone else. No father can believe for his whole family. No leader can believe for the whole group. When this is attempted, there is danger that individual belief will be lost in the collective formal acceptance of Christianity, as occurred in the Church at the time of Constantine the Great.

The Greek lexicographers, Liddell and Scott, tell us this word *pantes,* here translated "all," when used of the several persons in a number, means "every" and is equivalent to the Greek *hekastos.* *(A Greek-English Lexicon,* Seventh Edition, New York, 1889, p. 1160.) This word "all," then, could very well be taken to mean the individuals within the group.

Now, which group did this refer to? Of course, primarily it referred to those who came to the wilderness to hear the Baptist preach. But it extends further than that, to all the human race, to every man who has ever lived, to us as individuals. No one has a right to say that God never meant him to believe, for the application is to everyone within the human race. God's will and desire is that all might believe. As Paul says in I Timothy 2:4, "Who will have all men to be saved, and to come unto the knowledge of the truth." And then Peter says, "The Lord is . . . not willing that any should perish but that all should come to repentance" (II Pet. 3:9). This is the expressed will and desire of God, that every member of the human race may believe. But we know, both in the Scriptures and in our own experience with men, that many are called but few chosen (Matt. 20:16). Some will believe and some will not. But our

185

witnessing should be addressed to all, for we do not know who will accept and who will reject.

What does believing mean? Here it is used in an absolute sense. It does not say "believe on Christ" but simply "believe." But since the general subject in this passage is the Lord Jesus Christ, the eternal Word becoming flesh for our salvation, undoubtedly the word "believe" must refer to the acknowledgment of Christ as God incarnate for our redemption. It means accepting Him as our Saviour.

Interestingly, the verb "believe" in Greek is in the aorist tense (*pisteusoosin*). This refers to that initial experience when man under the influence of the Holy Spirit accepts Jesus Christ as his personal Saviour. That was the task of John the Baptist, to introduce Jesus Christ to those who had not experienced Him. In other words, he was an evangelist. Our witness to the unbeliever should also be evangelistic, for his greatest need is that initial experience of the new birth, of believing that Christ died for his sins and that he can be free from them by accepting the work of Christ on Calvary's cross.

This verse also tells us that God honors the testimony of His witnesses. "That all men through him might believe." Undoubtedly the word "him" refers to John the Baptist as a witness. The author of the Fourth Gospel is not speaking of the Baptist exclusively, but of his office as a witness for Jesus Christ. It shows the place of human instrumentality in God's plan to lead men to believe on Jesus Christ. God uses our witness for Him. Now, John the Baptist has no magic power in himself to make people believe. It is his witness to Jesus Christ that is referred to, since in this context the person of John the Baptist is spoken of. The same thing can be said of us as we bear witness for our Lord.

In verse 8 John proceeds to clear up a possible misunderstanding about John the Baptist. Some who heard him may have overestimated his work and witness and believed him to be equal with Christ, whose forerunner he was. That is why John states, "He was not that Light, but was sent to bear witness of that Light."

John the Evangelist here reverts to the verb *een,* which in this context we translate as "had been." It is the durative imperfect of the verb *eimi,* "to be," which, in the first 18 verses of John's Gospel, when used of Christ or the Word, refers to His eternity. Thus John tells us that John the Baptist had not always been the Light, for only Christ is the eternal Light. But didn't the Lord Himself say of John the Baptist, "He was a burning and a shining light" (5:35)? As we examine the Greek text, we find that an entirely different word is used from that in John 1:8. In speaking of Christ, John uses the word *phoos,* "light," which refers to the light of the sun or the day. It is the brightest light imaginable. But the word used for John the Baptist in John 5:35 is *luchnos,* which is a hand lamp fed with oil. A lamp is lit by the hands of another, and in this instance it is Jesus Christ. Men may rejoice for a season in its brightness, but then it must be extinguished. Though John the Baptist was a light that illumined the face of Jesus Christ, Christ the eternal One has always been the Light of the world. We who are witnesses are lamps lit by Him who is the Light.

John the Baptist could never do the work of Christ nor could he claim to be the Light. He came in order to witness to the Light. The fact that he himself was a lamp was proof of the truth of the Light and the efficacy of that Light to light the path of all who believe. May we, too, be true lamps of the true Light. Then others cannot help but see the Light through our shining.

CHAPTER 43

THE ETERNAL CHRIST COMING INTO THE WORLD

"That was the true Light, which lighteth every man that cometh into the world" (John 1:9).

A great French writer once said that from the Christian point of view the history of the world could be summarized in three phrases: Christ was coming, Christ is come, and Christ is to come again. The first of these phrases is the subject of John 1:9. However, as this verse is translated in the King James Version, it does not do justice to the thought in the mind of John, as we find it in the original Greek text.

In the first five verses of his Gospel, John has spoken of the eternity and infinity of the Word, Jesus Christ. He has called Him Word (*Logos*), Life, and Light. In verses 6 and 7 he has introduced John the Baptist as the forerunner of Christ's ministry as the Messiah. He appeared in order to tell others of the coming Christ. In verse 8, he has made it absolutely clear that we should not confuse the two, Jesus Christ and John the Baptist, since One was eternal and the other temporal. John the Baptist had never been the eternal Light, as Jesus Christ had been, but simply came to witness to the Light.

Now, in verses 9 to 12, John gives the purpose of Christ's coming and the reception accorded him by men. The literal translation of verse 9, in the exact sequence in which the words occur, is "He had been or was the light, the genuine (one), which illumines every man, coming into the world."

In order to understand this verse, we must first determine what its subject is. Clearly, it is the Word of whom John has been speaking all along. He spoke of His being the Light and of John the Baptist's coming to give witness to that Light. In further contrasting Jesus Christ with John the Baptist (or any other human being), John goes on to say what kind of Light the Word was.

It is noteworthy that the verb used here is *een*, which in this context is used exclusively to designate the eternity of Jesus Christ, and which for the sake of distinction we have translated "had been." Thus the first declaration of this verse is that "the Word, Jesus Christ, had been the Light eternally." This is a thought that has been previously expressed, but because of its importance it is emphasized again, and we believe it can never be stressed too much. Christ has always been the eternal Light.

But not only was He the eternal Light; He was also the true Light. The Greek word translated "true" in the King James Version is *aleethinon*, which John uses twenty-two times in his writings and which occurs only five times in the rest of the New Testament. This word is to be distinguished from a similar Greek word, *aleethees*. The first means "genuine, perfect in its make-up," while the second means "truthful in its expression." Here John was not declaring that Jesus Christ was truthful, but rather that He was the real, the genuine Light, not only in His substance and make-up, but also in His eternity. That, of course, did not imply that the light of John the Baptist was false, but rather that the One was original, like the light of the sun or the sun itself, and the other was borrowed, reflected light. John the Baptist had no light of his own, while Jesus Christ was Light. Herein consisted His genuineness and perfection. He was perfect in His originality, substance, and eternity. "He, the Word, Jesus Christ, had always been the Light, the genuine one."

The emphasis on the uniqueness of Christ in His genuineness precedes the declaration of the purpose of His incarnation. The Evangelist is telling us that Christ is the only One who can save man from sin. In Him salvation is genuine and perfect. Outside of Him there is no salvation. When people think they have salvation

189

outside of Christ, it is imperfect, and an imperfect salvation is no salvation at all. It is said that when one of the most noted English physicians was succumbing to a fatal disease, he went from one authority to another until he had reached the highest on the continent. Telling this man his trouble, he received the reply, "The only man who can save you is an English physician, Dr. Darwin of Derby." "Alas!" was the reply, "I am Dr. Darwin of Derby." He was the best, but he could not save himself. Even the best of us cannot save ourselves.

We believe the last clause of this verse ("that cometh into the world") actually refers to the first clause ("That was the true Light"), describing the Light, and that what lies between is a parenthetical statement. The first clause declares that Jesus Christ had always been the only genuine Light. But what concerns us is not only what Jesus Christ was in Himself in eternity, but His relationship to us and what He can do for us. A man may be good, but his goodness means something to us only when it is manifested as help and benevolence toward us. What this verse really states is "[The Word] had been the Light, the genuine one . . . coming into the world." Here we have the Creator of the world entering His own creation, the Infinite and Eternal One penetrating the finite and the temporal. In other words, the verb *een,* "had been," has two predicates referring to it. The Word was or had been what? First, "the Light, the genuine Light," and second, "coming into the world." The first marks the essence of Christ and the second its relationship to His creation.

But why does John say, "coming into the world" and not "came into the world"? What does he want to signify by using the participle *erchomenon,* "coming"? This is the present participle and may be called anticipatory. It refers to something that is about to happen. The Lord Jesus Christ from His eternity has been purposing to come into the world and now He is about to manifest Himself in His public ministry, which is to be followed by His death and resurrection. It is this public appearance of Jesus Christ

190

that John the Baptist was a witness to. He did not particularly come to declare the eternity of Jesus Christ, but the fact that eternity was to enter history actively and personally and change it decisively. It is as if John were shouting by what he did and what he said, "The Light is coming openly! You will see Him, for He is the Light!"

The Lord Jesus Christ was about to enter the world of human beings and physical forces. In a way, He was going to commit Himself to their evil intents and purposes in order to achieve their salvation through His death. Yet His entrance into this world was entirely voluntary, as evidenced by the participle *erchomenon*, "coming," which has no connotation of constraint but rather indicates willingness. But that is not the way we come into the world. We did not come from a prior existence, as Christ did. And that is one reason why this participle cannot be taken to refer to the word "man," which immediately precedes it in the text. Christ came into the world of men and of created things voluntarily and subjected Himself to their whims. Such an act could only be committed by God, or a fool: a fool because he knew no better than to fall into the hands of his enemies, but God because of His great love for us and to show us that, although He descended voluntarily to the lowest depths of humiliation, He also reached the greatest heights of exaltation in His resurrection and ascension.

Of course, another reason for believing that the durative imperfect verb *een*, "had been," and the present participle *erchomenon*, "coming," go together is that they indicate to us the eternal saving purpose of Jesus Christ. From the beginning, the Lord Jesus Christ had been going to come into this world to save it. That was His eternal intent. And this construction also shows the progressive revelation of God to His creation, through the prophets and through natural phenomena, as well as through the various theophanies of the Old Testament. All along, the Word in His eternity has been appearing as the Light of the world and has finally appeared in the person of the Son. As Hebrews 1:1, 2 says, "God, who at sundry times and in divers manners spake in time past unto the fathers by the prophets, hath in these last days spoken unto us by his Son, whom he hath appointed heir of all things, by whom also he made the worlds.''

CHAPTER 44

THE WORK OF LIGHT

". . . which LIGHTETH every man . . ." (John 1:9b).

———————

John has already told us in the first clause of this verse that Jesus Christ was the eternal and only genuine, perfect Light. In the third clause he says that this eternal and genuine Light was about to enter the physical world He had created. "[The Word] had been the light, the genuine one ; . . coming into the world," is the literal rendering of the first and third clauses. In between these clauses John tells us of the purpose or work of this eternal and genuine Light: "which lighteth every man." What does this mean? Does it mean universal salvation? Does it mean that the eternal Light becomes the possession of every human being? Nothing of the sort.

John here speaks of the practical value of this genuine and eternal Light. Its work is to light every man. In the Greek text, the verb used is *phootizee,* which is derived from the basic word *phoos,* meaning "light." This is a transitive verb, which means that its activity is passed on to an object—in this case to "every man." What the Light, the genuine, eternal Light is, it also enables man to become. One is the Source of Light and the other becomes the recipient of Light. What a glorious truth this is, that we mortals may acquire the Light of God, the Light that is God! But this is not because of any merit of our own. The initiative is taken entirely by Jesus Christ, who came into the world for that very purpose, to enable us to participate in His Light. He becomes our Light.

On a dark and stormy night, a little child was lost in the streets of a large city. A policeman found him crying in distress, and gathering enough from his story to locate the home, gave him directions after this manner: "Just go down this street half a mile, turn and cross the big iron bridge, then turn to your right and follow the river down a little way, and you'll see where you are." The poor child, only half comprehending, chilled and bewildered by the storm, turned about blindly, when another voice spoke in a kindly tone, "Just come with me." The little hand was clasped in a stronger one, the corner of a warm coat was thrown over the shoulders of the shivering child, and the way home was made easy. The first man had told the way; the second man became the way. This is exactly what the Lord Jesus Christ has done for us. From eternity He had told us the way, by letting His light shine, but we still could not find the way. He had to become our Light, and that Light is effective. It passes from Him to us without in any way diminishing His Light. What a glorious possibility this is, that we humans may receive eternal Light!

The tense of the verb *phootizee,* "lighteth," is arresting. It is the present indicative. You remember what we said about the verb *een,* "had been," referring to the eternal existence of Jesus Christ as the Light, the genuine Light. That's how verse 9 starts, with timelessness— a special emphasis on the fact that with Jesus Christ there is no beginning. And then the last clause of our verse uses the anticipatory participle *erchomenon,* "coming," referring to the imminent coming of the eternal Christ into the world in public ministry and activity. Here is timeless past, if we may call it that, and imminent future. In between stands a verb in the present indicative. That is what connects eternity with history, as far as the Lord Jesus Christ is concerned. John wants to stress through the use of the verb *phootizee,* "lighteth," in the present indicative, that the eternal Light of Jesus Christ has been illuminating all human beings in some way or another, in ways known and unknown, and possibly even unknowable.

A more correct rendering of this tense would be "has been illuminating." This would embrace the past, the present, and the future. Very well does grammarian William Edward Jelf say, "The present most usually signifies an incomplete action yet in course of performance, going on coincidentally with the time present to the speaker" (*A Grammar of the Greek Language,* Third Edition, Vol. II Syntax, 1859, p.58). This means that the revelation of the Light of Jesus Christ at the time John was speaking was still in progress. It had not been completed. It extended as far back as man could think and on into the future. This very strongly suggests the progressive revelation of the Light that is in Christ to the human race. Christ appeared as the Angel of the Lord in many instances in the Old Testament and now finally He was to appear in human flesh. This appearance of Christ in human flesh, however, in no way means that His light did not illuminate men in the past. It started in the past, it goes on now, and it will continue in the future.

It also seems to us that the present tense is used in order to give more emphasis to the fact that the saving work of Christ, at the time that John wrote and as long as this age of grace shall last, is always a present tense matter. John the Baptist was preaching the message of repentance, but it is inconceivable that he was urging those who wanted to find forgiveness right then and there to wait until some time in the future, when the work of the cross and the empty tomb would be physical accomplishments. The illumination of Christ, the eternal Light, is presently effective. There is no better and more effective time than the present. "Behold, now is the accepted time; behold, now is the day of salvation" (II Cor. 6:2). We are not to be like that cabin boy who, when pleaded with to give his heart to the Lord in Sunday school, used to say, "I will repent, next day after never." His steamer was lost at sea and he with it. The next day may well be the day after never. That's why our verse says that (the Word) *phootizee,* "lighteth," here and now; for after now may come never.

Alexander the Great, on being asked how he had conquered the world, replied, "By not delaying." Most of those who are not already saved are among those who in all probability intend to be saved. But so few of this class ever find salvation that it has become a proverb, "The way to hell is paved with good intentions." Every year leaves them less likely to be saved, for they have become more accustomed to the deceitfulness of sin; some hardness is added every year, every day, to their consciences. Soft sponges oftentimes become flints by a peculiar process. Sponges contain particles of flint or silex which continually attract particles to themselves, until in process of time the whole mass is an aggregate of flinty matter and the softness of the sponge has disappeared. It is exactly thus with our conscience; its sensibilities gradually give way to the hardening particles that are introduced by every sin we commit. There is no better time than now for us to open our hearts to the Light.

CHAPTER 45

WILL GOD ULTIMATELY SAVE EVERYONE?
". . . which lighteth EVERY man . . ."(John 1:9b).

In the original Greek, John 1:9 tells us that Jesus Christ "had been the light, the genuine one, which lighteth every man." We have seen that the Greek verb *phootizee*, "lighteth," is in the present indicative tense, indicating two particular things: (1) that this action of the Light upon men spans the past and the future, and (2) that it appeals to the present as the best and most appropriate time for its action and reception.

But there is still another reason, we believe, for its being in the present indicative. It indicates the continuous action of the Light. It precludes intermittence. The Light does not illuminate at one moment, then fail to shine for a time, and thus keep up a process of "light" and "no light." No, the Light of Jesus Christ has been shining and illuminating everyone from the very beginning of the creation, and will continue to the very end. Its action is constant and uninterrupted. No one, therefore, can excuse himself on the ground that the Light was not shining at any particular time, and thus put the blame for his lost condition on Jesus Christ. The method of this illumination and its intensity may have varied, but always the Light has been shining and illuminating, whether through conscience (Rom. 2:14-16), or through nature (Rom. 1:19-21), or through the direct revelation of Jesus Christ. There has been Light in the world, and its utmost intensity is now, the now of all times for the people of every time.

And there is yet another beautiful thought hidden in the tense of

197

this verb *phootizee,* "lighteth." Not only does it speak of non-intermittence, but also of continuity after the original illumination that led to regenerating enlightenment. Here is the Light of Christ shining upon every human being. Man decides to accept that Light. He then becomes an illuminated being. He possesses the Light of God. But this process does not stop there. Christ does not fill him with enough Light, so to speak, at the time of his new birth into the Kingdom of Heaven to last him for eternity. He has to receive a constant effusion of Light. Christ continues to illuminate him, and he must continue to receive His Light constantly if he wants to shine. Man is like the moon in this respect. In order for it to continue to be a luminary, it must constantly receive the light of the sun. How could we live one second without the Light of Christ? He illuminates us not only once but constantly.

A city missionary visited a poor old woman in an attic room who scarcely had sufficient money for her bare existence. He observed a strawberry plant growing in a broken teapot on the windowsill, and on subsequent visits remarked how it continued to grow and with what care it was watched and tended. "Your plant flourishes nicely; you will soon have strawberries on it." "Oh, sir, it is not for the sake of the fruit that I prize it, but I am too poor to keep any living creature, and it is a great comfort to have that plant living, for I know it can only live by the power of God; and as I see it live and grow day by day, it tells me God is near." This lonely Christian wanted something to remind her constantly that life in its continuance and growth was a direct result of God's activity. Would to God we realized it ourselves! It is true that we are luminaries, but it is because of the constant illumination we receive from Christ. We have no light of our own, and not for a single moment could we live and shine without receiving His Light.

But what is the real meaning of this verb *phootizee,* "lighteth"? Does it mean that Christ automatically saves everyone? Is the term equivalent to salvation? Here it is used transitively, so that it calls attention to the object upon which the light falls. The object here is man, every man. It is used, of course, in a spiritual sense, so that man here can be taken to mean the heart, the soul, the spirit, the mind of man — call it what you will. It is that immaterial part of man which God seeks to save and which lives eternally. But what does enlightening our spirits really imply? That we have appropriated that Light and made it ours? No, it does not, and for good reason.

Immediately after this verse, we are presented with two classes of people, those who rejected Jesus Christ and those who accepted Him. If the 9th verse taught universal salvation, how could we reconcile it with verses 10, 11, and 12?

Also, the verb in this verse is not in the passive voice, as it is in Ephesians 1:18, and Hebrews 6:4 and 10:32. The active voice indicates God's activity, but does not necessarily determine man's response to that activity. The eternal and genuine Light of Christ is shed abroad upon the soul of every man, but that does not mean that every man accepts that Light and is consequently illuminated in the sense of being saved or regenerated. As far as God is concerned, His salvation is universal; it is to every creature; it is to "whosoever" believeth on Him. But whosoever does not believe cannot blame God that His Light did not fall upon him. The Light falls upon everyone.

This enlightenment by Christ is the first step in the reconciliation of man to God. It is only as the Light comes down from heaven that man is enabled to see God and consequently to appropriate Him. Without this heavenly Light shining upon the earth, it would be totally impossible for any man to see and appropriate God.

As the Light descends from heaven upon man, it not only makes God visible, but it brings to light all that man is. All of us know the experience of groping in the dark. There is an object yonder, but we don't know what it is. One way to find out is to take a flashlight and shine a beam upon it. We thus illuminate the object and show what it is. That's exactly what Christ's Light has done as far as our spiritual natures are concerned. It has revealed how sinful, how bankrupt we are, how helpless and miserable. And in this respect no one can ever hide from God's revealing Light. Human vanity prompts us to admire our reflection in the mirror. But what would happen if we viewed ourselves under a microscope? We might see imperfections in our fine skin to be ashamed of. Instead of smoothness we would see irregularity, coarseness, even impurity. It is such revelations that the Light of God makes to us and to others as it falls upon us. Look at the mirror of the Word of God and you will see that there is nothing good in us that any should love us. Such, then, is the work of the Light of heaven falling upon us. It brings to light everything that we would like to have hidden about ourselves.

On whom does this Light fall? On "every man." Here we have an adjective, *panta* ("every"), and a noun, *anthroopon* ("man"). John does not say *pantas anthroopous*, "all men," but "every man." Why? Because he wants to emphasize the individual members of the class denoted by the noun following the adjective (Arndt and Gingrich, *A Greek-English Lexicon of the New Testament and Other Early Christian Literature*, The University of Chicago Press, p. 636). The word *anthroopos* is used here in its generic sense; it stands for the entire human race, all the humans who have ever lived or will live. But although John wants to show the all-inclusiveness of the human race as the objects of the eternal Light, he also wants to emphasize the individual within the universal. In other words, he declares that the Light of the eternal Christ shines on every individual human being, irrespective of time or space. God is interested primarily in the individual within His universe. It is individuals as individuals that He saves, and not groups as such. And we can only respond to that Light as individuals and not collectively. A collective response to the Gospel can be such only as it is made up of the aggregate of individual decisions. Let us make sure that each of us is not only the particular object of God's shining Light, but also the voluntary recipient of the salvation and life He gives.

After a mission service, the preacher of the evening was

200

hurrying away to a late train. He had just three minutes to catch it when he saw a man running after him. "Oh, sir," he said breathlessly as he came up, "can you help me? I am very anxious about my salvation." "Well," replied the preacher, "my train is just here, and it is the last one; but look up Isaiah 53:6. Go in at the first 'all' and go out at the last 'all.' Good night." The man stood staring after him until he had disappeared into the station and then he muttered, "Go in at the first 'all' and go out at the last 'all.' What does he mean?" When he arrived home he took down his Bible and turning to Isaiah 53:6 read these words, "All we like sheep have gone astray; we have turned every one to his own way; and the Lord hath laid on him the iniquity of us all." "Go in at the first 'all,'" he repeated. "'All we like sheep have gone astray.' I am to go in with that 'all.' Yes, I see. It just means that I am one of those who have gone astray. And go out with the last 'all.' 'The Lord hath laid on him the iniquity of us all.' I see. Yes, I am to go out free with those whose iniquity has been laid on Christ." And at last he realized his individual lost condition and his individual redemption. This is actually the message of John 1:9. The eternal Light of Christ illumines the individual souls within the totality. Blessed is the individual who responds affirmatively. "Go in at the first 'all' and go out at the last 'all.'"

CHAPTER 46

CAN MANKIND KNOW ITS CREATOR?

"He was in the world, and the world was made by him, and the world knew him not" (John 1:10).

Of you and me it could not be said, centuries before we were born into the world, that we were one day coming into it. That would involve our prior existence, on which the Scriptures are silent. But of Jesus Christ it was said that He was to come into the world voluntarily. When our existence in the world became a reality, it was not because of our will and action, but as the result of the will and action of others, our parents.

Though John speaks of Christ's "coming into the world" in the last clause of verse 9, he does not want us to confuse the historic appearance of Jesus Christ in the world with His eternal existence in the world. This is why he immediately declares in verse 10, "in the world he had been." When Jesus Christ came into the world physically, He stepped into it from a prior eternal existence. The coming into the world was physical, whereas His eternal existence in the world was spiritual. However, His physical appearance in the world of space and time did not abrogate His being in the world spiritually and omnipresently.

This is shown by the use of two different verbs in these clauses. In John 1:9c the participle *erchomenon,* "coming," is used; but in 10a the verb *een,* "was or had been," is used. This is the durative imperfect of the verb *eimi,* which in this context—the first 18 verses of John's Gospel—refers to timelessness, to eternity. In other words, the expression "in the world he had been" means "he

202

had always been in the world." The Creator of the world, as Jesus Christ is declared to be in this passage, has never divorced Himself from His creation. The world has not been left to chance or to its own choice and fate, but it is in the hands of the One who made it. Thus Jesus' coming into the world as the Son of Man was an historical event, but Christ's being in the world is an eternal fact.

What does John mean by the word "world"? In the Greek it is *kosmos,* from which we derive the English words "cosmic, cosmogony," etc. It has a variety of meanings, but here we believe it primarily refers to the sum total of the orderly universe. Since the verb *een,* "had been," is used, we could very well take this clause to read, "Before the world, the universe, was, Jesus Christ, the *Logos,* the Word, had been." He existed prior to the universe He created. And this is perfectly logical, since the Creator must exist before that which He creates.

Then John tells us that, after He created the universe, He remained in it as its sustaining force. How beautifully Paul expresses it in Colossians 1:17, "And he is before all things, and by him all things consist." That word translated "consist" is *sunesteeken,* which in its infinitive form means "to hold together, cohere." And as J. B. Lightfoot says, "He is the principle of cohesion in the universe. He impresses upon creation that unity and solidarity which makes it a cosmos instead of a chaos. Thus (to take one instance) the action of gravitation, which keeps in their places things fixed and regulates the motions of things moving, is an expression of His mind. Similarly in Heb. 1:3 Christ the *Logos* is described as *pheroon ta panta* (sustaining the Universe) *too rheemati tees dunameoos autou,* by the word of His power." (*Colossians and Philemon,* Zondervan Publishing House, p. 156.)

Thus John's declaration is threefold: (1) Jesus Christ had been in existence before the world, the universe, was created. (2) He created the universe. (3) He sustains the universe by being in it.

But let us not misunderstand this as pantheism. By Christ's

being in the world we do not mean that He is to be identified with His creation, as so many people unfortunately believe who call Him "Nature." Everything in the universe is not God, but God's force is in everything in the universe, for the universe could not exist for a single moment without Him. He who came to Bethlehem as man has always been the sustaining force of the universe.

We find further in the writings of John that *kosmos,* "world," is also used to mean the sum total of all beings above the level of animals. It is the sphere of human life as an ordered whole, considered apart from God. And this is the particular meaning that the word has in the third clause of verse 10, "and the world knew him not." This refers particularly to the human element of the universe rather than the universe in its totality.

But before we go on to examine this last clause of our verse, let us look at the second, "and the world was made by him." The verb used here is *egeneto,* "came into existence," which is the same verb used in verse 3. In the previous clause, in speaking of the eternal Christ, John uses the verb *een,* "had been"; but now, since he is referring to an historical event, to the creation of the universe, he uses the verb *egeneto,* "came into existence at a certain time in history." He "had been" before the world, and the world came into being through Him. But when He created the world, He remained in it as its only sustaining force.

"And the world knew him not." In the original Greek the order of the words is "and the world him did not know." What does that mean? Of course, the term "world," *kosmos,* must refer to the sum total of humans created. The rocks and water cannot know God, but only those of His creatures who have been endowed with the power of thinking and knowing.

It is important for us to determine the meaning of the verb *ouk egnoo,* "did not know." This is the second aorist tense, active voice, of the verb *ginooskoo,* "to know." This verb means "to know by observation," as distinguished from the verb *eidenai,* which means "to know by reflection." If we were to paraphrase this

204

statement, we would say, "And the human race did not know the eternal Christ by observation." And that is true, for until the coming of the Word in human flesh, mankind had no opportunity of observing God with its eyes. But in His coming into history as Jesus, man could observe Him. And the eternal Christ made Himself observable in human flesh so that man would be completely inexcusable for not recognizing and obeying Him. But sadly enough, even after He appeared in human flesh and mankind had an opportunity to observe Him, they still did not recognize Him.

The real meaning here of the verb *egnoo* is "recognize, acknowledge." Mankind as a whole never acknowledged Jesus Christ as its Creator and sustainer, either before His incarnation or after it, either before they observed Him or after His coming to live among them (I John 3:1, John 16:3).

The fact that this verb is in the active voice indicates that man of his own will and in his own power cannot recognize God. This is why God's revelation was needed, both before the incarnation and after it. Man cannot recognize Christ by groping. Christ has to reveal Himself to the human race, to you and me individually. He had to take the initiative and then give us the opportunity to respond to it. And of course our refusal to respond to it would be particularly inexcusable after He appeared in human flesh in history.

CHAPTER 47

THE CREATOR NOT WELCOMED BY HIS CREATION

"He came unto his own, and his own received him not"
(John 1:11).

When Jesus Christ came to this earth, He ought to have been ecognized by His creatures as God and as such their Creator. Almost everybody acknowledges that someone by the name of Jesus lived upon this earth. But the acknowledgment that Jesus merely lived is of no use to that person. It cannot transform him from a vile sinner into a saint. Christ has to be everything or nothing. That is why John, in the first 18 verses of his Gospel, masterfully presents Jesus Christ in His eternity and infinity as the Creator of all things, who as such entered the realm of history. His pre-existence makes His earthly existence meaningful and saving.

There is no doubt that John is referring to this definite historical fact of the incarnation in verse 11 by the use of the verb *eelthen,* "he came." This is the fulfillment of His "coming into the world" in verse 9. The same verb is used, but in verse 11 it is in the effective aorist, indicating here a definite and final act in history. For a long time, He was coming, but finally He came. That is history, and no one can deny it. We may deny the pre-existence of Christ, but as we look at His existence on earth, we are forced to examine His claims to pre-existence and deity.

Jesus Christ did not come to His world because He had to come. It was a purely voluntary act resulting from His grace and mercy. Many think that what God did and does for man He does simply because it is His duty. But this is an erroneous conception of

God's nature. What we see as duty, God considers as grace. How can we claim from God something which we do not merit? God came to this earth in the person of Jesus Christ through His own power and volition. Our sin did not force Him to come; but our sinful plight made Him feel so sorry for us that, in His great love, He came to save us.

A preacher tells us how one of his children said to the youngest, "You must be good or Father won't love you." He called the child to him and said, gravely and tenderly, "That is not true, my boy." "But you won't love us if we are not good, will you?" asked the child. "Yes, I shall love you always; when you are good, I shall love you with a love that makes me glad; and when you are not good, I shall love you with a love that hurts me." That's exactly what the love of God is toward us. He was not obliged to love us because we were either bad or good, but He did love us because of what He is— Love—and for that reason He came. His coming was neither forced nor deserved.

Jesus Christ "came to his own." This expression in Greek is *eis ta idia.* Fundamentally, the word *idios* is an adjective which expresses what belongs to an individual in contrast to what is public property. It refers to something which is exclusively for self. This is the word from which our English words "idiom" and "idiot" are derived. An idiom is an expression that has a particular, exclusive meaning, in spite of the fact that the words making it up may have other meanings. But here this adjective is used as a substantive in the plural neuter. It is as if John were saying, "He came to his own things." *Ta idia,* then, has come to mean "his own home, his homeland, his own possession."

We claim things as our right, sometimes, to which we have no right at all. In fact, we have no right to anything; and sometimes God impresses this upon us by taking things from us. Let us not be like that sick man to whom a benevolent gentleman had been giving a quart of milk a day. At last the time came for him to die, and of course the gift of milk was expected to come to an end. When the poor man was gone, the gentleman called upon the widow. "I must tell you, sir," said she, "that my husband has made a will and has left the quart of milk to his brother!"

This expression, *ta idia,* "his own," has two possible interpretations, both of which, we believe, can apply in this verse. The first is that "his own" refers to the world, the earth. This, of course, is the more generally held position and is in full agreement with what John has already said in the previous verse about God coming into the world in the person of Jesus Christ and not being recognized by the world. If we take this interpretation, we arrive at the following conclusions:

(1) That Jesus Christ considers the world as a whole His exclusive possession. He always had full rights to it and therefore came into it without asking permission from anyone. No one was asked if Jesus Christ could appear in history at Bethlehem. He came in spite of all human attempts to stop Him. Neither kings nor armies could prevail against Him. He has the title to this earth. The rulers of earth constantly fight over pieces of real estate, as if anything actually belonged to them. Hear God's Word concerning this matter: "For all the earth is mine" (Exod. 19:5). "The land shall not be sold for ever: for the land is mine; for ye are strangers and sojourners with me" (Lev. 25:23). "For all things come of thee, and of thine own have we given thee" (I Chron. 29:14). "The earth is the Lord's, and the fulness thereof; the world, and they that dwell therein" (Ps. 24:1) "For every beast of the forest is mine, and the cattle upon a thousand hills" (Ps. 50:10). "The silver is mine, and the gold is mine, saith the Lord of hosts" (Hag. 2:8). And God also has the right of possession over the souls of men. "Behold, all souls are mine; as the soul of the father, so also the soul of the son is mine: the soul that sinneth, it shall die" (Ezek. 18:4). And unfortunately all souls are under sin, therefore separated from God and dead, which is why God came into the world in the person of Jesus Christ to reconcile the world unto Himself.

(2) The fact that God, in Jesus Christ, entered the world He

had made indicates that in a sense He had been away from it. Christ had been in the world, declares the 10th verse. Yet the 11th verse implies that He was away, since He is now come through His incarnation. Is there a contradiction here? No, for one can be in the world and yet not be recognized by the world. Christ in His eternity was always in the world, not as Jesus the visible and tangible, but in His essential character and substance as Spirit omniscient. This is a particular and specific appearance of the infinite Christ as Jesus. As Infinity and Eternity, He was always in the world and was everywhere present before the world came into being; but as the human Jesus, as the Stranger of Galilee, He came into the world at a certain set time in history. As God, the Lord Jesus Christ was always in the world, but as God-man He came into the world. And that coming was the turning point of history.

When Christ came, He was surrounded by the world he had made. A young nobleman had been absent for a long time from his extensive domains and numerous tenants till he was a stranger to them. Having returned home, he was out hunting and wandered from his party. Lost and thoroughly drenched by the rain, he sought shelter and relief in the cottages of some of his tenants, but they did not recognize him as the lord of the manor and shut their doors in his face. Knocking at the cottage of a poor widow, he heard the invitation, "Come in, thou blessed of the Lord." She gave him a suit of dry though coarse clothing and spread before him the best food she could provide. He went away promising to return for his own clothes. The next day he appeared with his retinue and stopped before the poor widow's door. She discovered in the young lord her unknown guest. He thanked her for the kindness shown to a stranger and rewarded her with a better cottage and an annuity. She gave as the reason for her hospitality the fact that her own boy was away at sea and might be in need of shelter, and also that Christ had not where to lay His head, for "He came unto his own, and his own received him not."

True, Christ's creation shuts its door collectively and individually against Him, but His claim to the title of the world will never be given up. A day is coming when the world will fall at His feet. That will be the day of the Lord. "For it is written, As I live saith the Lord, every knee shall bow to me, and every tongue shall confess to God" (Rom. 14:11). "Who shall not fear thee, O Lord, and glorify thy name? for thou only art holy: for all nations shall come and worship before thee; for thy judgments are made manifest" (Rev. 15:4). No wonder the Lord laughs as he looks down from heaven upon the rulers of the earth as they fight over His property (Ps. 2:2-4).

CHAPTER 48

EXPECTED YET UNWELCOME
"He came unto his own, and his own received him not" (John 1:11).

———

It is only natural, when you are eagerly expecting someone, to welcome him with open arms. Just imagine the disappointment of a father returning to his family from the war to find out that he is unwanted. All along the family has been praying and waiting for his return, yet when he arrives he is not allowed to come in. There could be no greater shock to a father than that. A welcome by one's own family is the instinctive hope of all. When the author is away from his family for any length of time, he can hardly wait until he gets back home. As he travels homeward, he constantly visualizes the open arms of his wife and children waiting to welcome him.

But John 1:11 tells us that this was not the case with Someone who was long expected. "He came unto his own, and his own received him not." John speaks of Christ, who from His eternal abode, heaven, came to His temporal world. Man had been longing to see God with his own eyes, and now his longing was to be fully satisfied. God walked on earth in the person of Jesus Christ, yet He was unwelcome to the very men who had so eagerly expected Him. This is the picture we have of the incarnate God among men. And undoubtedly the primary and more general meaning of this verse is that the eternal Word, the *Logos*, came into the world and the world received Him not. Since they did not recognize Him (verse 10), it was natural that they would not receive Him. Recognition is essential to reception. And we have already seen how the

211

expression *ouk egnoo,* "knew him not," in verse 10 means, "did not recognize him." They recognized Him not as God, but merely as a great man. Therefore they did not receive Him as the One to satisfy their longings. When Jesus Christ is recognized only as man by man, He is impotent to help man in any way. Only as God incarnate can Jesus Christ be of help to man, in saving him and keeping him in eternal fellowship with Himself.

In our previous study we saw that the first and more general interpretation of the expression *ta idia,* "his own," in the first clause of verse 11, "He came unto his own," is that it means "the world" which He made. But the more particular interpretation is that it means the land of Palestine, the land of Israel and the people of Israel. This is the place in which Jesus as God-man made His visible appearance. He had been in the whole world, as verse 10 told us, but now He enters a particular part of it — Israel — to make Himself known particularly to His ancient chosen people, the Jews. The land of Israel and the people of Israel were the door through which the Lord Jesus appeared to the rest of the world. God calls Israel His peculiar people (Deut. 26:18). In Exodus 19:5 the Lord says, "Ye shall be a peculiar treasure unto me above all people: for all the earth is mine." And then in Deuteronomy 7:6 God says, "For thou art an holy people unto the Lord thy God: the Lord thy God hath chosen thee to be a special people unto himself, above all people that are upon the face of the earth." For over a thousand years the people of Israel had lived in constant expectation of their Messiah. He was coming. Now He has come; He is here among them.

At the time when Jesus came into the world, the Jews were under Roman slavery. They wanted to be free from this foreign yoke. They expected the Messiah to be not only their foretold deliverer in a spiritual sense, but their political and national liberator as well.

"And his own received him not." This is probably the saddest declaration in the entire New Testament. An expected liberator

212

unwelcome. Jesus Christ did not desire the Jews merely to understand Him, but also to welcome Him, not only to recognize Him, but also to take Him as their very own possession. Christ's claim on them was reciprocal. Oh, if we could only take advantage of our rights to God in response to His coming to us!

It is interesting to note that the verb translated "received" in verse 11 is from the same Greek root as the verb translated "comprehended" in verse 5. It is *katelaben* in verse 5 and *parelaben* in verse 11. The difference is in the prepositions by which the verb *elaben*, "received," are prefixed. In the present indicative, the first one means "to seize, to capture, to understand." Man in his sinful condition could not understand and capture the eternal light of Christ. But here in verse 11 John uses the verb *parelaben*, "did not receive or welcome." More was expected of the Jews, as God's own peculiar people, than of the people of the world in general. They were not only expected to have an understanding of who the Light was that shone in their midst, but an attitude of immediate acceptance of that Light.

Here comes the father home from the war, of whom we spoke at the beginning. His wife or child opens the door and looks at him. Two reactions are possible. One is for the wife or child to say, "Oh, you are my husband, my father!" But the father surely expects something more than that, especially since he knows that he has been eagerly awaited. He expects a welcome. He expects his family to say, "It's good to see you, Daddy! Come right in. This is your home." The first attitude is that of *katelaben*, "comprehended" (verse 5), and the second attitude of exuberant welcome and reception is that of *parelaben*, "received" (verse 11).

The idea behind this compound verb is that of delivery. The Jews and generally everyone were expected to receive something handed down, something offered. Jesus Christ came into the world as a gift to the human race and especially to the Jews, for He was their own in a very special way. He was offered to His people as a free gift, and yet He was refused. No tragedy could be greater than

213

this — for the Jews to have God incarnate as their Lord and King and yet to refuse Him! And now that the veil of partition between Jew and gentile is torn down, it is equally tragic for anyone to refuse Him.

An only son, a boy of no ordinary promise, was the idol of his parents' hearts. They could talk of him by the hour. As the years went by and he grew to manhood, he suddenly became a raving maniac and had to be placed in a mental institution. His sorrowing mother made frequent visits to see him. On one occasion, as the attendant unlocked the door of his room, the boy met the eye of his weeping mother, who had so long suffered and endured hardships for him. No sooner had he glared at her than he cried out, "Take her away! Take her away! She is a witch come to torment me!" The attendant tried to explain to the boy that it was his loving mother, his best friend on earth; but he persisted and refused to allow her to come in and minister to him. The attendant locked the door and led the heartbroken mother away. Her son did not recognize her and receive her as she had expected him to. Yet she was his own mother. What a disappointment! And can the disappointment of God be any less when we do not receive or welcome Him?

And finally, let us note that the "him" in verse 11 refers to Jesus Christ Himself and not to anything about Him. It does not refer merely to the light, because then the word used would have been *auto*, "it," which is neuter, instead of *auton*, "him," which is masculine. Christ does not want us simply to accept certain ideas about Him, but to accept Him as a person.

The expression *hoi idioi*, "his own," in the second clause of verse 11, is not in the neuter gender, as in the first clause, but in the masculine plural. It is used to stress the fact that the Jews as a whole did not welcome the Lord Jesus Christ. Some Jews as individuals accepted Him as their Lord and Saviour, but not the Jews as an entity — even to this day. *Hoi idioi*, "his own," could actually be translated "his relatives," meaning His human relatives as man — the Jews. How close they were to Him — and yet how far!

214

CHAPTER 49

IS CHRIST A RESPECTER OF PERSONS?

"But AS MANY AS received him, to them gave he power to become the sons of God, even to them that believe on his name" (John 1:12).

———

John 1:11 speaks in a general way of the eternal Christ coming into the world and not being welcomed by His creation. In a more restricted and specific sense it speaks of His coming to His homeland, Palestine, and not being welcomed by His own people as a group. It refers to the welcome attended by pomp and circumstance that Jesus Christ should have received from Israel as a nation and from the world in general. All this is implied by the compound verb *ou parelabon,* "did not welcome or receive Him," which is used here.

In contrast to this corporate refusal to welcome God in Christ into the world, verse 12 tells of an acceptance — not by the world in general, or by the Israelitish nation, but by individuals belonging to the world and also to Israel. Thus in verse 11 we have the corporate rejection by man of Jesus Christ in His incarnation, and in verse 12 we have Him individually accepted by various men. Although in one manuscript and in the writings of some Church Fathers the particle *de* ("but") is missing, we believe its presence in the majority of manuscripts is significant and correct. Exegetically it provides for a vivid contrast between the two verses. He, Christ, came to His own home—that home being the world and particularly Israel — but His own creation and peculiar people Israel did not welcome Him. But those who received Him, to them gave He

215

authority to become the children of God. The contrast is apparent and vivid — corporate rejection in one verse and individual acceptance in the other.

John 1:12 is one of the most important and pivotal verses of the entire Bible and thus requires our detailed and careful study. In the King James Version it reads, "But as many as received him, to them gave he power to become the sons of God, even to them that believe on his name."

The first Greek word that arrests our attention is *hosoi,* which is here translated "as many as." It would be more accurate and much clearer if we were to translate this pronoun "all who," as Arndt and Gingrich indicate in their *Lexicon* (p. 590). Thus this pronoun would include the totality and the individuality at one and the same time. First of all, it is inclusive of all who accept Jesus Christ by believing on His name. All who accept Christ by believing become the children of God. Not a single one has ever been disappointed by believing and then not becoming a child of God. This speaks of the absolute trustworthiness of the promises of God. He has promised that, when we believe and thus accept Christ as the eternal Son of God, we become children of the Father.

A pastor who visited an old man held fast to his chair by rheumatism found him with his Bible open in front of him. The minister noticed that the word "proved" was written continually in the margin. He turned over a few pages and found, "God is our refuge and strength, a very present help in trouble." "Proved." And so it went on through the Book. Next to John 1:12 he had written "Proved." He had received Christ by believing and had indeed become a child of God. He had proved that promise of God's Word. And millions of other born-again believers could write "proved" next to this verse. There isn't a single one who has put this promise of God to the test who has been disappointed.

A certain printer stamps each package that leaves his shop with his name and the words, "I never disappoint." This trademark is also upon each promise of God. All who have believed on the Lord

Jesus have become something that they were not before — the children of God. This is the first meaning we take from the pronoun *hosoi*, "all who."

But there is also an individuality within the totality. Though the pronoun refers to all who have accepted or received Christ, it does not speak of their having received Him en masse but as individuals. Among all of the people of the world, whether they be gentiles or Jews, there are individuals who have accepted and still accept Christ. These individuals can belong to any ethnic group; their skin can be any color; their tongue what it may, their religious background varied. The door is open to every one who will enter. This is the "whosoever" of the Gospel of Jesus Christ, which speaks of the individual believing in a universal context. Thus the Gospel is an individual Gospel and at the same time a universal one. Christ is not the Saviour of the white man or the negro, of the Greek or the American. He is the Christ of all those who receive Him by believing on His name. This is basic to the understanding of the Gospel and what makes it unique.

A little girl was helping to care for a sick gentleman whom she loved very much. He said to her, "Ellen, it is time I should take my medicine. Measure just a tablespoon and put it in a glass." She quickly did so and brought it to his bedside. He made no attempt to take it from her but said, "Now, dear, will you drink it for me?" "Me drink it? What do you mean? I am sure I would in a minute if it would make you well all the same, but you know it won't do you any good unless you take it yourself." "Won't it really?" "No, I am sure it will not." "But if you cannot take my medicine for me, neither can I take your salvation for you. You must go to Jesus and believe in Him for yourself." The dear old saint of God had been trying to explain to his young nurse that she could not be saved on his account and by serving him, but rather through her own acceptance of Jesus Christ as her Saviour. This brought it home to her so vividly that she made her own individual appropriation of Christ.

217

There is nothing in this pronoun *hosoi* to restrict it to the Jews, even if we take the previous verse as speaking exclusively of the rejection of the eternal Word by Israel as a nation. If there were, as Frederick Louis Godet very aptly says (*Commentary on the Gospel of John,* Grand Rapids: Zondervan, p. 264), it would have been qualified with the amplification *ex autoon,* "of them." In other words, it would have read, "all who received him from among them," that is, the Jews. No, the "all who" of *hosoi* is completely unqualified and therefore non-restrictive in its meaning. The Gospel's "whosoever" includes each one of us, no matter who we are or how great sinners, whatever our nationality and religion. A nobleman after his conversion said, "Praise the Lord, I have been saved by an M." It was not clear what he meant until he recited I Corinthians 1:26, "Not many mighty, not many noble, are called." "It's good," he continued, "that it did not say 'not any noble.' " The Gospel excludes no one, but each person as an individual must accept it by faith.

CHAPTER 50

WHAT DOES IT MEAN TO RECEIVE CHRIST?

"But as many as RECEIVED him . . ." (John 1:12a).

———————

A gentleman residing in the fashionable part of London, and thoroughly carried away with the follies of society life, was walking down the street one day with a Christian woman of his acquaintance when he turned to her and asked, "How is it that you religious people are always trying to rob us of our pleasure? I enjoy life, and I can't see why you should be forever trying to rob me of what pleasure this short life affords." "You are greatly mistaken if that is what you think," replied the woman. "We do not want you to give up anything, but to receive." The gentleman kept thinking of the word "receive." It refused to leave him. Not long after, he called on the woman, and told her his life was miserable, and asked what he must do to receive peace of soul and joy of heart. She led him to the Saviour, where he found pardon and comfort he had never known before.

The Gospel of Jesus Christ is predominantly not a Gospel of doing but a Gospel of receiving. It is receiving Christ. But is Christ an article of merchandise or a gift to be received? How can man receive Jesus Christ?

The Apostle John declares in his Gospel, "But as many as received him, to them gave he power to become the sons of God, even to them that believe on his name" (1:12). Here, of course, John speaks of Jesus Christ, the eternal Word, who penetrated the realm of humanity on Christmas Day in Bethlehem of Judea. Some people living in Jesus' physical lifetime had the blessed privilege of

219

receiving Him into their homes.

The language used here is spiritual and concerns a spiritual reception. Jesus Christ, before He came to this earth, was Spirit — Spirit eternal, infinite, omniscient, omnipresent. But when He voluntarily and of His own power limited Himself to human form, He did not cease to be what He was before he came to this earth; and having left this earth He continues to be the same eternal and infinite Spirit. It is as Spirit that Jesus Christ can be in many places at once and in the hearts of many men at the same time. But that which is not possible as far as the human body is concerned is possible with the eternal Spirit called God, the Word, the Life, the Light. Thus the word "receive" applies to spiritual realities. And realities can be spiritual; they are not limited only to the material.

To receive Christ, then, is to receive His Spirit into your spirit, to receive Him as a spiritual Person. And as such He can fully occupy your whole being. After all, the real self is not the few chemicals that constitute the human body, but the spiritual "I" that makes up the personality. It is that which thinks, feels, loves, and consciously acts. To receive Christ is to allow His Spirit to be the Spirit of our spirit. When one receives Christ, he knows it. It is not an unconscious experience.

There are three words used in this context of John 1:1-18 which come from the same root. One is the word *katelaben*, translated "comprehended" in verse 5. "And the light shineth in darkness; and the darkness comprehended it not." And then in verse 11 we have the word *parelabon*, translated "received," which rather has the connotation of "welcoming." "Unto his own household he came, and his own people did not welcome him." And finally, in verse 12 the word is used in its simple form in contrast to the compound forms used in verses 5 and 11. Here it is *elabon*, "received," which basically indicates more activity and accord on the part of the one receiving. It could be translated "to take hold of, to grasp." Of course, this is when the object is a thing. But here the object is a person; it is the Lord Jesus Christ in His infinite and eternal Spirit. In this case, the word should be understood in the sense of recognizing someone's authority. (See Arndt and Gingrich's *Greek-English Lexicon of the New Testament and other Early Christian Literature*, p. 465.) Thus, when we speak of receiving Jesus Christ, we mean recognizing His authority in all that He is and all that He came to do in this world. We acknowledge Him as Saviour, as King, as Master of all.

Why is it that the verb *elabon*, "received," is in the second aorist tense and not in the present indicative? Why does John say "all who received him" instead of "all who receive him"? Does he mean that this is something of the past and that it is not valid and possible today and at all times? In the Greek, the aorist is often used to speak of the whole span of time in one view (nomic aorist). In other words, the aorist is used to take in the entire past, present, and future. It demonstrates something that happened, happens, and will happen. And this is precisely the meaning which John wishes to convey here, that in the past there were those who received Christ; there are those who receive Him now, and there are those who receive Him in the future. Salvation in Christ never had any chronological limitation placed upon it. (See W. E. Jelf's *Syntax*, pp. 69-71).

Also, this aorist is an ingressive aorist (A. T. Robertson, *Grammar of the Greek New Testament*, p. 834). In other words, it takes us back to that initial step when man receives Jesus Christ. It refers to the initial faith of appropriating Christ as one's own possession. Here we have that step taken by man when he says in faith believing, "Lord Jesus, come into my heart." And that surely is the most important step of faith, when man recognizes Jesus Christ as his Lord and Saviour.

But this verb *elabon*, "received," not only refers to that initial action of man, but shows that it is an action that is taken to completion. This means that, once we have taken that initial step by God's grace, we can rest assured that the desired purpose will be accomplished, that we shall have Christ as our very own. Christ

221

will not disappoint anyone who takes that first step of faith, for it is He, through the Holy Spirit, who enables him to take that first step in response to His invitation. Actually, we start to receive Christ, but it ends with His receiving us. It is illuminating to watch the action and reaction between a child and his father. Here is my little child putting forth his hands to touch me, to receive me. What do I, a loving father do? I respond. I put out my arms and take my child into them to hug and love him. The child starts the process and I finish it. That's exactly what happens in this matter of receiving Christ. We put out our arms of faith. Without faith, and the object of faith, Christ, however, we could not initiate the stretching out of our arms toward Him. As in the case of my little boy, if there were no father toward whom to stretch his arms, there would have been no stretching. Christ sees them and responds. His everlasting, infinite arms immediately take hold of us and complete the process of union with Him. If it were up to us to hold on to Christ, it would never work because our faith is too weak, but He is strong and will let no one snatch us out of His hands.

CHAPTER 51

IS IT ENOUGH TO RECEIVE CHRIST AS SAVIOUR?

"But as many as received him . . . even to them that believe on his name" (John 1:12:a, c).

————————

"Accept Christ as your Saviour" is a common admonition heard in evangelistic meetings and over the radio. We may look for this expression diligently in the New Testament, but we shall not find it. We shall find many instances where Jesus Christ is referred to as Saviour, but these simply serve to describe the principal work for which He came to earth. Nowhere are we told to accept Jesus Christ as Saviour only. We are rather commanded "to receive Him." Note carefully what John 1:12 says, "But as many as received him, to them gave he power to become the sons of God, even to them that believe on his name." It does not say "as many as received him as Saviour," but "as many as received him"—and for a very good reason, we believe. It is true that we are expected to receive Jesus Christ as Saviour, but as more than that, as the Lord and King of our lives. It may be that if we stick to Biblical terminology we shall not give men the idea that all they need is to be rescued from eternal destruction and punishment. This would assign to man a selfish motive in seeking Christ. There is more to it than that. There is the enjoyment of Christ.

Christ's salvation of man's soul and life is just the beginning of a series of constant activity on his behalf. Christ does not merely offer a rescue operation. Have you ever seen a rescue operation on the beach? There stands the lifeguard. He sees the frantic hand of some swimmer struggling in the water. That's a danger signal. He dives in and saves him. He brings him out. The moment the saved

223

swimmer can manage on his own, the lifeguard quits. He leaves him alone. But this is not all that Christ does for us swimmers among the billows of life. He does just as much, or even more, after He saves us as at the moment He rescues us from the sea of iniquity in which Satan would drown us. He continues to save us from all the dangers and attacks that we encounter. He becomes the director of our lives. No man would like the lifeguard who rescued him to continue to direct every moment of his life thereafter, would he? Perhaps if he knew that his rescue would involve the enslavement of self and will, he would not have allowed himself to be rescued. Many want to be rescued from impending destruction, especially knowing that it is eternal, but they resist enslavement to the Saviour. It is the duty of us who preach to declare the whole counsel of God by telling people what is involved in this rescue operation from sin. It is not just a matter of arriving safely on shore, but it is voluntarily living thereafter for the One who has saved us.

There are many who seem content just to sneak into heaven, instead of starting to live as citizens of heaven the moment they receive Christ. A preacher went to see a dying old man who was very anxious about his soul. After a few visits by the preacher, the truth dawned upon him, and through repentance and faith he experienced the joy of forgiveness and the assurance of eternal life. Just before he died, he said to the preacher with obvious regrets, "I feel such a sneak because I've served Satan all my life and only now at the end have I yielded my heart to God." His conscience told him it was a mean, despicable way to serve his Master and Redeemer.

What happens when we receive Christ? We are given authority to become the children of God. This is a great declaration, indeed, but before we deal with it in detail we must look at the third clause of our verse, "even to them that believe on his name." The first and third clauses are inseparably connected in meaning, and we must look at them together. "All who received him . . . even to them that believe on his name." This third clause gives us the medium by which man receives Christ.

It is instructive to note that the verb in the Greek is not in the present indicative as the King James translation would indicate. It is the present participle, *tois pisteuousi*, which correctly and literally translated would be "to the ones believing." The time to which the present participle refers is relative and is usually determined by the main verb in the sentence. Here the verb is *elabon*, "received." We have said that although this is in the aorist (past) tense, it refers to all events of all time—past, present, and future—to those who received, receive, and will receive Christ. But what was and is the medium by which men receive Christ? It is faith. One can only receive if he believes. I am offered a hundred dollar bill. You tell me, "Take it; it is yours for the taking." Before I will stretch out my hand to take it, I must believe you. I must have faith that you are telling me the truth. My faith in you causes me to accept your offer. This is the situation that is presented to us here. Christ is offered to sinful men in the eternal plan for their salvation. In order that we sinners may receive Him, we must believe Him. Christ cannot be ours without faith. "For by grace are ye saved through faith; and that not of yourselves: it is the gift of God" (Eph. 2:8). Both grace and faith are the gifts of God to us enabling us to appropriate Christ.

This faith, this believing, is simultaneous with, not necessarily prior to, receiving Christ. Believing and receiving Christ are two aspects of the same thing. At the same time that we believe, we receive Christ. We cannot do the one and not the other. The two go together. Believing is receiving and receiving is believing. A person who believes will receive Christ, and a person who has received Christ has believed. Our verse does not say *tois pisteusasi*, "to those who having believed," but *tois pisteuousi*, "to the ones believing"—believing at the time they received Christ. (See A. T. Robertson's *Grammar of the Greek New Testament*, p. 891.)

Furthermore we must observe that this participle is in the present tense and is preceded by the definite article. It is *tois pisteuousi* and not *tois pisteusasi* ("those who did believe"), nor is it *pisteuousi* ("believing"), *tois* being the article. Now the present participle, even with the article, often has the iterative sense (*Ibid*, p. 892). This faith is not something that occurs once and for all, but is continuous. Faith is something that is consciously active every moment. It is part and parcel of one's nature as a believer. The believing one means the believer, and the believer is one who believes uninterruptedly, constantly. Every moment of his life he has conscious belief in Christ. He doesn't just believe initially and then stop believing. Belief becomes natural in place of the unbelief one had before accepting Christ.

CHAPTER 52

WHAT IS IT TO BELIEVE ON CHRIST'S NAME?

". . . even to them that believe on his name" (John 1:12c).

————

The Apostle John in his Gospel uses the verb "believing" (*pisteuein*) ninety-nine times, but not once does he use the noun "belief" or "faith" (*pistis*). Why is that? The Gospel of John is the Gospel in which the divine is brought in touch with the human in a very special way. John never speaks of faith as an abstract thing. He always speaks of it as part and parcel of the human heart and mind. Belief is associated with man as his reaction to the love of God for him. For John, faith has a subject and an object. It is believing in somebody or something. The one who believes is man, and the One to be believed on is God in Jesus Christ. John, therefore, puts faith in context. Faith is believing by someone on somebody.

It is thus that John speaks of the believing ones in John 1:12. "All who received him, to them gave he authority to become the children of God, *to those believing on his name*" (literal translation from the Greek). The King James Version interpolates the word "even" in the third clause of this verse, which may lead some to come to the erroneous conclusion that there were those who received Christ in some other way than by believing. However, when we understand that this is the archaic use of the word "even," emphasizing identity, we see that the translators were simply making "as many as received him" synonymous with "those who believe on his name." Those who believe and are in the act of believing receive Christ. That is what miraculously happens the moment that a person believes on the name of Christ: he receives

227

Christ. The two are totally interwoven—the receiving and the believing. One cannot receive Christ without believing, and one cannot believe without receiving Christ. So whether we exhort the sinner to receive Christ or to believe on Christ's name, it is one and the same thing, for the one presupposes the other as a simultaneous experience.

What does it mean "to believe," when the subject is man and the object is "the name of Christ"? In the New Testament we often find the expression "in the name of Christ." The name of a person stands for what a person is. This is Mr. John Jones. We know that the name John Jones stands for a certain person. Now in Hellenistic Greek, which was the Greek used between 300 B.C. and A.D. 300, the expression "in the name of someone" was used extensively, both in legal and commercial language. It is still used in Modern Greek and in English. "Deposit this in my name" means "deposit it in my account." Or "draw this in my name" means "draw this from my account." Isn't that what would happen if I were to write out a check for you? You would take it and present it to the bank. You would cash it. But the money would come out of my account because my name was signed on the check. You would actually have cashed something in my name. You would have had to believe that I had money in the bank and that that money could become yours; otherwise you would never have presented the check to be cashed. Thus, through faith in my name, you would have made my account yours in the amount that I had made it available to you.

That's exactly the transaction that takes place between God and man. He has the resources which we need. He is Life and Light. Especially do we need these in a spiritual sense for our spiritual existence. They are made available to us in the measure that we need them, because we ourselves are bankrupt. Our name isn't worth anything at the source of Life and Light. But the Lord Jesus Christ has available what we need. It is available with God His Father, with Himself as God, and with God the Holy Spirit. He it is who became man so that we in His name might bank at the eternal Bank of Salvation. Thus in the name of Christ we can come to God. When we believe what He is and what He can do for us, He becomes ours. Believing in His name, we receive Him.

Or take another expression found in the New Testament, which is incorporated in the great commission, "Go ye therefore, and teach all nations, baptizing them in the name of the Father, and of the Son, and of the Holy Ghost" (Matt. 28:19). In this expression the concept of dedication is highly significant. Baptism signifies that the one who believed became the possession of the Trinity—of God the Father, the Son, and the Holy Spirit. He came under the divine protection. Therefore the one who believes in the name of Christ may be said to be one who is completely dedicated to Christ. Belief, then, involves dedication to the name of Christ.

Believing in the name of someone is the same as having confidence that that person bears his name rightfully, that he really is what his name declares (Arndt and Gingrich, *A Greek-English Lexicon of the New Testament,* pp. 575-6). Christ thus far has been presented by John as the Eternal Word, the Life, and the Light of the World. He is presented as God. And only as we look at Christ in His incarnation as God will His name have any saving power as far as we are concerned. He came and He was known by two names in particular: Jesus, which means Saviour, and Emmanuel, which means God with us. If He had been a mere man, He could never have been the Saviour of the world.

An evangelist was holding special meetings for boys and girls. One day after the children's meeting, little Helen came home, rushed into her father's study, threw her arms around him, and said, "Daddy, I am a Christian!" "Well, Helen, I am glad to hear that," said her father. "When did you become a Christian?" "This afternoon, Daddy," she replied. He asked her to tell him what had occurred. "Oh," she said, "the evangelist told us that Jesus Christ was there in the room and that, if we would receive Him, He would come in and live in our lives and make us His own: that He would receive us." "Well," he said, "go on; tell me what else happened."

"Why," she said, "I received Him and Jesus took me in." "But how do you know that when you received Jesus He took you in?" the father persisted. She gave him a look which he would never forget as she answered, "Why, Daddy, because He said He would!" That's exactly what it means to believe in the name of Christ—to believe what He is and what He said He would do for us when we receive Him. It is so simple that explanations only serve to complicate it.

The name of Christ, then, stands for Christ Himself. We are not told here that we should merely believe certain things about Him, but in His name, in Him. Many people are content to seek the periphery of God instead of the center of God. When they come to God, they seek His blessings instead of Himself. It is the same as marrying a person for his money or his name, for what he can give instead of what he is.

And finally we should consider the relation of the tense of the verb *elabon,* "received," to "believing." It is in the aorist indicative, which denotes certainty of receiving. What does that mean? That believing in the name of Christ absolutely and surely enables you to receive Christ. It makes Christ your very own. With a "Yes" of faith, Christ, the eternal God, becomes yours. A woman came up to an evangelist after hearing him preach and said that she could not understand salvation. The evangelist asked, "Mrs. Franklin, how long have you been Mrs. Franklin?" "Why, ever since I was married," she replied. "And how did you become Mrs. Franklin?" he asked. "When the minister said, 'Wilt thou have this man to be thy wedded husband?' I just said, 'Yes.' " "Didn't you say, 'I hope so,' or 'I'll try to'?" asked the evangelist. "No," she replied, "I said, 'I will.' " Then pointing her to God's Word, he said, "God is asking you if you will receive His Son. What will you say to that?" Her face lighted up and she said, "Why, how simple that is! Isn't it queer that I didn't say 'Yes' long ago?" That is the simple believing the Bible calls for—for you to say "Yes" and God will receive you as long as you come in the name of Christ—in what

He is and what He did for you on the cross of Calvary, redeeming you from sin.

CHAPTER 53

GOD'S GIVING

"But as many as received him, to them GAVE HE POWER to become the sons of God, even to them that believe on his name" (John 1:12).

Are all men the children of God? This verse would definitely indicate that they are not. God gives the authority to become His children only to those who receive Jesus Christ by faith. Two very clear teachings are implied in this verse:

1. That since man can become a child of God, he must not have been one previously. This, of course, would immediately destroy the much-talked-about doctrine of the universal Fatherhood of God. Many people seem to think that God is the Father of all. They mistakenly assume this to follow from the fact that He is the Creator of all. We are all creatures of God, but we are not all His children. There is a difference.

Man was originally created in the image of God, but he chose to follow Satan rather than obey his Creator. In consequence of his disobedience he fell from the favor of God. Man chose to become the child of the devil rather than the child of his Creator. The fact that God is not the Father of all men is not God's fault but entirely man's.

One day the Lord Jesus Christ was discussing this very subject with the Jews of His day. They spoke up, even as people today, saying, "We have one Father, even God" (John 8:41). But Jesus told them, "Ye are of your father the devil" (v. 44). True, in Adam we were children until we decided to become prodigal children; then we became estranged children. An estranged child does not

232

endeavor to please the Father whom he has voluntarily left, but rather the one he has decided to follow. Thus we are the children of the devil, if we are still in the realm of sin and disobedience.

2. The second truth found in our verse is that it is possible for man in his estrangement once again to become a child of God. This, however, is as a result of God's initiative and His revelation that He in His infinite love and mercy will receive the prodigal again. This is clearly brought out by the verb used in the verse, "To them gave he power to become the sons of God." In the original Greek text the verb is *edooken,* which is in the aorist tense. This takes us back to the past, but it also applies to the present and the future. Ever since man in Adam estranged himself from his Creator, God in Christ has given him the authority to return. After man left the Father's house, God did not close the door behind him, so to speak, but left it open so that man might have the opportunity of returning.

The story is told of a girl who turned her back on her widowed mother, who had worked so hard to bring her up, and left home without telling her where she was going. Night after night the mother waited for the girl, but she did not come back. In her perplexity and sorrow the mother went to her pastor to ask his help. He suggested that she have some pictures taken of herself and bring them to him, which she did. Then he asked her what message she wanted to send her lost girl. In tears the mother said, "All I want to tell her is 'Come back.'" "Write that on each picture," said the minister, and then he proceeded to send these pictures to places of amusement in other large towns which he felt the daughter was most likely to frequent. He requested that the picture be posted on the bulletin board where it could easily be seen. One night the daughter came to one of these places and was attracted by something familiar about the picture on the bulletin board. Little did she imagine that it could be her mother's picture. She came closer to it, and there it was—her own mother, looking much older than when she had left. Then she saw what was written on it,

233

"Come back," and knew it was addressed to her. She could not proceed with her plans for that night. With a heart burning with remorse, she went back to her room, packed her clothes, and took the first train home. Arriving in the early hours of the morning, she was surprised to find the door of the little apartment open. In she went. There was her mother in tears, not sleeping, but sitting up, praying for her prodigal daughter. She threw her arms around her, and the first thing she asked when she could speak was, "Mother, why did you leave the door open?" "Oh, Louise, the door has never been closed since the day you left. It has been open all the time expecting your return. I didn't want you to find it shut when you came back."

That is actually what God did. Ever since we decided to leave the Father's house, the door has been left open for our return. He gave all those who believe and accept Christ the opportunity to come back and once again claim all the privileges and responsibilities of sonship. Irrespective of what we do, the door is open, has always been open, and will remain open till the day of grace expires. As far as God is concerned, He has given man the authority to come back at any time. In God's giving of this authority, He has placed no time limit on it, but in our appropriation of that authority we are faced with the limitations of time. One day we may want to go back and not be able to. God did His part once and for all. He gave those who believe the authority to become the children of God. He left the door open. It is up to us to arise and go to Him—an act which makes us once again His children. In going, however, we must recognize our sin. To say one is a sinner is a humiliating experience, but it is necessary for the restoration of the privilege of sonship with God.

The son of a rich father forsook his fine home for a life of crime and immorality, bringing disgrace to his family and causing his father many years of deep sorrow. One day he learned of his father's death and decided to return home at once. He wanted to be present at the reading of the will, to see if he had been left anything.

He thought possibly his father out of kindness had bequeathed him something. Together with other members of the family he assembled at the lawyer's office to listen to the reading of the will. The first part of it was a long recital of his own sins. Father had set them down carefully, one by one, expressing the grief of heart which he had borne for so many years. The son became more and more restless as he heard that sad story of his evil doings. He began to fidget and fuss in his seat, obviously disgusted with the whole proceedings. Finally, he could stand it no longer and grabbed his hat, rose to his feet, stomped out of the room, and slammed the door behind him. But he left too soon. For the second part of the will said that his father had left him $25,000. He could not subsequently be located and thus never got the money, for the simple reason that he refused to hear about his sin, and he would not confess it. So he lost his inheritance.

CHAPTER 54

YOU CAN BECOME SOMETHING NEW

". . . to them gave he power TO BECOME the sons of God . . ."
(John 1:12b).

———————

To those who receive Christ by believing on His name, God has given the authority to become His children. This and a multitude of other Scripture verses make it very clear that it is God who always takes the initiative in the matter of salvation, and everything else, except sin. Man has no authority of his own. He is impotent in himself.

The verb translated "gave he" in this verse, *edooken* in Greek, comes from the same root as the words *dosis* and *dooron,* meaning "gift." Therefore *edooken* in this context has the implied notion of giving freely. There is no restriction to God's giving. Divine authority can become ours freely, without restriction in its outflow and without the necessity of our having to pay for it. It comes generously and without price. And this exactly describes the attitude of God towards us in our sinful state. It is sin which has made us the children of the devil. No matter how great our sin, God's giving of grace is sufficient to meet it.

A little girl and her mother were reading the New Testament one morning when they came to John 3:16, "For God so loved the world, that he gave his only begotten Son, that whosoever believeth in him should not perish, but have everlasting life." (The word "gave" in John 3:16 is the same as in John 1:12.) Stopping for a moment in the reading, the mother asked, "Don't you think it is wonderful?" The child, looking surprised, replied in the negative. The mother, somewhat astonished, repeated the question, to which the little daughter replied, "Why, no, Mommy, it would be wonderful if it were anybody else, but it is just like God." And the little girl was absolutely right. It is God's nature to give freely of His grace and of His authority.

We don't have to pay for this authority to become the children of God, because God Himself paid for it through the sacrifice of His Son, the Lord Jesus Christ. The wages of sin is death; and it is through His death that the Lord Jesus purchased our salvation so that now we can be given the authority to become the children of God without price. The good news of the New Testament and the Christian religion is that salvation is free. There is no other religion like it.

In one of his large meetings, while D. L. Moody was explaining that salvation is free, a man jumped to his feet and, oblivious of his surroundings, exclaimed, "Oh, it is beautiful! I always thought I had something to do, but now I see I have something to take!" "The gift of God is eternal life through Jesus Christ our Lord" (Rom. 6:23).

The King James Version translates the Greek word *exousia* as "power." "To them gave he power to become the sons of God." This noun comes from the verb *exesti,* meaning "it is free, it is allowed." Thus the word *exousia* actually refers to the permission, right, liberty, power to do anything (Hermann Cremer, *Biblico-Theological Lexicon of New Testament Greek,* p. 236). In this word we have two ideas combined, that of right and might. It does not describe mere ability, but legitimate, rightful authority, derived from a competent source, which includes the idea of power (Brooke Foss Westcott, *The Gospel According to St. John,* Vol. I, Grand Rapids: Wm. B. Eerdmans, 1954, p. 16). In this instance, we can hardly separate the idea of might from right. God first gives the right, the privilege, to man to become His child. But that right is not merely an academic one. In it there is the ability to become that which you have the right to become. In other words, it is an executive right God gives, so to speak. When Jesus Christ says

237

"Come unto me," He also gives you through His Spirit the enablement, the strength to come.

Again, this right is not something that is inherent in man. It is something that is given to him by God. He did not have it before. He acquires it through faith in Christ. This is not a spark within that is made to grow through our own efforts of positive thinking or action. This is a right that we ourselves could not work for and could not bestow on ourselves. We could not possibly have it if it were not for the work of Jesus Christ on our behalf. Without the right, there could be no might. With the right Christ gives us, comes the might also. We should be so conscious of the origin of the grace we possess that we should pray the prayer of that saint of God who said, "O Lord, give me grace to feel the need of Thy grace; give me grace to ask for Thy grace, and when in Thy grace Thou hast given me grace, give me grace to use Thy grace."

Being given the ability to go to God does not necessarily mean coercion on the part of God. Observe the way this verse runs. "But as many as received him, to them gave he *exousia* [the right and the might] to become the sons of God." Man is given the right and the might to become something which he is not. This involves the acquisition of a new nature. It is the nature of the child of God. John does not tell us that, when we receive Christ by believing, we do certain things, but that we become something. We do not perform Christian acts and thus become Christians, but we become Christians and then instinctively perform Christian acts. This deponent verb *genesthai*, "to become," must not be interpreted as if man had the ability on his own to become a child of God. It is God who gives it to him, and he receives it through faith. This is all done through the mysterious operation of the Holy Spirit in the heart of man. It is God who makes man become His child through faith. A complete transformation of man is involved.

Queen Victoria once paid a visit to a paper mill. The foreman showed her and her attendant over the works, without knowing who his distinguished visitor was. She finally went into the rag-sorting

238

shop, where men were employed in picking out the rags from the refuse of the city. Upon inquiring what was done with this dirty mass of rags, she was told that, sorted out, it would make the finest white paper. After her departure, the foreman found out who it was that had paid the visit. Some time later, Her Majesty received a package of the most delicate white stationery, having the Queen's likeness for a watermark, with the intimation that it was made from the dirty rags she had inspected. That illustrates Christ's work in us. He takes us, filthy as we are, and makes us into new creatures. Receiving Christ is becoming Christ's. After receiving Him, we are as different from what we were before as pure white paper is from the filthy rags from which it was made.

This verb *genesthai*, "to become," is the infinitive of the second aorist tense, which in this context refers to two things. First, that this is an event that definitely takes place. It is something that happens within time and space. There is a time when man changes from a child of the devil to a child of God. He knows it and others know it. It is not a delusion but an accomplished fact. A preacher was once asked, "Where were you born?" "I was born in Dublin and Liverpool," he replied. The man with whom he was conversing thought there was some misunderstanding. "How can a man be born in two places at once?" he asked. But the preacher meant that he had been born in the flesh in Dublin and born again in the spirit in Liverpool. The second birth is just as definite an experience as the first. With the first birth man becomes a creature of God; with the second he becomes a child of God.

Secondly, the tense of this verb implies finality. When you become a child of God, it is not like acquiring something which you can lose. You may be weak and your growth slow or defective, but nevertheless you are a child. You have become a living organism, even as a child when it is born into the world. Of course, the process of growth has to be realized all through life, but this experience is the beginning of a new life. But the life that you possess when you receive Christ by faith is complete. There is no congenital

239

deficiency. Any deficiency in later growth is not due to God's bestowal of life but to our negligence in not acting as children of God. True, we are babies when we become children of God, when we are born into the Kingdom of God, but we are whole and complete—constitutionally perfect if we may use that expression.

Another truth found in the tense of the infinitive *genesthai* is that this act of becoming cannot be repeated. It happens once and for all. You cannot become a child of God many times in your life. That happens once. There is a definite parallel between man's first becoming as a natural being and the second becoming as a spiritual being. You come into the world once and you come into the Kingdom of God once. The Kingdom of God is not like a house which you keep entering, leaving, and re-entering. The new birth is not like a garment you wear and discard at will. It is a transformation so complete and final that it can happen to you only once. A child can be born only once—whether naturally or spiritually.

CHAPTER 55

WHO ARE CHILDREN OF GOD?

". . . to them gave he power to become THE SONS [CHILDREN] of God . . ." (John 1:12b)

———————

The Apostle John tells us that, when we receive Jesus Christ by believing on Him, we are given the authority, the right, and the power to become the children of God. We are thus enabled to become something that we were not before.

It is definitely wrong to say that we humans are all children of God. It is anti-Scriptural. Paul standing in Athens and speaking to the philosophers of his day proclaimed that all are the offspring of God (in the sense that all originated with Him), that we are all descended from Him, that we owe our life to Him, but to be a child of God is something different (see Acts 17:28).

True, God's love extends to every human being, and His expressed desire is that everyone may become His child (see John 3:16). But John makes it very clear in his Gospel that man is not born a child of God but that he becomes a child of God after he is born into the physical world. "But as many as received him, to them gave he power to become the sons of God, even to them that believe on his name." (1:12).

There is a marvelous agreement between the verb *genesthai,* "become," and the noun *tekna,* translated "sons." This should be translated "children" rather than "sons," for the Greek word *tekna* refers to both the male and female. This word *tekna* comes from the verb *tiktein,* which means "to give birth, to bear." What is implied here is that, when we receive Jesus Christ by believing on Him, we become newborn creatures. We are just like little babies born into a

241

special world, the world of the Spirit, the Kingdom of God. This concerns an entirely new beginning. It is not a matter of some repair work being accomplished by Christ, but the creation of entirely new beings. One time when a former drunkard was praising God for taking away all his appetite for liquor, a physician remonstrated with him, saying that he would have to have a new stomach in order to have the appetite for liquor removed. "Praise God!" said the former drunkard. "I knew I had a new heart, but this is the first time I knew I had a new stomach!" "Therefore, if any man be in Christ, he is a new creature: old things are past away; behold, all things are become new" (II Cor. 5:17). Thus we see that when one receives Christ it is not the same old person doing new things, but a new person created within, a spiritual child born.

Very interestingly, the Lord Jesus Christ is never called *teknon Theou,* "a child of God." but always *ho huios tou Theou,* "the Son of God," or *ho huios tou anthroopou,* "the Son of man." Why? Because the word *teknon* ("child"), which comes from the verb *tiktoo,* meaning "to give birth," would not apply to Jesus Christ in His eternity and infinity. God the Father never gave birth to God the Son. If one had given birth to the other, one of the two would have had to be less than God. They were eternally in fellowship with each other, as is declared by the second clause of John 1:1, "And the Word was with [or toward] God [the Father]." (See our study in the booklet entitled *God in Man.*) *Teknon,* "child," denotes derivation from, while *huios,* "son," denotes fellowship with or relation to. This is very important to remember. Jesus Christ in His eternity was not derived from God the Father, because then He would be inferior to Him, but He was eternally "toward" the Father, or in eternal relationship and fellowship with Him. This is why He is never called *teknon Theou,* "a child of God," but always *ho huios tou Theou,* "the Son of God" implying the fellowship of two co-equal and co-eternal personalities.

When we believe on the Lord Jesus Christ and accept Him in our hearts, we do not simply establish a relationship with Him, but

242

we are actually born of Him. What occurs is not the mere union of the human and the Divine, but the entrance of the divine nature into the human personality. We become something that we were not before. We are not simply adopted by God, as would be suggested if the word *huioi,* "sons," had been used here, but through the mysterious and mystical operation of the Holy Spirit in the new birth we actually become children of God, in the same way that we become the children of our parents through physical birth. As by nature we acquire the characteristics of our parents, so through our spiritual birth we acquire the nature and character of God. This is a real miracle, that man by believing in Christ becomes a child of God with all the privileges and responsibilities of a child.

Furthermore, the word *teknon,* "child," has special connotations of endearment and tenderness, whereas the word *huios,* "son," speaks of legal standing. John wants us to realize that through believing we become not simply heirs of eternal life but very dear and tender children of God. We come to the place where in a very real way we experience God as our Father. God does not want us to think only of how we can benefit from Him, but He wants us to enjoy Him and His love to us, irrespective of what He gives us. Have you ever noticed how miserable family life is when the tie that binds the various members is merely what each can get from the other? If my little son considered himself my son only for what he could get out of me, he would be missing a great deal of the father-son relationship. Let us not become children of God just for what we can get from our Father, but let us seek to enjoy Him for what He is.

An elderly man was walking along the street when a tramp approached him and said, "Mister, please give me a dime." But as soon as he took a good look at the man, he recognized his own father. He exclaimed, "Father, don't you know me?" And the overjoyed father threw his arms around the tramp saying, "I have found you; all I have is yours." You can imagine how the tramp felt when he heard these words. Oh, that we might realize the position of the one who, believing, receives Jesus Christ and becomes the child of God. To realize that everything that God is and has belongs to us through our new birth into the Kingdom of God is staggering and beyond human comprehension.

Dr. Guthrie, attending a Ragged School gathering, followed a speaker who had referred to poor neglected children as "the scum of society." This roused the indignation of Dr. Guthrie. Taking a clean sheet of paper and holding it up, he said, "Yes, this was the scum of society once, only filthy rags, but they can be cleansed and made into spotless white paper, on which you may write the name of God."

CHAPTER 56

CAN HUMAN EFFORT SAVE MAN?

"Which were born, not of blood, nor of the will of the flesh, nor of the will of man, but of God" (John 1:13).

For centuries, many able theologians and commentators have been puzzled over John 1:13. Their difficulty springs from the possibility of its being related either to the verse that precedes it or the verse that follows it. If it is related to verse 12, then it refers to those who receive Christ by believing on His name. Thus the thought of the two verses would run as follows:

"But as many as received him, to them gave he power to become the sons of God, even to them that believe on his name: Which were born, not of blood, nor of the will of the flesh, nor of the will of man, but of God." If these two verses are taken in conjunction, then the idea in verse 12 is that the new birth by which man becomes a child of God is entirely an act of God; and the declaration in verse 13 is that this miracle of becoming a child of God is not by human descent, or desire, or power.

If, however, verses 13 and 14 go together, then the thought expressed would be as follows: "Which [referring back to the word "he"—Christ—in verse 12] [was] born, not of blood, nor of the will of the flesh, nor of the will of man, but of God. And the Word was made flesh, and dwelt among us, (and we beheld his glory, the glory as of the only begotten of the Father,) full of grace and truth." In this case, these two verses would refer to the incarnation of God in Jesus Christ. Verse 13 would proclaim the virgin birth of Jesus, and verse 14 would refer to His incarnation.

Both sides have their arguments, which would take too long to enumerate here. We believe, however, that it would be advantageous to present both interpretations and for us to receive the benefit of both. The author is personally persuaded that the second relationship, namely, that between verses 13 and 14, is the correct one and that verse 13 declares the virgin birth of Jesus Christ. We shall see the reasons later as we examine the verse more carefully.

What does verse 13 mean if it is related to verse 12? "Which were born, not of blood, nor of the will of the flesh, nor of the will of man, but of God." Naturally, it would refer to those who received Christ by believing on His name. We are told in verse 12 that they have the right to become the children of God. This is a positive statement.

But John also wants to give us a very clear idea of the means by which we cannot become children of God. First, he says in effect, here is how you *can* become children of God. But second, to dispel any misapprehension, here is how you *cannot* become children of God. And he tells us this in three negative phrases:

1. You cannot become children of God by "bloods." This is the correct translation of the word *haimatoon* in the original Greek text. It is plural and not singular, as it appears in most translations. What does John mean by this? That we cannot be born again, born into the family of God, by any natural means. Human beings give birth to human posterity. But spiritual beings do not necessarily give birth to spiritual beings. You are not a Christian because your father and mother may have been Christians. Of course, you have a far better opportunity of becoming a Christian if you have had a Christian upbringing; but the fact that you were born of Christian parents does not in itself insure the result.

Unfortunately, this is one of the great misapprehensions of our day. Religious affiliation is determined by our parents' religious beliefs. The children of Jews are Jews, and the children of Catholics are Catholics, and the children of Protestants are Protestants. But the New Testament makes it very clear that the children of Christians are not necessarily Christians. And by

246

Christians, of course, we mean not Christians in name only, but true children of God who have received Christ by believing on Him and His work on Calvary's cross. Christianity is not inherited but is appropriated by faith. Christian ancestry predisposes toward but does not determine the faith and personal behavior of posterity. No man, therefore, should depend upon the fact that his parents or grandparents were true Christians. The only way he can become a Christian is by believing in the same way they did.

2. The second means by which man cannot become a child of God is "the will of the flesh." This means the natural desire of man, his physical appetites. These never push him toward God, but rather away from God. This clearly shows that the initiative is taken by God Himself and never by the natural inclinations of man. Man is degenerate and depraved. There is nothing good in him nor any desire for good. Any spiritual desire of man is the result of God's Spirit visiting his spirit. But there is always a struggle between what is "flesh" in man and what is "spirit" in him (I Cor. 2:9-12).

It is the clear and unmistakable teaching of the New Testament that man does not have the will to save himself. And even if he had, he could not accomplish his salvation. In our natural state, we do not want God, and even when He tells us that our only hope is to let Him save us completely, our natural will is so degenerate that we do not want His will for our salvation imposed upon us.

Evangelist Gypsy Smith said that once, when a group of gypsies were forced to cross a swollen stream, a great number of men were drowned. One young man made a desperate attempt to save his mother, who kept clinging to him. Several times he pushed her away, saying, "Let go, Mother, and I can save you." But she would not heed him and was lost. At the funeral, the son stood by his mother's grave and said over and over, "How hard I tried to save you, Mother, but you wouldn't let me!" These are the tragic words that we shall hear Jesus Christ say to many in eternity one day, "How hard I tried to save you, but you wouldn't let me. Your will was the great hindrance." May God save us from our own natural and fallen will and, through the Holy Spirit, enable us to will God's will for us.

3. The third means by which man cannot become a child of God is "the will of man." In the original Greek, this does not mean man in the generic sense, because then the word used would be *anthroopou,* but it is *andros,* which refers to the male, to man as contrasted to a woman. It is the use of this word, as we shall see later, that tilts the scale of our judgment in favor of taking this entire verse as referring to Jesus Christ and His virgin birth rather than to the believer. Jesus Christ was not born through the desire or will of a husband, of a male. He was born of the Virgin Mary without the intervention of a man, as has been the case with all other conception of human life.

But if this verse is taken to refer to the believers who received Christ, then it means that no man can be saved through the desire, or effort, or power of any other human individual. Not only are we not desirous of God as individuals, but no other man can of his own power and volition make us children of God.

And finally there is the positive declaration of how the believers did become children of God. They were born of God Himself. He takes the initiative, even as our human parents take the initiative in our physical birth. Being born into the spiritual Kingdom of God is entirely a work of God. That work, in some mysterious way, includes His making us willing to be willing to receive Him through faith.

CHAPTER 57

IS THE VIRGIN BIRTH OF CHRIST SCIENTIFIC?

"... born, not of blood, nor of the will of the flesh, nor of the will of man, but of God" (John 1:13).

———

The Gospel of John is predominantly the Gospel of the deity of Jesus Christ. John wrote this Gospel for the express purpose of proving that the Jesus of history was the Christ of eternity. His life did not begin in Bethlehem (He was simply manifested there as man), but He had always been God.

It would be very strange indeed if the Gospel of John did not say anything about the virgin birth of Jesus Christ, thus proving right from the outset that He had a supernatural nature. We believe that John 1:13 does refer to the virgin birth of Jesus Christ, as we shall proceed to demonstrate from the evidence.

First, we must look at the evidence of the ancient manuscripts or codices. This we cannot do in detail here, because it involves the matter of textual criticism of the various manuscripts.

The original reading of John 1:13 appears specifically in the writings of Tertullian, who lived A.D. 155-222. He is the earliest, and after St. Augustine the greatest, of the ancient Church writers of the West. In his treatise "On the Flesh of Christ," chapter XIX, he goes into detailed argument to prove that the original manuscript of this verse had the principal verb in the singular and not in the plural. This is how the verse should read according to Tertullian: "Who [referring to the eternal *Logos*, Jesus Christ] was born not of bloods, nor of the will of the flesh, nor of the will of man, but of God." The argument here is that if *egenneethee,* "was born," is the word used in the original Greek text, then it must refer to Jesus

249

Christ and not to the believers, because these are spoken of in the plural.

Tertullian also gives us some of the historical background which made him set forth so explicitly his arguments concerning this verse. He was fighting the same battle as Irenaeus, that most distinguished theologian of the second century, against the doctrines of the Gnostic philosophers, the Valentinians. Around the year 140 this sect changed the original singular *egenneethee* ("was born") to *egenneetheesan* ("were born"). This was easily done by adding the suffix *san*. The Valentinians believed that there was a special class of people in whom was infused a spiritual element that had nothing to do with matter. By saying, therefore, that these people were not born of bloods, which is matter and therefore evil, or of the will of the flesh, which again involves matter, or of the will of man, which again involves matter, they separated the spirit completely from matter.

Now very interestingly the Occidentals held to the singular rendering (*egenneethee*, "was born") until the third or possibly the fourth century. The Alexandrians, who were more affected by the Valentinian Gnostic philosophy, were ready to adopt the plural rendering (*egenneetheesan*, "were born") and had done so by the end of the second century.

When the Alexandrians changed "was born" to "were born," they did not incorporate at the beginning of the verse the Greek relative pronoun *hoi*, meaning "these who" (plural). This was inserted later for the purpose of connecting the believers of verse 12 and verse 13. And then this relative pronoun *hoi* ("these who") found acceptance also in the Occident.

Ordinarily, the determination as to which reading is the most correct in the various manuscripts is made by comparing the readings in the various codices and accepting the one which only the best and most reliable codices support. But in this case it is different. The historical evidence of the existing doctrines of the Valentinians ought to be taken into consideration, as well as the writings of Tertullian, Irenaeus, and others in relation to this verse and the dispute that existed with the Gnostic Valentinians. We must also take into consideration the trend of thought and the exegesis of the verse in its entire context. We believe that the exegesis, the declarations contained in the verse, provide the weightiest argument in support of the proper reading being, "Who was born, not of bloods, nor of the will of the flesh, nor of the will of man, but of God." If we were to try to make this refer to the believers of verse 12, even if the verb *egenneetheesan* ("were born") were accepted, the exegesis of each of these three negatives would be forced. It would not make sense. We therefore believe that this verse refers to the eternal *Logos,* who is the predominant subject of this entire passage of John 1:1-18. It was not necessary for John to mention the word *Logos,* "the Word," again, even as he did not in the beginning of verse 9 when he declared that He "was the true Light." In verse 14, he will tell us about the fact of the incarnation of the eternal Word, but before he does this, he wants to speak of the method of the incarnation: Here is how it happened. Since the fact of the incarnation is supernatural, the method of the incarnation is also supernatural, and that is what he declares in verse 13. He, the eternal Christ, was born into the world of history — not of bloods, nor of the will of the flesh, nor of the will of man. It was not your and my desire that brought the eternal Christ to this earth, but purely His will and power.

But how can we in this scientific age accept such a scientific improbability? The virgin birth was thought in ancient times to be so essential to those who claimed to be supermen, or gods, or great deliverers, that it was often asserted they were virgin born. But these were false claims. None of these pseudo-gods ever lived a life comparable to that of Jesus Christ, or worked the miracles He did, or rose from the dead never to die again. To make claims is one thing, but to substantiate them with evidences of one's deity or characteristics transcending humanity is another. We quote Dr. J. Wilson Sutton regarding this: "Those who would have us give up the Virgin Birth on scientific grounds only succeed in leading us into serious scientific difficulty. Since the beginning of the world, millions upon millions of children have been born of human mothers through the agency of human fathers, and never has it been known that the union of human father and human mother brought into the world other than a human person. But Jesus Christ is a Divine Person and to claim that He came into the world in the way that human persons come into it is to take a thoroughly unscientific position. . . . Our Lord has a human mother because He has a human nature; He has a Divine Father because He is a Divine Person. His human nature was brought into being and united with His Divine Person through the operation of the Holy Spirit because, while a human father in union with a human mother could have produced a human nature, and have brought into the world a human person, a human father in union with a human mother could not possibly have brought into the world a Divine Person, except by running absolutely counter to the natural law of which people make so much. I am not prepared to say that God could not have brought His Divine Son into the world through the agency of St. Joseph and St. Mary. I am prepared to say that if He had done so He would have violated the recognized and universally scientific law that the union of human father and human mother brings into the world a human person and that in so far this law would have been discredited." (As quoted in *The Modern Mind and the Virgin Birth*, by G. W. McPherson, Yonkers, N.Y.: Yonkers Book Company, 1923, pp. 20-22.)

We firmly believe that John wants to show us in this verse that Jesus Christ the man had no human father, that He was born into the world of the Virgin Mary through the miraculous intervention of God.

CHAPTER 58

IS SPIRITUAL BIRTH POSSIBLE
BY PHYSICAL MEANS?

"Who [the eternal Word] was born, not of bloods, nor of the will of the flesh, nor of the will of man, but of God" (preferred reading of John 1:13).

———————

Now let us go deeper into the reasons for believing John 1:13 to refer to the virgin birth of Christ and to be related to verse 14 rather than verse 12.

The Greek connective conjunction *kai,* meaning "and," is most important in leading to a clear understanding of the trend of thought of a certain passage. In this connection we observe that verse 14 begins with "and." "And the Word became flesh, and dwelt among us, (and we beheld his glory, the glory as of the only begotten of the Father,) full of grace and truth."

In his series of declarations concerning Jesus Christ in the first 18 verses of his Gospel, John has masterfully used the conjunction "and" to combine related thoughts. Nine times prior to verse 14 he has used the word "and," as follows:

"In the beginning was the Word, *and* the Word was with God, *and* the Word was God" (v. 1). The subject spoken of here is the Word, the three statements about Him being united with the conjunction "and."

Then John continues, "All things were made by him; *and* without him was not any thing made that was made" (v. 3). The "and" here naturally combines the two thoughts, one positive and the other negative, concerning creation.

And then, speaking of Christ as the originator of life and light,

John says, "In him was life; *and* the life was the light of men. *And* the light shineth in darkness; *and* the darkness comprehended it not" (vv. 4, 5).

Then, in verse 10, we have a new paragraph, which does not begin with the conjunction "and." "He was in the world, *and* the world was made by him, *and* the world knew him not." This expresses the complete thought of Christ's coming into the world and His rejection by the world.

And that the tragedy of His rejection may be made clear, John goes on to tell us that, in spite of the fact that the world as a whole and people as individuals rightfully belong to God as His creation, they did not welcome Him. "He came unto his own, *and* his own received him not" (v. 11.).

Then John proceeds to tell us in verse 12 what those who receive Christ are entitled to become, that is, the children of God. "But as many as received him, to them gave he power to become the sons of God, even to them that believe on his name." This verse is connected naturally with verse 11. Verse 11 speaks of those who did not receive Christ, and verse 12 speaks of those who did receive Him. Since there is a contrast of attitudes here, it is expressed by the conjunction *de*, "but." "But as many as received him. . . ."

Now we come to the crux of the matter, which is that verse 14 begins with a conjunction, the word "and." But what does it connect? It could not begin a new thought, because in this passage John has never introduced a new thought by the conjunction *kai*, "and." This would completely contradict both the practice here and general practice.

Also the conjunction "and" would not be used to connect two unrelated thoughts. The "and" with which verse 14 begins would have to connect the thought in verse 13 with the thought in verse 14. But if we take verse 13 as referring to the believers not born of blood, nor of the will of the flesh, nor of the will of man, then somehow verse 14 must also be interpreted as referring to the believers, which is impossible in view of its very clear declaration concerning the incarnation of the Word. "And the Word became flesh." In verse 13 we would have the regeneration of the believers, while in verse 14 we have the incarnation of the eternal Word. The first happened at all times and especially at the time of John's writing, and the other, the incarnation, happened at a certain set time in history. Thus there would even be diversity of time in these two verses. If these two occurrences were related either in thought or in time of occurrence, they would be connected by "and." If they were opposite in meaning (which they are not), they would be connected by "but." Therefore we conclude that there must be a very definite relation between verses 13 and 14, because of the connective "and" with which verse 14 begins. Since verse 14 deals unmistakably with the incarnation of the eternal Word (that is, with the *fact* of the incarnation), then verse 13, with which it is connected by the conjunction "and," must also refer to the incarnation (which it does, that is, the *method* of the incarnation).

Immediately another question arises, and that is, why would John need to refute the spiritual regeneration of man through physical means? Since verse 12 really refers to the believers who receive Christ, and John very clearly tells us that this is an act of faith, by believing, why would he go on to make what would seem to be the ridiculous claim that spiritual birth cannot be accomplished by means of physical procreation and generation? Was such a view ever held—that people could be spiritually born through their physical ancestry by procreation? Nobody in the Christian Church has ever supposed that regeneration was a physical act. Even the Gnostics, and especially later on the Valentinians to whom we made reference previously, fully rejected matter as sinful and hence, according to them, the material means of generation could never account for the spiritual state of man. Hence John did not need to refute them on this score. When Nicodemus came to Jesus Christ, he was told that he needed to be born again, from above. He knew perfectly well that this new birth could not be accomplished through his re-entrance into his mother's womb and his physical

255

rebirth. Thus there was no doctrine to which verse 13 would be the refutation, if it were taken to refer to the believers and their spiritual birth.

In view of all this, we must conclude that John 1:13 refers to the virgin birth of Christ, rather than constituting a denial of the spiritual birth of man through physical means. Who ever put forth such a view, that John should attempt to refute it?

CHAPTER 59

DID JESUS CHRIST HAVE THE BLOOD OF A HUMAN FATHER?

"Who was born, not of bloods . . ." (preferred reading of John 1:13a).

In our previous study we gave the reasons why we believe that the text of John 1:13 as referred to by Tertullian should be accepted. Also the "b" manuscript of the 5th century, the Old Latin Version, gives *qui natus est* ("who was born"), the verse being in this way a reference to the virgin birth of Christ. We are fully aware of the fact that this Western reading, so called, is not generally accepted, but there is no really satisfactory reason why it should not be. Of course, we could never venture to change any of the text, if a variant text did not exist making this verse refer to the virgin birth of Christ. Although this text is generally not the most trustworthy, in this particular instance it seems to be, especially in view of the arguments concerning the connection of thought, as well as the difficulty of determining the correct exegesis of verse 13 if it really refers to the believers. Also, this reading, which makes verse 13 refer to the virgin birth of Christ, is the older one.

This original Western reading of our verse does not begin with a relative pronoun, either plural (*hoi,* "these who") or singular (*hos,* "he who"). Therefore, the verse in the Western text reads, "Not of bloods, nor of the will of the flesh, nor of the will of man, but of God he was born." And this refers to the human birth of the eternal *Logos,* the Word. This is the most natural explanation and follows the most natural sequence of thought. As we proceed to examine every word in this verse, it will be made clear that the arguments are

257

all on the side of the Western text referring to the virgin birth of Christ.

The first expression found here is "not of bloods." All the manuscripts agree that the word is in the plural, *haimatoon*, meaning "bloods," and not "blood" as most of the English translations have it. The latter translation is definitely incorrect and was possibly done to support the belief held by most commentators that this verse referred to the believers of verse 12 rather than to the mode of the incarnation of Christ. Remember, then, that this first phrase of John 1:13 reads "not of bloods."

Now, why "bloods" and not "blood"? In Leviticus 17:11 we read, "For the life of the flesh is in the blood; and I have given it to you upon the altar to make an atonement for your souls: for it is the blood that maketh an atonement for the soul." Blood is symbolic of the corporeal part of man, of his physical element, and it stands for the total physical body in contrast to the soul, which is the non-physical element of the individual man. Now, if this verse is taken to refer to the believers, the most probable thing that John would have said is, "These believers were not born of blood," blood as we have said being the symbol of the corporeal part of man. Spiritual birth is not generated by anything physical. But this would be more or less absurd, for no one believed that spiritual life was the result of any physical agent.

Paul, in speaking to the Athenian philosophers, told them that God had made all nations "of one blood," using the singular and not the plural form to indicate that all men of all nations, no matter what their outward color, have the same origin; that their blood is the same—human. Paul did not want to bring out the fact that human procreation necessitates the participation of a man and a woman, and that is why he used "blood" instead of "bloods."

But the fact remains that John says "bloods." Undoubtedly he wants to differentiate the sources of the blood as the symbol of the physical element of life. In using the plural "bloods," it is as if he were referring to the two corporeal sources involved in human procreation. It is not actually the blood itself that is contributed by the father and the mother that goes into becoming the fetus which ultimately develops into a human being. But it is absolutely essential for the procreation of man that a male contribute the sperm and a female contribute the ovum. Neither of these contain any actual blood, in the form of red cells, but they are the carriers of the genes which determine the various physical characteristics of the new individual and which are capable of producing organs which will produce blood in a new individual. So ultimately it is the blood of the father, or more specifically his contribution of the sperm cell, and the blood of the mother, or again more specifically her contribution of the ovum, which when united serve to form a new individual. This new individual later becomes capable of producing his own blood.

Thus we conclude that the term "of bloods" refers to the two different sources of the physical elements necessary for physical procreation, and not to the substance itself, that is, human blood. What verse 13 declares is that Jesus of Bethlehem did not have both a human mother and a human father, as did every other human being ever born. From the human side, only the physical body of Mary the Virgin was involved in the development of Jesus' human body. His body did not have two corporeal sources but only one, that of His mother.

This is unmistakably spoken of by Matthew in his Gospel. "Behold, a virgin shall be with child, and shall bring forth a son, and they shall call his name Emmanuel, which being interpreted is, God with us" (1:23). In the Greek text, the word translated "virgin" is *parthenos,* which does not mean simply a young woman, but a virgin or a young woman who has not known a man. This Greek word is even used of men who are similarly chaste, who have not known a woman. Thus the stress is on virginity. And that is what John means when he says that Jesus Christ as man was born "not of bloods." His physical body owed its being to the Virgin Mary. He was not the son of Joseph who later became her husband.

259

The skeptic asks, "How can this be possible?" Humanly it seems impossible. From man's standpoint it is a miracle. But from God's standpoint it is just part of His creative work. To us the whole creation is a miracle, and yet it is a fact. God, according to the Scriptures, created the first man without that man's having a mother. And He created the Second Man, Jesus Christ as man, without His having a father. Why accept Adam's motherless beginning and not Jesus' fatherless birth? The only mystery that goes beyond the comprehension of man's mind is God Himself. Once we accept Him, there is no difficulty in accepting anything that He decides to bring about.

A young man who was studying medicine could not accept the doctrine of the supernatural generation of Jesus Christ. He went to a preacher, who reasoned with him and left him in greater perplexity than ever. When he had finished his medical studies, he went to practice medicine in a rural community. One Sunday he decided to go and hear a backwoods preacher, not thinking for a moment that such a man could change his viewpoint on the virgin birth of Jesus Christ. But this humble preacher knocked more skepticism out of the doctor in half an hour than he had accumulated in all his years of medical school. He said, "If there is anybody here troubled about the mystery of God becoming man, I want to take you back to the first chapter of Genesis and the first verse, 'In the beginning God.' " He looked down into the audience very searchingly. The doctor was so self-conscious that he felt the speaker was looking directly at him: Then the preacher continued, "My brother, let me ask you this: Do you believe God was in the beginning? That is to say, that before the beginning began, God was? Somebody had to be to start things off. Science tells us how things evolve and grow, but not how they first started." And the doctor whispered to himself, "Yes, I believe that." "Now," the preacher said, "if you believe that God was ahead of the beginning, you believe the only mysterious thing of this universe." "If I believed that, God knows I could believe anything else in the world," thought the doctor to himself. And then his conclusion that

260

memorable morning was, "I had gone to college and traveled through the mysteries of the theory of reproduction and cell formation, and had come out to realize that I was just a common fool; that if God was in the beginning, that was the one supreme mystery of all mysteries of this mysterious universe of God."

It would be far more difficult to understand and explain the life, death, resurrection, and ascension of Christ, if we did not believe in His deity than if we did. And if we believe that the Word was God from the beginning, why could He not declare from the very time of His entrance into the realm of history, through His virgin birth, that He was no mere human being and therefore that it was to be expected that what He was and did would be far more than any man could do or be? As man Jesus Christ was born of the Virgin Mary only, through a miracle of procreation, and as God He was well capable of such a miracle, since all things were made through Him.

CHAPTER 60

WAS THE DESIRE OF THE FLESH INVOLVED IN THE PHYSICAL BIRTH OF JESUS?

"... born, not ... of the will of the flesh, nor of the will of man ..."
(John 1:13).

All of us know that the procreation of man is made possible by the union of a man and a woman. This union originates in a desire for one another, a desire that has its instinct and basis in our physical make-up. Procreation has to do primarily with our flesh rather than with our spirit.

There was a unique exception in the history of all the people born into this world, and that was the Lord Jesus Christ. His conception had nothing to do with the desire of the flesh. Nevertheless, He was a physical being just like you and me, yet without sin. He had a human mother but not a human father.

This is made clear by the second and third negative phrases of John 1:13. Speaking of the incarnation of Christ, John says, "born, not ... of the will of the flesh, nor of the will of man [husband]." John is narrowing down in his statements about the virgin birth of Jesus Christ. The first declaration is that there was no union of two bloods, meaning two individuals—a woman and a man—in the conception of Jesus Christ as man. Of course, there is no actual union of drops of blood, but the term blood is used here as symbolizing the material element in man.

And then he goes on to explain further. He builds a narrower platform. And standing on this he tells us that physical desire had nothing to do with the conception or birth of Jesus Christ the man. Of course, by this statement concerning Christ's unique birth, John

262

leaves it to be assumed that such is the case with every other human conception and birth. It is the result of "the will of the flesh." And the flesh here refers to both the will of the female as well as the will of the male. John emphatically declares that Mary's conception of Jesus had nothing to do with physical desire.

Of course, let it not be thought that there is any sinful implication in this God-appointed method for the procreation of the human race. God has instituted these natural desires as well as their honorable and rightful manifestations. It is God who made male and female, and it is He who has instituted the holy union of marriage and commanded us to be fruitful and multiply and replenish the earth. There is great sanctity in this divinely instituted ordinance, despite the fact that unregenerate man in his estrangement from God has completely perverted it. All we are saying here is that physical desire played absolutely no part in the conception of Jesus Christ by the Virgin Mary.

The word translated "will" in the Greek text is *theleematos* (the genitive of *theleema*), which here has the connotation of physical desire, even as it does in I Corinthians 7:37. "Nevertheless," Paul writes, "he that standeth stedfast in his heart, having no necessity, but hath power over his own will [the same Greek word *theleematos* referring to physical desire], and hath so decreed in his heart that he will keep his virgin, doeth well." And in Ephesians 2:3 the same word is used. "Among whom also we all have our conversation in times past in the lusts of our flesh, fulfilling the desires of the flesh [here the same Greek word *theleemata* in the accusative is used]. . . ."

This word *theleema* has also the suggestion of pleasure associated with it. (Cremer, *Biblico-Theological Lexicon of the New Testament*, p. 728). We believe that what is implied here, in this connotation, is that this was one conception that had no pleasure associated with it, either on the part of the man or the woman. Physical pleasure, then, is completely excluded as having had anything to do with the conception of our Lord.

263

A second distinct implication of the word, coming from its cognate root verb *theloo,* is that it means more than mere theoretical desire in the mind. It is will passing on to action; it is will realized. Thus we conclude that in the conception of Jesus Christ there was neither the will as thought nor the will translated into action in the flesh. There was neither the thought nor the act of physical union or pleasure. How holy and beyond the realm of the purely human, indeed, was the conception of Jesus Christ by the Virgin Mary. A far higher will than the will of human flesh was involved here. It was the desire of God to save sinners through the birth and consequent sacrifice of His Son. This brought pain to the heart of the Triune God instead of pleasure to the flesh of any human being.

John closes in still further in the third negative statement he makes. He stands on a narrower platform this time when he says that the human Jesus was not born "of the will of man."

Not of bloods,
nor of the will of the flesh [either man's or woman's],
nor of the will of man [male].

The Greek word translated "man" in this third phrase is *andros* (genitive of *aneer*), which stands in contrast to a woman. It is not *anthroopou* (the genitive of *anthroopos*), which is the generic word for both man and woman, but it is the word that definitely refers to the male, and in this context it could really be translated "husband." Thus the third declaration of John as he speaks of the conception and birth of Jesus the man is that He was not born "of the will of a husband or a male." If this verse were taken to refer to the believers spoken of in verse 12, we would have great difficulty in finding an adequate and satisfactory exegesis for it. What would it mean if we were told that the believers were not born spiritually of the will of a male? But it does make sense when referring to the virgin birth of Jesus Christ. What John stresses in unmistakable terms is that Jesus Christ did not have a human father. Joseph was not His father.

John, of course, takes it for granted that his readers are already aware of the details as found in the Gospels of Matthew and Luke, in existence prior to the writing of this Fourth Gospel. Thus we can correctly say that his axiomatic statements in the first 18 verses of his Gospel have their narrative counterparts, not only in the body of the Gospel of John, but also in the Gospels of Matthew and Luke. At least the details of the virgin birth of Jesus Christ are given in Matthew and Luke and only these axiomatic statements about the mode and fact of His incarnation are given in John 1:13 and 14.

CHAPTER 61

THE BIRTH OF JESUS CHRIST, A SUPERNATURAL PHENOMENON

"Which [was] born, not of blood, nor of the will of the flesh, nor of the will of man, BUT OF GOD" (John 1:13).

———

We now come to the fourth statement in John 1:13, this time a positive one. It tells us how Jesus Christ was born as man. "But of God he was born" is the literal translation here. The preposition used in all four phrases of this verse, the three negative ones and this positive one, is the Greek word *ek*, a causal preposition denoting the source or origin of something. But *ek* has the distinct meaning of immediate cause, while *apo*, meaning "from" or "of," is more remote (Jelf, *Greek Grammar*, Vol. II Syntax, p. 289). Why do we mention this? Because first of all John wants to tell us that the immediate and direct cause of the conception and birth of Jesus Christ as man was not human bloods, or the will or desire of either man or woman—of any flesh, particularly that of a male— but was absolutely and directly an act of God. John wants to leave no ground for anyone to think that God was merely the indirect cause of the conception and birth of Jesus Christ as man. He wants to exclude the possibility of anyone's thinking that, in the birth of Jesus, God was the ultimate cause, but that He ordained some human means, such as Joseph. The Virgin Mary was found with child as a result of the direct miraculous intervention of God Himself. In other words, it was *ex nihilo*, out of nothing, that He created something, as in the case of the original creation of the world.

Is such a statement contrary to science? Can a scientifically

266

oriented mind accept it? Science demands proof of everything before it is accepted. But many things are accepted in spite of the fact that there is no adequate explanation for them. Science usually deals with the physical, not with the metaphysical or the supernatural. It can tell us absolutely nothing about the original creation of the world. Science simply takes the world and its laws as they are, and works on them, and learns about them, but it is silent as to their origin and destiny. Yet even the greatest scientists will readily acknowledge their limitations. Dr. Gustaf Stromberg, Staff Astronomer of Mt. Wilson Observatory, wrote, "I believe that behind the physical world we see with our eyes and study in our telescopes, and measure with instruments of various kinds, is another, more fundamental, realm which cannot be described in physical terms. In this non-physical realm lies the ultimate origin of all things, of energy, matter, organization and life consciousness. I am convinced that our consciousness is rooted in a world not built of atoms, and that our mind in its facets reflects some of the fundamental characteristics of its origin." (*The Faith of Great Scientists,* A Collection of "My Faith" Articles from *The American Weekly,* p. 42).

If we do reject the virgin birth of Christ simply because there can be no biological explanation of it, then we must reject a great many other facts of life which remain inexplicable. Take sleep, for instance. If we were to stay awake to ascertain what sleep is, or why we go to sleep, or why we awaken, we would no doubt die of sleeplessness. But we accept sleep as part of life, whether we have a full explanation of it or not. The same thing is also true about food. The mystery of body metabolism has not been fully explained. We study it constantly and doubtless know a great deal about it, but there are more unanswered questions concerning our body metabolism than those we have been able to answer. In the meantime, we do not go hungry until we fully figure out or understand this mysterious process of metabolism.

So it is with the virgin birth of Christ. It is an historical fact, fully attested. And God who originally made it possible for a tiny sperm and a tiny ovum to be joined in a perfect human organism, with all its mysterious intricacies, can certainly bring forth the person of Jesus Christ as man into this world without the use of one of the two, without a human sperm, or by creating one without the instrumentality of a man. This was a supernatural phenomenon, even as it was in the case of the original creation of man. The first man was created without a mother, and the Second Man, Jesus Christ from eternity, entered history without the intermediary of a father. Thus there was something uniquely distinctive about the first Adam and something uniquely distinctive about the Second Adam. God who produced the first could produce the second.

CHAPTER 62

BORN OF "THE GODHEAD"

"Which [was] born . . . of God" (John 1:13 a, d).

———————

In order to get a clear picture of the incarnation, we must now examine two words in the last clause of John 1:13, "Of God he was born." The first is the word "God." In the original Greek, this is the genitive case, which in English is expressed periphrastically as "of God." It is interesting to note that the definite article is not used here. John does not say that Jesus as man was born of *the* God (*ek tou Theou*) but of God (*ek Theou*). Again we remember what grammarian William Edward Jelf says about the omission of the definite article. "The effect of the omission of the article is frequently that the absence of any particular definition or limitation of the notion brings forward its general character." (*A Grammar of the Greek Language,* published by John Henry, and James Parker, 1859, p. 124.). Here John, by omitting the definite article, is speaking generally of Divinity, of the entire Godhead, and not particularly of any one of the Three Persons of the Triune God. Jelf goes on to say, "Some words . . . without the article . . . signify the general notion conceived of abstractedly, and not as in actual existence; with the article the objective existence is brought forward, as Theos (God), the Divinity; Ho Theos (The God), the God we worship" (*Ibid,* p. 124). Thus the second clause of verse 1, in which the word God is preceded by the definite article, "and the Word was toward the God," could be translated as "And the Word, Jesus Christ, was or always had been toward the Father God." Consider also I John 5:20, which translated literally reads, "And we know that *the* Son of *the* God [the Son of the Father, bringing out clearly the distinction between the two personalities without robbing the Son of His deity], and he has given us understanding so that we may know the true one [the genuine one], and we are in the true one [genuine], in *the* his Son Jesus Christ. This one is the true [genuine] God, and life eternal." When John says that Jesus Christ is the true, genuine God, using the definite article, he refers to the distinct personality of Jesus Christ as God.

And now in John 1:13 we are told that Jesus as man was born of *God* and not of *the* God. In other words, John wants to tell us that the human Jesus, who came into the world through the virgin birth, was born of the entire Godhead and not only of the Father. It is the Divine making His appearance in the human. It is the entire Godhead that was in Jesus Christ down here on earth. This was not the incarnation of the eternal Father only, or the eternal Son, or the eternal Holy Spirit, but the incarnation of God—the Divine becoming human.

There is evidence in the New Testament that where the one eternal personality of the Godhead is, there the other two may be also. And this is entirely possible in view of the fact that we are dealing with the infinite, the spaceless, and the limitless. Of Jesus Christ while here on earth in the form of man it was said by the Apostle Paul, "In him [Jesus Christ] dwelleth all the fulness of the Godhead bodily" (Col. 2:9). Thus we find that the entire Godhead played a part in the incarnation of Jesus Christ, the eternal *Logos;* and in the same manner, when a person receives Christ, he receives the entire Godhead. When we remember this, it is easy to understand the words of Jesus in John 14:23, "If a man love me, he will keep my words: and my Father will love him, and *we* will come unto him, and make *our* abode with him." We can see, therefore, that there is an interaction between the personalities of the Godhead that transcends human understanding. The omnipresence of the Three Persons of the Trinity explains their separate yet united activity. The Holy Spirit also had a part in the incarnation of the eternal Christ. "And the angel answered and said unto her [the

270

Virgin Mary], The Holy Ghost shall come upon thee, and the power of the Highest shall overshadow thee; therefore also that holy thing which shall be born of thee shall be called the Son of God" (Luke 1:35).

Thus, when we are told that Jesus was born of God, we are told, not that God acted in a paternal fashion, similar to the way that a human father acts in the conception of a child, nor as a substitute for a human father, but that it was the Godhead, the Infinite God in the eternal Father, Son, and Holy Spirit, that used the Virgin Mary as an instrument for the incarnation of God in Jesus Christ. But Mary could not have conceived Jesus Christ without the direct creative action of God. It is significant that the name of the Virgin is not mentioned here, as if to give more emphasis to the fact that Jesus was born, not of a human being, but of God through the choice vessel of the Virgin Mary. The principal point is that man did not in the real sense of the word initiate the birth of Jesus. He was of God. Being God, He became man of His own volition and power and in His own time.

Then finally we come to the word *egenneethee*, "was born." This is the first aorist passive of the verb *gennaoo*, which originally meant "to beget" and was used of the father's part in procreation, but later was used of the mother's part also. This denotes a new commencement of the personal life of the eternal Word, of the eternal Christ. The Divine begins to live as human. This does not involve the beginning of the personality, but a new beginning in a new form. The eternal Christ is born as man. He was born as man only, and not as God, for He had always been and never ceased to be that.

The fact that this verb is in the first aorist passive indicates that it refers to a definite historical event complete in itself. Jesus Christ was born of God through the Virgin Mary at a fixed time in history. But this could not be said of Him as the eternal Word. That, as we saw in these verses of John under study, He had always been. Jesus Christ had no beginning as God, but He did have a beginning as

271

man. It is only as man that He has a birthday, and not as God. The Eternal cannot have a birthday.

CHAPTER 63

THE NEED FOR A CLEAR AND UNAMBIGUOUS TESTIMONY

"John bare witness of him, and cried, saying, This was he of whom I spake, He that cometh after me is preferred before me: for he was before me" (John 1:15).

Beginning with John 1:15 we are introduced to the direct testimony of John the Baptist concerning the person of Jesus Christ. We have already been told in verses 6 and 7 who he was and what was the purpose of his life. In verse 8 a possible misunderstanding is cleared up, lest anyone mistakenly think that John the Baptist had any light of his own to offer the world. He was just a reflected light of Jesus Christ, an instrument through whom the eternal light of Christ might shine into the world.

The author of the Fourth Gospel, however, considers a direct quotation from John the Baptist essential further to avoid any misunderstanding of the role he came to play· in relation to the person and work of Jesus Christ. This testimony must have been given by John the Baptist time and time again throughout his ministry as the forerunner of Jesus Christ, and possibly even later. Here then, in verse 15, we have a direct quotation ascribed to John the Baptist, the last of the prophets and the first of the disciples.

The Jewish Sanhedrin (the high ecclesiastical ruling body) sent a delegation to observe John the Baptist in his work and to question him about the Lord Jesus Christ. Naturally he refused to claim that he was the expected Messiah. He told these Pharisees that the Christ of the prophecies had already come, but that he himself was not the Christ. And then, the next day, as the Baptist looked upon

273

the Lord Jesus Christ coming unto him, he fully identified Him by saying, "This is he of whom I said, After me cometh a man which is preferred before me: for he was before me" (1:30). This is one very definite occasion on which these words were utilized. Let us continually bear in mind what was said at the beginning of these studies on John, that these first 18 verses are in all probability an epilogue instead of a prologue, as is commonly believed. Internal evidence would indicate that John wrote the incidents of the life and teaching of the Lord Jesus Christ from 1:19 to the end of his Gospel, and then came back to give us an axiomatic summary of the whole.

John 1:15-17 is in the nature of a parenthesis. The three main verses of this passage of John 1:1-18 are 1, 14, and 18, which are all closely related as we have already seen through careful examination. Between verses 1 and 14 there is a long parenthesis, and between verses 14 and 18 another parenthesis. Having already covered the first parenthesis, let us go on to the second.

It begins thus: "John bare witness of him, and cried, saying, This was he of whom I spake, He that cometh after me is preferred before me: for he was before me." There is no connective conjunction between this verse and the preceding one, verse 14. The verse does not begin with "and" but with the word "John." There is an independence of thought in verse 15 which allows us to conclude that John meant the thought included in verse 14 to be considered as complete in itself. Verse 14 deals succinctly but completely with the incarnation of the eternal Word. Verse 15 deals with the Baptist's direct testimony of the pre-incarnate existence of Jesus Christ. Thus verse 15 is also indirectly related to verse 1, which deals with the eternity of the Word. The absence of a conjunction at the beginning of verse 15 detaches it in a peculiar way from its immediate relationship with verse 14 and connects it with the whole passage of the first 18 verses. The entire thesis here is the eternal existence of Jesus Christ and His appearance in human form in time and space. His appearance in the world, however, is not to be understood as taking place at the expense of His eternal existence.

There is no doubt that John the Evangelist is speaking here about John the Baptist, the forerunner of Jesus Christ as far as His earthly ministry is concerned. The witness of John is valid, not only because he knew Jesus Christ intimately, but also because he initiated Him into His public ministry. There were two reasons, therefore, why the Evangelist presented the testimony of the Baptist: first, to avert a misapprehension concerning John the Baptist (that is, that he could in any way usurp the work of salvation that Jesus Christ came to accomplish exclusively), and second, because his testimony was trustworthy.

"John bare witness." In Greek it says, *Iooannees marturei,* which literally translated is "John testifies." This verb is in what we call the historic present. The tense form is the present, but it speaks vividly of an historic event in the past. When the Evangelist wrote these words, the testimony of John the Baptist was actually a past experience. And yet it is presented as continuing by the writer of the Gospel. We believe there are two reasons why the present is used instead of the past. First, the testimony of the Baptist must have been so clear, loud, and unmistakable that it still resounded in the ears of the Evangelist as he wrote this Gospel. It was as if the Baptist were right there repeating these words, in spite of the fact that he had been dead for many years. That is how our testimonies should be given, in a clear and unmistakable way. Let us do away with dubious and ambiguous statements for gaining personal popularity and pleasing our listeners. We must be fearless and faithful in all our declarations concerning the person and work of the Lord Jesus Christ.

A minister felt that for some reason the words he spoke from Sunday to Sunday were not bearing the fruit they should. One Saturday morning after he had finished writing his sermon, the thought occurred to him, "Perhaps I shoot too high. I will go down and see if Betty can understand it." Betty was a trusted kitchen helper. He went to the kitchen and called her to come and hear his sermon. She hesitated. He insisted. She came.

After he had read a few sentences he asked, "Do you understand that?" "No," she replied. He repeated the idea in simpler language and then asked her if she saw it. "I see it a little," she said. Again he simplified it. She saw it more clearly and showed deep interest but said to him, "Plane it down a little more." And once again he simplified. Then she exclaimed with ecstasy, "Now I see it! Now I understand it!" He returned to his study and rewrote his sermon in the simple style that Betty could understand.

On Sunday morning he went to church in fear and trembling lest his people should be contemptuous of his sermon, but fully resolved to try the experiment. What was his surprise to find that he received better attention than ever before and that there were tears in the eyes of many of his congregation. From that time on he changed his style of language and had no further cause to feel that his work was unsuccessful. Clarity of thought and expression do not rob our testimony of its depth and significance. When a man is really profound, he can speak in such a way that even the most lowly can understand him. A witness for Christ need never fear oversimplification.

CHAPTER 64

SHOULD WE ADAPT OUR TESTIMONY
TO A CHANGING WORLD?

"John bare witness of him . . ." (John 1:15a).

———————

John the Baptist gave an unequivocal testimony concerning the person and work of the Lord Jesus Christ. There was nothing doubtful or ambiguous about it. And our testimony, too, must be clear and unmistakable; it must take sides. No doubt, by virtue of its truthfulness, it will needle some people. But one cannot accomplish anything by sewing without a needle! If the thread of our testimony is going to be used to bind back men to God, it must be preceded by the needle. Of course, we must never purposely needle people out of a heart filled with resentfulness. But we will find that the truth in our testimony will always needle those who are in error. This needling is necessary for the repair of the error and the good of all.

"In hearing my orations," said Cicero, "the people admire my intellect and my art, and interrupt me with applause." Demosthenes replied: "True, indeed! You employ the audience for yourself; I occupy it only with the things of which I speak. Your hearers admire you. My hearers forget me, attentive to my purpose. They praise you; they are too absorbed in what I say to praise me. You are ornate, but there is little ornament in my speeches. They are composed of precise, strong, clear reasons which are irresistible. You make the audience cry out, 'Ah, how eloquently he speaks!' I make my audience exclaim, 'Come on, and let us march against Philip!' "

We can truly say that John the Baptist in his preaching was a

277

Demosthenes rather than a Cicero. He did not lead people to follow himself but Christ. He plainly stated all that he was not and all that Christ was. This cost him his head but gained faithful followers for Christ. That is why the Evangelist, when speaking of him in John 1:15, says that his testimony still rings in his ears, as it still rings in ours after all these centuries. That is his first reason for using the historic present tense in this verse, "John testifies."

The second reason, we believe, is to show that the same testimony will continue through the centuries, that it is not subject to change. The passage of time cannot affect the testimony concerning the person and work of Jesus Christ. We may use different methods of giving our testimony, but the content of the testimony, if it is to be effective in accomplishing the purpose of Jesus Christ, must not be changed. We are preaching a changeless Gospel in a fast changing world. Time travels, but eternity does not. There is an eternal quality about the testimony concerning the eternal Christ. Let us not be afraid to give the same testimony about Christ as Scripture gives. Everything should speak of Him, no matter what man thinks of Him.

Someone told G. Campbell Morgan that the preacher must catch the spirit of the age. Immediately this great preacher answered, "God forgive the preacher who does that. The preacher's business is to correct the spirit of the age." And may we add that a witness for Christ must endeavor thoroughly to understand the spirit of the age—without conforming to it—in order to know what to correct.

A minister, on taking a new church, was highly complimented on his first sermon. A number of people told him it was just what the congregation needed. The next Sunday he preached well again, but the congregation was greatly puzzled because he preached the same sermon as before. The third Sunday, when the same sermon was preached again, the session waited on the preacher for an explanation. He said, "Why, yes, it is the same sermon. You told me the first Sunday how much you needed just that, and I watched all week for some change in your lives, but there was none; so I preached it again. I watched all next week; still no change; and I don't see any yet. Don't you think I'd better prepare to preach it again next Sunday?"

And thus it was with John the Baptist. His testimony was unchanging though it cost him his life. He tried to please no man, only God; he feared no man, only God. I wonder whether our testimony to the Gospel is so changeable because of our desire to please man rather than God, because of our fear of man rather than God. It is only the unchangeable testimony to the changeless Christ in a changing world that will go down in history as having changed the world—though at great cost to the witnesses who gave it. John still testifies. "He being dead yet speaketh" (Heb. 11:4).

But not only must our testimony be unchanging; it must also be relevant. Unfortunately, the testimony of many preachers today is out of order. They speak about everything under the sun except what they should. In a court of justice, a judge will usually rule out any irrelevant testimony. He is concerned with nothing that does not have a direct or indirect bearing upon the establishment of the truth about the case before him. Our testimony in the proclamation of the Gospel of Jesus Christ must concern Christ and His work.

Someone once came to a preacher and said, "Sir, you have but two subjects—yourself and myself—and I am sick of both." This could well be said of many who pose as witnesses for Christ. Christ is left out. It is myself and yourself, I and thou, what I can do for you and what you can do for me; instead of what Christ can do for us all.

When the Evangelist wants to summarize the witnessing of John the Baptist in John 1:15 he says, "John testifies of him" (literal translation). The "him" here, of course, is Jesus Christ; not only Jesus Christ the man, but Jesus Christ the eternal God who became man. That is why, we believe, verse 15 is not directly connected with verse 14, which specifically speaks of the incarnation of the eternal Christ. John gives his witness about a person who is more than a man. He is God who became man. He is the God-

279

man whom John came to know intimately during His earthly sojourn. Verse 15, we believe, speaks both of verse 1, which deals with the eternity of Christ, and verse 14, which tells of this eternal Christ becoming flesh for us. John does not stress the manhood of Jesus Christ more than His deity, as so many modern preachers do. If He were not God, then as man He would not have been much different from many of us. But because He was God, His manhood is important as well as unique. The two must go together and they must be presented in their proper sequence and importance.

Thus, the writer of the Fourth Gospel speaks of the Baptist as giving his witness of "him," the Him referring to the God-man, the eternal Christ who made His appearance in history nearly 2,000 years ago. Let us not leave Him out of our testimonies and lives.

A Sunday school teacher had taught her class about David and Goliath, especially stressing the word, "The Lord was with David." One little boy was greatly impressed with this thought. He went home and got out his nursery pictures to find the one of David and Goliath. After studying it for some time, he took it and started for his father's study. The father, who was pastor of the church, was busy getting out his evening sermon, but the boy persistently rapped on the door and was finally admitted. Showing the picture to his father, he said, "Papa, they left the Lord out."

The father went back to his sermon, but he could not finish it. He saw that he had been preaching from the Word of God but had left the Lord Jesus out completely. He tore up his sermon and fell on his knees. That night he talked about the Lord Jesus Christ. The centrality of the Christian message should be Christ.

James Inglis was a graduate of Edinburgh University, learned and eloquent. He became the most popular preacher in Detroit, Michigan. Eager listeners filled his church to overflowing. One day, when he was preparing sermons for the following Sunday, it seemed as though a voice said to him, "James Inglis, whom are you preaching?" Startled, he answered, "I am preaching good theology." "I did not ask what you are preaching, but whom you are preaching." Inglis answered, "I am preaching the Gospel." Again the voice said, "I did not ask you what you are preaching; I asked whom you are preaching." Silent, with bowed head, the preacher sat for a long time. Then rousing himself he cried, "O my God, I am preaching James Inglis. But henceforth I will preach Christ and Him crucified." Inglis went to a chest of drawers in his study, took his eloquent sermons from the files, and burned them one by one. From that day he turned his back upon popularity and gave himself wholly, by life and testimony, to the task of lifting Christ before men. And God honored his consecration by giving him ever widening influence.

CHAPTER 65

HOW OUTSPOKEN SHOULD OUR TESTIMONY BE?

"John bare witness of him, and cried . . ." (John 1:15 a, b).

———————

John, the writer of the Fourth Gospel, has said that John the Baptist gave an unequivocal testimony, a trustworthy testimony, a relevant testimony—and now he further characterizes the testimony of the Baptist by saying, "John testifies of him, and cried . . ." At first it would seem peculiar that one verb is in the present indicative (*marturei*, "testifies") and the other is in the perfect tense (*kekragen*, "has cried"). But it is to be noted that "has cried," although in the perfect tense, is one of those perfects of the Greek language which have the force of the present tense. It is an intensive, dramatic, historical present perfect. (*A Grammar of the New Testament*, by A. T. Robertson, Fourth Edition, Doran, pp. 894, 896). But one wonders why John should use a verb in the present perfect instead of one in the present indicative that would agree with *marturei*, "testifies."

We believe that what John is trying to bring out here is first that this testimony of the Baptist, as far as time is concerned, belongs to the past. It was given during the lifetime of the Baptist. He was not there with John to give it in person while John was writing, nor is he here to give it to us today. There is a completeness about the testimony of the Baptist, although he himself, as he died in prison, may have thought that his testimony was cut short. His heart cry may well have been, "Oh, for a few more years to serve the Lord!"

We know, however, that his testimony was complete and perfect; it had reached its goal when he was cruelly beheaded. The

282

perfection of our testimony for Christ does not always consist in the completion of our own plans, sacred though they may be, but in God's actual appointments for our lives. John the Baptist is not here to cry out his testimony; but his testimony is complete, nevertheless, and continues to be heard. This is a testimony that was given faithfully in the past but which extends with force to the present. Such is the continuing effectiveness of our testimony if it is a faithful one as to the person and work of the Lord Jesus Christ. The truth of our testimony will surely outlive us.

During the time of the persecutions against the early Christians, a man came to Tertullian, the great and fiery Church Father, and complained to him about his business difficulties as a result of his Christian testimony. "What can I do?" he asked. "I must live." "Must you?" responded Tertullian. The sacrifice of life as a result of our testimony, as in the case of the Baptist, will mean a continuation of the effectiveness of our testimony, but a mere continuation of life at the expense of our testimony for Christ may bring the Gospel into disrepute. To be true to Christ is more important than to live.

Dr. Adam Clarke, the great Biblical scholar, lies in Westminster Abbey. On his tomb is a candle burned down almost to the socket, and around it these words: "In burning for others I myself, also, have been consumed." Has he? No, it was just his life that was consumed, but his testimony still lives on and cries out. So it was and is with the Baptist.

The verb *krazoo,* from which *kekragen* is derived, means "to cry out, to scream, to shriek, to cry with a loud voice." In other words, what we are told here is that the Baptist was not afraid to shout out his testimony about Christ. What a difference between him and some of us. We are the loudest when we speak of ourselves, but ever so quiet when speaking of Jesus Christ. This is not just empty crying, the shouting of a demagogue, but the strong voice of conviction and compassion for the souls of men that they may see and follow Christ.

283

An Indian had attended services one Sunday morning. The sermon, which contained very little in the way of spiritual food, had been rather loud in spots. The Indian, a good Christian, was not impressed. When asked how he liked the sermon, he said, "High wind, big thunder, no rain." The Baptist's crying as he gave his testimony surely watered the hearts of thirsty souls who heard him. And it is still watering millions of souls. Of him it could be said, as Richard Baxter said of the ideal preacher, "He preached as though he'd never preach again, and as a dying man to dying men."

"How can I get crowds to attend my services?" asked a young preacher of John Wesley. Replied Wesley, "Get on fire and people will come out to see you burn." It is pathetic that we have so many sleepy preachers and noiseless sermons. Henry Ward Beecher used to say, "If a man sleeps under my preaching, I do not send a boy to wake him up, but I feel that a boy had better come and wake me up." We need resounding preaching and testifying, so that everybody can hear and that some by the grace of God may heed. This verb certainly knocks out the pious pretensions of many who say that God's work and God's testimony should always be done and given in a quiet and unobtrusive way. No, we are to shout from the housetops what God has done in us, without fear and without hesitation.

It may be that some will think us out of our minds if we speak thus loudly. In fact, this verb *krazoo* does imply just that. What we declare concerning the person of Jesus Christ in a loud, clear, and convincing way may be thought of as the cries of crazy people. But let's not be disturbed by that. Paul was not crazy, and yet people who had their conscience pricked under his outspoken ministry thought so. Peter, as he preached with a loud voice on the day of Pentecost, was thought to be drunk and therefore talking nonsense. Nevertheless, 3,000 souls were saved. God can use our outspoken testimonies to His glory and the salvation of souls.

By what we have just said, however, we do not want to imply that testimony has virtue simply by reason of loudness. No, it must

284

be both reasonable and logical. We are people of sound minds and healthy, clean hearts, and at all times we should behave accordingly. Our loudness in giving testimony comes not from mental derangement but from real enthusiasm resulting from the absolute knowledge of what Jesus Christ has accomplished in our hearts and lives. This is logical shouting, if you will. And this is demonstrated by the participle used immediately after *kekragen* ("has cried"). It is the participle *legoon*, commonly translated "saying," which nevertheless comes from the noun *logos*, implying logic, intelligence, and refers to the sanity of the mind. The words that we speak are not merely loud; they are meaningful. They are not words of fools but words of those who have been filled with the Spirit of God, with divine power and compassion for the souls of men. Let us not be illogical or irrational in our testimony, then, but as ardent and fiery as we can. We should not fear arousing the anger of some. Anger may be what they need to wake them up.

Dwight L. Moody once saw a man in the streets of Chicago freezing to death. Moody could not just talk this man into warmth. He pounded him with his fist and got him real mad. The man began to pound back and then got up and ran after Moody. That saved his life. Our loud and outspoken witnessing may make people angry, but at least it will waken them from their frozen stupor.

CHAPTER 66

NO USURPING OF THE DIVINE

". . . This was he of whom I spake, He that cometh after me is preferred before me: for he was before me" (John 1:15c).

When a man gives a witness on behalf of someone else, he must be very careful not to make himself the center of attraction. We find that this was the scrupulous attitude taken by John the Baptist in his witness for Jesus Christ. This is confirmed by his direct quotation given to us in John 1:15: "This was he of whom I spake, He that cometh after me is preferred before me: for he was before me."

We believe that John the Baptist gave this testimony very often concerning Jesus Christ. In the narrative portion of the Gospel of John it appears in verse 30. "This is he of whom I said, After me cometh a man which is preferred before me: for he was before me." In this verse he certainly implies that he had given this testimony at least once before, if not frequently. This was his testimony to all who asked him what his relationship to Jesus Christ was. Many of them had incorrectly thought John the Baptist to be the true Messiah, Christ, but he would leave no one under such a misapprehension. This is who I am, and this is who Christ is. Let's get the record straight. We must have no confusion.

There is, however, some difference in the words and tenses used in verses 15 and 30. So that we may be fully aware of the differences, let us look at the literal English translation of both verses—which, while it is awkward, is illuminating.

Here is verse 15 in the original Greek wording: "This one was ["had been," *een*] of whom I said, the one coming after me has been before me, for he had been first of me." Note that the verb *een* is

286

used here—the same verb that John has used right along in the first 18 verses to demonstrate the eternity of Jesus Christ.

And here is verse 30: "This one is [*estin*] about whom I myself said, after me cometh a man [a male] who has been before me, for he had been [*een*] first of me."

It is the tense of the same verb used in both passages—*eimi*, "to be"—which we want to call to your attention in these two verses which are similar in meaning but not completely identical. In verse 15, it is the durative imperfect of *eimi* which is used and which has been used consistently in this context of the first 18 verses of John's Gospel to indicate the eternity of Jesus Christ—that He was co-equal and co-eternal with the Father from the beginning.

Undoubtedly, John the Baptist must have said many times, when pointing to Jesus Christ in the presence of others, "This One is the very One of whom I have been telling you right along that He was coming. Here He is. It is He." It was natural for him on these occasions to use the straight present indicative of the verb *eimi*, which is *estin*, or just plain "is." But when it came to the statement in John 1:15, the Gospel writer decided to keep the same pattern as in the whole context and therefore used the verb in its durative imperfect form, *een*, as he had from the beginning of this passage. "This one had been the one of whom I told you." It was as if once again the Evangelist were emphasizing the eternity of Christ in contrast with the humanity of the Baptist. It is an interpretative quotation, if we may call it that. John had no scruples about doing this, since later on in the record of the incident itself he gives the verb within the context of the present happening. In verse 30 we have the quotation in its historical setting, while in verse 15 we have it in its eternal implications of thought. Also by the use of the verb *een* in verse 15 John refers to the repeated thought he had expressed in various ways concerning the eternity of Jesus Christ; while by the use of the verb *estin* in verse 30 he refers to a single historical utterance at the time when it was made.

Now what did John the Baptist mean by saying, "He that

287

cometh after me is preferred before me: for he was before me"? For the sake of clarity we must remember some fundamental facts of chronology as to the Baptist and the human Jesus. The Baptist was born about six months before the birth of the Lord Jesus. Thus, physically, Jesus came into the world after John. And in one sense that is what the Baptist meant by "He that cometh after me." Also John the Baptist began his public work of preaching and baptizing before the Lord Jesus began His public ministry. This is why the Baptist is called the Lord's forerunner. He was His forerunner in age and in work.

It is apparent, then, that the adverb *opisoo,* "behind, after," although primarily an adverb of place, is in this instance an adverb of time. It is as if the Baptist were actually saying, "He who is coming later on, in a little while." There is no difficulty, then, in understanding this first clause of the statement.

In this connection we should note the participle *erchomenos,* "coming," which was used of the genuine Light of Christ, in verse 9. In verse 30, on the other hand, the present indicative of the verb is used, *erchetai,* "comes." *Ho erchomenos* is a participle used as a substantive, indicative of the imminent coming of the eternal Christ, the Messiah, in the flesh in the form of man. We believe the reason the participle is used in verse 15 and the present indicative is used in verse 30 is that in verse 15 we have a declaration in its eternal setting, while in verse 30 we have it in its historic setting. In eternity, Christ was the coming One, at all times. It expressed the ever present desire and hope of the Israelitish people actually to have their Messiah come to them. But in verse 30 we have the Baptist's declaration to those who were sent by the Sanhedrin at that time to ask him whether he was that Messiah whom they were expecting. No, he said to them, here He is; He comes; He is almost here. I do not intend to usurp Him. I am only His forerunner.

The difficulty in this verse, however, is with the two statements that follow. Since John declared that Jesus Christ was coming after him in age and work, why did he immediately add, "He has been before me, for he had been first compared with me"? We shall see in our next study.

CHAPTER 67

IS IT WORTH SPEAKING OF CHRIST IF HE WAS MERELY A SUPERIOR MAN?

"... He that cometh after me is preferred before me: for he was before me" (John 1:15c).

How can anybody come later and yet be said to have come before? This seems to be a paradox. One cannot be both a successor and a predecessor.

Yet there was One who could be exactly that. This was Jesus Christ in His relation to John the Baptist. The latter, speaking of Christ, said, "The one coming after me, has been before me, because he was first compared with me" (literal translation from the Greek).

We saw in our previous study that the adverb "after" in the first clause refers to time and not to place. Jesus was born after John the Baptist and He began His public ministry later than John.

In the second clause we find another important adverb, *emprosthen*, meaning "in front, ahead, before, forward." Unfortunately, in the King James Version it is rendered "is preferred before," which we believe to be completely unwarranted. No comparison of rank or importance of work is involved here, but of time. *Emprosthen*, "in front," is the opposite of *opisoo*, "after, behind, later." Therefore these adverbs, coming together in this conjunction, must both be taken to denote time—the one later and the other earlier. The announcement which the Baptist makes is that, although Jesus Christ the Messiah was born later than he and started His work later, He was actually in existence before John. How can one be born later and yet have been in existence before some predecessor of his?

There is only one explanation—that Jesus Christ, before making His appearance as man in Bethlehem, had been as God eternally. This has been the testimony of John the writer of the Fourth Gospel thus far, and it is now strengthened by the testimony of John the Baptist.

Perhaps some fanatical followers of the Baptist wanted him to have the pre-eminence over everyone else who was to come later. After all, age is important. They admired John and they could not countenance anyone else coming in and putting John's ministry and importance to one side. The Baptist, however, wants to stress that, although Jesus Christ as man is younger and came later than he, yet Jesus Christ is the Creator of all things. He is first. None of the other three evangelists (Matthew, Mark, and Luke) states the supremacy of Jesus Christ in relation to John the Baptist in just the way that John mentions it. This is significant. John's Gospel was written so that the eternity and deity of Jesus Christ might be established and not just His superiority over other men. (See Matt. 3:11, Mark 1:7, Luke 3:16, and also John 1:27). In the Synoptic Gospels there is actually no parallel to John 1:15. What we have referred to are parallels to John 1:27 and not to John 1:15. The latter verse is unique to the Gospel of John, the Gospel of the deity of Jesus Christ.

The verb which is used in the second clause of our verse is different from the verb used in the first clause. It is not the verb *erchomai,* "come," in any form, but the verb *gegonen,* which is the perfect tense of the verb *ginomai,* "to become, to begin to be." This verb can have either an absolute or a relative meaning. Absolutely, and when referring to persons as here, it means "to become." Relatively it means "to become something" and has an adverbial limitation or predicate. "To become" absolutely, then, means "to come into being, to be myself"; and relatively it means "I become something," such as "I become a doctor, I become a teacher." Here, in the absence of a predicate or an adverbial limitation, the verb is used in an absolute sense. Correctly and literally translated, then, *gegonen* would be "He is become." It refers to our Lord's essential existence as God and not to His acquired existence as man. Therefore what the Baptist is declaring is that Jesus Christ, in His essential existence as God, was before him. It was only as man that He came after him. This is perfectly clear.

Furthermore, the verb *gegonen* (the perfect active intransitive of the deponent verb *ginomai*) implies that Jesus Christ in His eternal existence was not the result of the creative act of someone else. John the Baptist, however, owed his existence to his parents and only ultimately to God. In other words, Christ in His eternity and deity was not made by anyone, but He came into being by His own power and volition. He was not created but is self-existent. He is not a creature. This is one of the main points brought out repeatedly in these axiomatic declarations of John in the first 18 verses of his Gospel. As God, Jesus Christ was never born, for eternity cannot give birth to eternity. There is a differentiation between the Father and Son in eternity, but only as personalities, without a time differential of their existence. Of course, we human beings, limited by time and space, cannot possibly understand the workings of eternity. What we are told here, then, is that Jesus Christ came to be, and that He came to be before John the Baptist.

The final and conclusive explanation of the first two clauses is given by the third. How is it possible for the successor also to be the predecessor? Because "He has been first compared with me." John does not speak here of the superiority of rank or achievement or prestige. This adjective must also refer to time, as did the two adverbs ("after" and "before"—*opisoo* and *emprosthen*) in the previous statements.

In spite of the fact, however, that two persons are compared here, the Baptist and the Messiah, it is not the common *proteros* ("prior") which is used as would ordinarily be the case, but *prootos,* which should be translated "first." He is the First One, the beginning of all things, the originator of all things. As Jesus, He came later than I, but as Christ, the eternal *Logos*, He is the Creator, the First Cause; He is God.

This adjective *prootos*, "first," is superbly matched with the verb *een* which is again used to demonstrate the eternity of the existence of the Lord Jesus Christ. He had been the first, the One who gave birth to all, but who Himself, in His eternity and deity, was given birth to by no one.

John the Baptist did not actually need to speak about the pre-eminence of the rank and work of Jesus Christ. Once His deity and eternity were established and proclaimed in the minds and hearts of his listeners, the superiority of Christ's rank was self-evident. If Jesus Christ is God, He has to be Master of all; He has to be superior to all His creatures. To compare God favorably with man is to do the obvious and redundant. This is why we should never preach the superiority of Jesus the man over mere men of history. Unfortunately, however, this is what many preachers do. They preach Christ the superior teacher or the superior man, but we must preach as did John the Evangelist and John the Baptist of old, Christ the God who became flesh to enable us men to become the sons of God. He is the first compared with John and everybody else. He is the First among all, for He is the Maker of all.

Two infidels once sat in a railroad train discussing Christ's wonderful life. Even infidels cannot escape thinking of Christ. One said, "I think an interesting romance could be written about Him." The other replied, "And you are just the man to write it. Set forth the correct view of His life and character. Tear down the prevailing sentiment as to His divineness and paint Him as He was—a man among men." The suggestion was acted upon and the romance was written. The man who made the suggestion was Colonel Ingersoll; the author was General Lew Wallace, and the book was *Ben Hur*. In the process of constructing it, General Wallace found himself facing the unaccountable Man. The more he studied His life and character the more profoundly he was convinced that He was more than a man among men; until at length, like the centurion under the cross, he was constrained to cry, "Verily, this was the Son of God." That's exactly the testimony of John the Baptist. He says, "The one coming after me, has been before me, because he was first compared with me." He was and is God. When that is accepted, then there is no difficulty in understanding either His character or His miraculous works.

CHAPTER 68

WHAT IS THE "FULNESS" OF CHRIST?

"And of his fulness have all we received, and grace for grace" (John 1:16).

———

The testimony of John the Baptist in John 1:15 was that Jesus Christ "was before" him, although He came after him; not merely in the sense that He was a greater man, or achieved more than John did, but because He was God, the First, the Creator of all things. Without Jesus Christ, who was God, neither John the Baptist nor anyone else could have come into existence.

Then in verse 16 the Gospel writer proceeds to give us a second reason why he testified of Jesus Christ as he did. He was impressed not only with what Jesus Christ was, but also with what He did. What emanated from Christ's life proved what He was. He could not have done what He did if He were not what He was and hence claimed to be. Because in Him dwelt all the fullness of God, all the fullness of God could flow from Him to us.

A person is known for what he really is by what he is able to give. The Baptist implied through his testimony that if Jesus Christ's existence began at Bethlehem, then He could not have given us all that He did. Only as God eternal could He have given us of His fullness and grace for grace. It is only logical, therefore, that the declaration of what Christ does follows the declaration of what He is.

In the best manuscripts, verse 16 begins with *hoti*, meaning "for" or "because," as does the last clause of verse 15. These two uses of *hoti* follow one another. Here is how the thought runs, first presenting the testimony of the Baptist in verse 15, followed by the resumption of the statements of the Gospel writer:

"He, Jesus Christ, was before me,
For he was first,
For of his fulness have all we received,
and grace for grace."

Verse 15 is simply a parenthesis, an insertion of the actual testimony of the Baptist, for support of the Evangelist's statements concerning the person of the Lord Jesus Christ. The same procedure is followed here as in a court of law where an attorney seeks to prove his claim. The attorney speaks first. He interrupts his presentation to introduce an actual witness and then resumes his presentation. John the Evangelist here (in the first 5 verses) speaks first, presenting the Lord Jesus Christ as the eternal God. Then in verses 6 to 8 he simply makes reference to the person of John the Baptist as an actual witness, reserving the right to present him for a personal testimony later on. From verses 9 to 14 he resumes his argument concerning the person of the eternal Word. Then he pauses to present John the Baptist in his very own words, which were, "This was he of whom I spake, the one coming after me, has been before me; because he was first compared with me" (literal translation of verse 15). The Baptist personally identifies the person about whom the Evangelist has been speaking, saying in effect, The eternal Word is the same person who was born six months after me and who was baptized by me. He says that the historical Jesus is really the eternal Word of God having come to dwell with us as very man as well as very God, so that there shall be no misunderstanding about it at all.

This is followed by a resumption of the argument concerning the person and work of the Lord Jesus Christ by the Evangelist himself, in verse 16. Remember, then, that in verse 15 we have the words of the Baptist, but in verse 16 we have a continuation of the statements of the Evangelist. When he says, "We have received of his fulness," he includes himself.

But of course, as a masterful attorney in his presentation of the case of the Lord Jesus Christ, he links the direct testimony of John the Baptist with his own. He satisfies the court, so to speak, by allowing the Baptist to say that the Jesus who was born after him really existed before him, because He was God. Then he himself proceeds to tell what this God in the person of Jesus Christ did for the human race, for him and others.

Thus we see that there is a very definite connection between verse 14 and verse 16. We get the full impact of this by letting the two verses stand together without the parenthesis of verse 15. "And the Word became flesh, and dwelt in us, (and we beheld his glory, the glory of the only begotten of the Father,) full of grace and truth . . . For of his fulness have all we received, and grace for grace."

Two of the words found in the last clause of verse 14, "fulness" and "grace," are found in verse 16 also. In verse 14 we are told that Jesus Christ is full of grace and truth, and in verse 16 we are told that He does not keep this grace to Himself but that He gives it to us; we can receive it. Grace is an altruistic word. It concerns a person's makeup, indicating that that person does not wish to keep everything good he possesses for himself, for he wants to share it with others. Grace is the externalization of goodness. It is one thing to be rich and another to share one's riches. To be full of love is inconceivable without that love being demonstrated to others. Love that is concentrated in self should be called something other than love, for love like grace is an altruistic word; its object cannot be the same as its subject; it must be other than self.

But what does verse 16 really mean, "For of his fulness have all we received, and grace for grace"? What is the fullness of Christ? When a person says he is full of something, he may mean either of two things:

1. That he is like a cup which someone else has filled. In this case fullness means the act of filling, or that with which a thing is filled. This is one of the relative meanings of the word. If there is water in one's cup, then when he speaks of the fullness of his cup he

means water—the content of his cup.

2. It may also mean the complement of something. It is that with which anything is made complete or is filled. For instance, this is the word used to indicate the patch put upon the rent in a garment (see Matthew 9:16 and Mark 2:21). Here a man's cup is half full. That which is added to complete it, to make it full, is the fullness of the cup.

But both of these meanings are relative. There is, however, an absolute meaning of the word, especially when it refers to the person of Jesus Christ. And in these cases the meaning is always passive, as the word basically is in use anyway; i.e., the cup is the passive receptacle of the water. Just what fullness it is that John is speaking about is amplified and made clear by what Paul says in Colossians 2:9, "For in him [Jesus Christ] dwelleth all the fulness of the Godhead bodily." What the Apostle meant by these expressions is that, when men saw Jesus Christ in bodily form, they actually saw all that there was of the essence of God. They did not see just part of God but God in human form. The human body of Christ was the receptacle of the full, complete, absolute being of God. Fullness here stands as the opposite of part. And this goes to demonstrate the mystery and at the same time the truth of the Trinity, that God the Father is all of God, that God the Son is all of God, and that God the Holy Spirit is all of God. When we speak of the Father, we do not speak about just part of God, even as we do not when we speak of the Son or of the Holy Spirit. It may seem to us that this defies logical explanation, that no one can really understand it. And this is true. That is why we find no explanation of it in the Bible. No human language is adequate to explain this transcendent truth. How can the finite understand the infinite? How can the temporal understand the eternal? Revelation was necessary because of the limitations of logical human understanding. (For an exhaustive discussion of the word *pleerooma*, "fulness," see *St. Paul's Epistles to the Colossians and to Philemon*, by J. B. Lightfoot, Zondervan, pp. 257-273.)

An eminent naturalist believed in a Supreme Being but found it impossible to believe that the God who had created the wonders of the universe could be known by man. One day, as he was walking in his garden, he came upon an ant hill covered with a swarm of ants that seemed greatly agitated as his shadow fell upon them. "If only these ants knew how kindly I feel toward them," he thought, "they would not be disturbed at my presence." Following this line of thought, he found himself wondering if a man could ever communicate his thoughts to ants. "No," he decided, "that is impossible. For a human to teach an ant what he is like, and to convey to it his thoughts, he would have to become an ant." Then like a flash of lightning came this thought: "That is it exactly! The God of this universe, infinitely high as He is above us in His being and in His thoughts, had to become a man to teach men to know Him, and to know His thought." And there, in the quiet of his garden, one who had long rejected the Gospel record bowed in the presence of the Lord Jesus Christ, exclaiming in holy awe with Thomas of old, "My Lord and my God!" But the scientist can not become an ant, because he has never made an ant and he never will. He is not a creator of beings or things; he is simply a manufacturer having to use the raw materials God created. But God the Creator could very well descend to earth as man in the person of Jesus Christ His Son, so that we might be able not only to behold the fullness of God in Christ, but also to appropriate it. As John says, "And of his fulness have all we received, and grace for grace."

CHAPTER 69

HOW MUCH OF GOD CAN WE RECEIVE?

"And of his fulness have all we received . . ." (John 1:16a).

When John speaks of the fullness of Christ in chapter one, verse 16, he refers to the total essence of God. Christ was all that God is, and not one iota less. He was completely God in Himself. His Godhead was inherent and innate, not something that was acquired. We must clearly remember that "fulness" (*pleerooma*) does not refer to that with which Christ was filled by someone else. He was not just full of divine virtues and attributes. "Fulness," when referring to Christ and to deity, means the sum total of God, all that God is inherently and not by acquisition.

Of this fullness, John declares, we have all received. And first of all by "fulness" he means Christ's Godhead, His deity, His eternity. We acquire *part* of His fullness, *part* of the full nature and essence of God Himself. John refers, of course, to those who have received Christ by believing on His name, as mentioned in verse 12. "All we" means each one of us who believe on Christ and not all men, irrespective of whether they believe or not. By becoming a child of God we acquire the nature of God, because we as men are partakers of the Word. However, we do not cease to be men. This is what John wants to amplify in this 16th verse. "For of his fulness have all we received, and grace for grace."

The Apostle John does not want to give the impression that he is alone in this receiving of the fullness of God in Christ. That is why he does not say, "Of his fulness have I received myself" but rather "have all we received." He constantly lived in the consciousness that he was among many who received the same fullness of

300

God, who had God in them. It is most dangerous to one's well-being to think that he has God exclusively. Some Christians find it difficult to recognize that others have an equal or greater share of God than they. We like to think of ourselves as being the closest to the heart of God, forgetting that there may be someone closer. So many of us are like that person who recognized just three persons: I, Myself, and Me. The selfishness of such people is illustrated in a little poem:

"I had a little tea party
This afternoon at three;
'Twas very small—
Three guests in all—
   Just I, Myself, and Me.
Myself ate up the sandwiches,
While I drank up the tea.
'Twas also I who ate the pie
   And passed the cake to Me."

No, John does not in any way want to give the impression that he was alone in receiving the fullness of God in Christ in his heart and life. He says, "Of his fulness have all we received." He does not exclude himself, but at the same time he includes many others, like John the Baptist whose testimony he had just finished giving. How little of the "I" it becomes us to use and how much of the "we." Let us not be like that man who, in writing his own biography, put the printer in a very difficult position because, having to set the type by hand, he ran out of "I's" and had to go borrow some from his brother printer.

The more of the fullness of God we have the more we recognize His fullness in others. It is very difficult to see in others something we ourselves do not possess. Aesop tells an instructive fable about a gnat that had been buzzing about the head of a bull, at length settling himself down upon one of his horns. Then the gnat begged the bull's pardon for incommoding him. "If my weight at all inconveniences you, pray say so and I will be off in a moment."

301

"Oh, never trouble your head about that," replied the bull, "for it's all one to me whether you go or stay, and to say the truth, I did not know you were there." Aesop adds, "The smaller the mind the greater the conceit." The greater the fullness of God in us the more we recognize it in other believers.

The adjective *pantes,* translated "all" in Greek, emphasizes the individual members of the class of believers. It could be rendered as "every" or "each" for the sake of emphasizing the individuality within the totality, without of course excluding the totality. Every one of us who has believed and received Christ, excluding none, has received of the fullness of God—a share of His total nature, essence, and characteristics. We have become the children of God. We now belong to His family. In other words, John does not stress here the collective acceptance of Jesus Christ but the total number of those who accepted Christ individually.

We must also note that the believer does not receive all the fullness of God, for then he would become God. Verse 16 tells us that we receive part of God, for *ek*, translated "of," has a partitive meaning, as if a part were taken out of the whole (William Edward Jelf, *Greek Grammar,* Vol. II, Syntax, p. 289). "*Of* his fulness have all we received," our verse says, not merely "His fulness have all we received."

We conclude, then, that when we receive Christ we actually receive part of God into our being. His Spirit is born in us, for God is Spirit. A complete transformation takes place as a result of God entering our hearts and lives. It is good to remember also that the entrance of God in us does not put an end to our individual physical natures. We are what we were, plus—plus part of the fullness of God.

Furthermore, there is a sense in which, as God becomes part of us, we become part of God. The relationship is mutual. It is distinctively clear in the New Testament that not only does God become ours by believing, but we become His. We become His children and He becomes our Father. The Fatherhood of God to the believer is equally as precious a doctrine as the adoption of the believer is to God. We receive of the fullness of God in Christ, and He receives us. We constitute the fullness of His body, the Church. "And hath put all things under his feet, and gave him to be the head over all things to the church, which is his body, the fulness of him that filleth all in all" (Eph. 1:22, 23).

The verb that is used here is *elabomen*, "received," the same verb, in the same tense, as was used in verse 12, and therefore what we said in our study of the word in the context of verse 12 applies here also. But in verse 16 the verb places the accent on the result of the action more than on the action of receiving itself. (A. T. Robertson, *A Grammar of the Greek New Testament*, p. 829). It is as if John were saying, "Look what we have as a result of believing and receiving Christ. We have part of the fullness of God in us. God is within us. We are different; therefore we act differently. God has come to dwell within us, because by faith we have looked at Christ, the God-man on the cross."

Two little children, a boy and a girl, who played a great deal together both received Christ and were converted. One day the boy came to his mother and said, "Mother, I know that Emma is a Christian." "What makes you think so, dear?" "Because she plays like a Christian. If you take everything she's got, she doesn't get mad. Before, she was selfish, and if she didn't have everything her own way she would say, 'I won't play with you; you are an ugly little boy.'" That's what the world sees, the result of our possessing part of the fullness of God. If we have God, then we must act like Him.

But why does John use the expression, "Of His fulness have all we received"? Why does he not simply state, "Of Him have we all received"? It would seem that, although it is only part of God's fullness that we receive, it is still fullness to us. God fully occupies our lives, changes us radically; our carnal nature is subdued, and the nature of God within us has full sway and dominance. His fullness becomes our fullness. And since we are full of God when we receive Christ, there is no room for the world or for anything that is foreign to Him.

A Scotch girl was converted under the preaching of Whitefield. She was asked if her heart was changed and gave the beautiful reply, "Something I know is changed; it may be the world, it may be my heart. There is a great change somewhere, I'm sure; for everything is different from what it once was." The Scotch lassie was right. The change within is so complete that the total perspective of life without changes. It is the inner condition of our souls that determines the appreciation and estimate of things without.

The verb *elabomen,* "we received," has an active sense. It means "to take, to take hold of, to seize." This always indicates man's part in the process of his salvation by the Lord Jesus Christ. And yet it should never be thought that man either merits this salvation or takes the initiative in its process. It is as if I had a piece of candy to offer to my child. It is my offering that prompts his receiving. My little boy would not say, "Daddy, give me that," if "that" were not there. Or here is a spring of water. I am thirsty. I can take a cup and fill it with water to satisfy my thirst. My cup would be absolutely useless if there were no possibility of getting it filled. Or I am sick. Medicine is available which the doctor prescribes for me. It is up to me to take it or leave it, and my choice would determine the consequences. But I, the patient, could never boast that it was my receiving the medicine that cured me. My receiving was actually nothing more than an active passivity— obedience and submission to the doctor's advice. No man, therefore, who is given the privilege of receiving of the fullness of God in Christ can boast of it, for without the offering and the giving there would have been no receiving. But on the other hand the offering and the giving would do a man no good if he did not receive it.

We note that this verb is in the second aorist tense, which ordinarily would refer to some definite act in the past. We received

304

of the fullness of Christ. But did we receive once and for all, or is there a continuing process? There are two clear teachings that we can derive from the use of this tense.

First, this is a gnomic aorist, as is the same verb *elabon* in verse 12, and it is used to take in the whole span of time, past, present, and future. In other words, it speaks of those who at any time receive of the fullness of Christ. It is not a privilege that belonged only to those who lived in apostolic times, but it is a privilege that is ours also, and it will continue to be ours till the day of grace is over.

Second, this tense intimates that the receiving of the fullness of God is not a once-and-for-all affair, but that we are constantly being filled with his grace. No matter how hard the world tries to occupy part of us, as children of God, after our initial experience of being filled with His grace. No matter how hard the world tries to divine filling. God's filling us is something that continues throughout our entire Christian life. A child experiences the process of breathing for the first time when he is born but continues to breathe throughout life. God's fullness for the believer is like the air around us: it is ever present and ever available for us to receive, constantly and uninterruptedly. Indeed, without the fullness of God, we could not live spiritually one single moment.

CHAPTER 70

HOW MUCH WILL GOD GIVE US?

". . . and grace for grace" (John 1:16b).

In the Gospel of John (1:14) we are told that Jesus Christ is full of grace and truth. In our study of that statement we indicated that grace was mentioned before truth to set forth to man the good news of the grace of God before His justice. The truth is that sin, the sin of man, must be paid for by death, his own death. Truth requires justice. But since this was satisfied in the person of Jesus Christ when He died for the sins of mankind, the Gospel is free to present predominantly the grace of God. Before being told that without Christ it would have been necessary for us to die for our sins, we are told that because Christ died we can have grace extended to us— that we don't need to pay the penalty for Adam's sin or our own. Merit that we do not deserve, life that we do not merit, are ours in Christ.

In verse 16, which deals with the result of receiving Christ, we are told that we partake of the fullness of God. But John goes on to give us another essential insight. After God becomes part of us, we continue to need His grace. The second part of verse 16 reads "And grace for grace." Naturally, the verb *elabomen*, "received," which precedes this clause, must refer to it also. We "received" grace for grace.

Let us go back to what we said about the verb *elabon* in verse 12. There it is in the third person plural of the second aorist tense of the verb *lambanoo*, "to receive," while in verse 16 *elabomen*, "we received," is in the first person plural of the same tense of that verb. This aorist is used to take in the span of time, to include all those

306

who believed in the past, who believe now, and who will believe in the future. Also, this does not refer exclusively to the grace which we received initially when we first believed in Christ, but also includes the grace which we continually receive from God.

Some people have the idea that once the relationship is established between God and man, nothing more is needed. This is a mistake. When a child is born it has the general nature and characteristics of its parents, but does it not continue to need their loving care? It could not live without it. And so it is with us and God. He gives us of His nature, His fullness; we become His children, but we need Him constantly and uninterruptedly if we are to go on living spiritually. Our lives as Christians cannot be maintained at all unless it is He who maintains them. This is unlike our earthly parent-child relationship in one sense, however, for in our relationship with God we never outgrow our need to be dependent on Him. Our children cannot wait for the time to come when they can cut the last apron string that binds them to us, their protectors. They want to be free to live their own lives as soon as possible. And though, in the New Testament, Christian maturity is enjoined upon all believers, this process of spiritual growth never brings us to a point where we may become independent of God. We are given to understand that our relation to Him is always that of children. Woe unto anyone who ceases to be a child of God in his own estimation and thinks he has grown up sufficiently to be independent of God!

Thus, if we were to paraphrase verse 16 to include its widest grammatical and exegetical implications, we would say, "For of his fulness do we constantly receive, and grace for grace." Those who once received of the fullness of God never ceased to be filled continually by Him and His grace, and those who do now receive of the fullness of God will continue to be filled, and those who at any future date will receive of His fullness will continue to receive it. In other words, there is a constant infilling of man's emptiness by God.

307

But why is this necessary? Simply because the God who comes into our beings should not be kept for self only, but should be externalized and shared. Man is not a Dead Sea, constantly receiving and holding the fresh water of God, but like a river must give in the same manner that he receives. Only as man shares the fullness of God which he receives will he be filled with more. And who would not desire a fresh visitation of God every day and every moment of his life? We are not referring simply to the benefits of God, but to God Himself. Too often we construe God as a Giver instead of considering Himself as the Gift.

A little girl used to visit her father's study often, knowing that he kept a bag of sweets there. Invariably she would ask for candy and receive a piece or two. But once she looked in and, when asked what she had come for, replied, "Nothing. I've just come to see you, Daddy."

Isn't it significant that "truth" is not mentioned here as it is in verse 14? There we are told that Christ is full of grace and truth. Here we are told that we receive "grace for grace." What happened to "truth," in the sense of the justice of God? Christ took care of that once and for all. Not only are our original Adamic sin and guilt under His blood, but also our sins while we are partakers of the fullness of God. When we receive of the fullness of God in Christ, it is apparent that we do not become absolutely sinless thereafter. Naturally, we do not voluntarily sin or find pleasure in sin; but we continue to fail God in many ways. We can never be exactly what God wants us to be, and this falling short of God's expectations of us is sin. And what about the sin James mentions? "Therefore to him that knoweth to do good, and doeth it not to him it is sin" (James 4:17). In our Christian lives, once we have received Christ and of His fullness, we are constantly under grace. Our sins are under Christ's blood, and sin will not overcome us, for His grace is sufficient.

"And grace for grace" is actually an explanatory addition to the previous statement that we all received of the fullness of God in

308

Christ. (See A. T. Robertson, *A Grammar of the Greek New Testament*, p. 1181). God's fullness in us entails the constant demonstration of His grace toward us. Even after our salvation, we constantly need the grace of God. Even as His children we do not merit either His fellowship or His benefits. Whatever we are, and have, come to us as the result of His love and mercy. Man neither merits his salvation nor acquires any merit as a result of it. As Paul says, "For who maketh thee to differ from another? and what hast thou that thou didst not receive? now if thou didst receive it, why dost thou glory, as if thou hadst not received it?" (I Cor. 4:7). And as John says, "A man can receive nothing, except it be given him from heaven" (3:27).

But what does the phrase "grace for grace" actually mean? The preposition translated "for" in Greek is *anti,* which could readily be translated "in place of." The idea is that when one supply of grace is used, there will be another to take its place. There is constant and uninterrupted replenishment of the grace of God for the believer. Thus his sins are never exposed; they are under the blood of Christ all the time. Let us not hesitate, therefore, to invoke God's grace upon us constantly. God never wants us to be lacking in His grace. We must have His fullness. Let us not be afraid that we shall ever exhaust the grace of God. In Him there is an inexhaustible supply.

But the intimation here is that, if we as believers do not manifest grace to others, we shall not experience a fresh replenishment of the grace of God within ourselves. God has filled us for a purpose. But many of us seem to be afraid that we do not have enough of His grace to share with others, that we had better go on accumulating more and more before we try to give it out. We are afraid lest God's supply in us may be exhausted. That idea makes a Christian utterly selfish. But which is better, to be like a standing lake which has neither inflow nor outflow, or to be like a running stream which, even as it empties itself, is filled anew? Would we not rather have the inflow and outflow? The believer will always be full of the grace of God, but this grace is fresh every day. The measure in which it fills us will be determined by the measure in which—in God's love and for the benefit of others—we empty ourselves toward our fellow human beings. As we forgive, we experience forgiveness. As we feed, we are fed. As we teach, we are taught. As we give, we receive. And God's measure is always bigger than ours.

And one more thing. This grace is undeserved mercy. We may say of someone, "But this man is not worthy of forgiveness. This person does not deserve help." Stop and think. God did not and does not give us what we merit. And it is a good thing. If He did, we would starve—both physically and spiritually. We would be the most miserable of creatures. He would have to execute the death penalty on us for our sins. But instead He gives us life—which we do not deserve. We, in turn, must confer undeserved benefits on others, if we expect God to fill us with His grace. He did not love us because we were lovable, so what right do we have to expect others to be lovable before we show love to them? If we expect grace from God (something we ourselves do not deserve), then let us give with grace to others, whether they deserve it or not.

And finally, it is worth noticing that it is only "grace for grace" we are promised and not "truth for truth". Truth involves the exercise of justice. It would mean that we were to do unto others as they deserve—love the lovable and shun the sinner. But as we do not want God to exercise His justice toward us, let us not insist on exercising it toward others. God chose to deal with us in grace by allowing Christ to bear our punishment. This brought pain to His heart. It is not without pain that we exercise grace toward others, but it is all worth while, for it proves that we are full of God in Christ.

CHAPTER 71

WHY DID GOD INSTITUTE THE LAW?

"For the law was given by Moses, but grace and truth came by Jesus Christ" (John 1:17).

———

John the Baptist stood between the Old and the New Testaments. He gave his faithful witness that the Lord Jesus was indeed the Christ of prophecy, the One to whom the entire Old Testament was pointing. His direct testimony was given in John 1:15. The Lord Jesus was the active beginning of all things; He is the Creator; that is why He is spoken of as first by John the Baptist, His elder.

Then in verse 16, as a natural consequence of what Christ was, we find what He came to do. He came to give of His fullness of grace.

But what about the law of Moses, the Old Testament? Are we to forget it? Are we not to acquaint ourselves with it? Are its precepts binding upon us? Isn't grace possible through the Old Testament law? These are questions that have perplexed many Christians through the centuries.

We now come to verse 17, which we believe is in further explanation of verse 16. The Lord Jesus Christ, being God, permitted us to acquire His divine nature through grace. And both verse 16 and 17 actually refer to verse 14, which deals with the incarnation of the Lord Jesus Christ. "And the Word became flesh . . . full of grace and truth." Through God's becoming flesh, we human beings were enabled to behold Him and His glory. But how? This beholding, as we saw in our study of verse 14, was not a mere physical observation but a supernatural perception. We recognized in Jesus Christ who walked the streets of Palestine the glory of

311

God, God incarnate. But how could we gain this insight? Only through receiving of His fullness, of His divine nature. It is He in us who enables us to recognize in Him all that He is. In other words, it is impossible for man to recognize God in Christ unless he has Christ within his heart and life. This is why verse 16 begins with *hoti*, "for" or "because."

Benjamin West, the great painter, speaking of Gilbert Stuart, a brother artist famed for his beautiful coloring, used to say to his pupils, "It's no use to steal Stuart's colors; if you want to paint as he does, you must steal his eyes." When we are baffled in our efforts to live as Christ lived, we feel that the record of His life, however wonderful it is, will not enable us to be like Him. What we need is His heart, His nature. Only divinity within us can recognize divinity without. Without His eyes, we cannot see Him as He is, God.

An unbeliever who was present at an evangelistic service was invited to go forward to the altar and seek Christ. He was an "intellectual" and could not possibly, as he thought, accept the doctrine of the deity of Christ. "If I do not believe Him to be God," he objected, "how can He save me? I've got to see Him as God first." It was suggested that he should test Him by prayer. He went to the altar and poured out his test-prayer. "O Christ! if Thou be God, reveal Thyself to me." He had not prayed long before he sprang up with new convictions, exclaiming, "He is God! He is God!" That conviction of the deity of Christ did not become a reality until he received Him.

"We beheld his glory as the glory of the only begotten of the father . . . (v. 14).
Because we received of his fulness" (v. 16).

How beautifully these two verses fit together. We must also look at the converse of this statement, which would be, "Those who did not receive and do not receive of the fullness of Christ, those who do not become believers and therefore the children of God,

312

cannot possibly recognize God in Christ." Thus, when we meet anyone who rejects the deity of the Lord Jesus Christ, we can safely conclude that that person has not received God within his heart, has not believed on Christ, is not a Christian. This is how fundamental the doctrine of the deity of the Lord Jesus Christ is, and this, of course, is the subject of these first 18 verses of John's Gospel.

In further explanation of both verses 14 and 16 we have verse 17. "We beheld his glory," says verse 14; that is, we recognized God in Christ, not only because we received of His fullness, but also "Because the law was given through Moses; the grace and the truth came through Jesus Christ" (v. 17, literal translation).

What does John mean by this verse? Well, how do we know that the sun exists? We say, "I feel the warmth of its rays and see the brightness of their light." This is subjective proof. We know something exists because of what it does to us personally. We know the Lord Jesus is God because of what He has done for and to us and because He now lives within us.

But Christ is not simply an idea formed within our minds. He is not only a subjective reality but He exists apart from us. And it was absolutely necessary for John to make this statement lest anyone think that Jesus Christ and the new birth He gives His followers are merely the products of their imagination. This is why John puts the name of the Lord Jesus alongside that of another historical character, whose existence in this world no one ever doubted, Moses. It is as if he says that the Lord Jesus Christ is just as historical as Moses. He is not merely a religious idea but a person outside of ourselves who can change us. On the one hand (in verse 16), this is what He has given us—of His fullness; He has made us new creatures. And on the other hand, remember that while He is within us He is also without us as an objective reality. This is why we as Christians claim to have Christ within us and yet pray to Him as an independent being outside ourselves, which, of course, He is. He was received by us (v. 16) "because" (a second use of the word

313

hoti, "for, because," with which verse 17 begins) He existed and He exists as an independent personality outside of ourselves, even as the sun exists. Unfortunately, there are those who believe only in a subjective religion, one that permits men to believe anything as long as it will do them good, whether it is real or imaginary. No, John says, Christ is real. He has objective reality. He enters man and converts him, revolutionizes him, saves him.

The law was given by Moses. Why does John make this statement? To show the relationship that existed between the law and Moses. This verse is not meant to portray a contrast between Moses and Jesus Christ, between law and grace, but to show the relationship of the law to Moses and the relationship of grace and truth to Jesus Christ. What the law was to Moses, grace and truth were to Jesus Christ. There was no reason for the Apostle John to be occupied with the controversy of the relationship between law and grace, for it seems that the problem was solved through the lengthy dissertations of the Apostle Paul written prior to the writing of this Gospel.

Undoubtedly by the word "law" John refers here to the entire set of laws which God delivered to Moses on Mt. Sinai. The law was a set of moral and ceremonial rules which the people of Israel were to keep. Why did God give Moses the law and not grace in the first place? Because that is what man chose for himself in Adam. God told Adam and Eve what would befall them if they disobeyed Him. They did disobey Him. This was an affront to God. It was as if man were saying to his Creator, "We can manage our own lives. You had better keep out." This is just what many say today. God in His wisdom respected the will of man and did not force Himself upon him. But there was one thing that God could not allow, and that was for man to be free to choose the consequences of his choice. God could not allow man to choose sin and at the same time to determine that the wages of sin would be life. No, God sets His own irrevocable consequences. This is what law actually is. It determines what is wrong and imposes a punishment for wrongdoing.

The law cannot force anyone to do good, but it can impose punishments for transgressions. God could not allow man to sin without spelling out for him what the consequences of his sins would be. That is the law of God given by Moses.

CHAPTER 72

ARE WE TO KEEP THE LAW?

"For the law was given by Moses . . ." (John 1:17a).

———

The law was not the greatest blessing that God ever gave to man. The law was necessary because man chose to disobey God, to sin. That is when law is applied and becomes necessary. If man had never disobeyed God, the law as a code would never have been necessary. The law was not of God's choice, but the consequence of man's disobedience to God.

That God was the giver of the law there is no doubt. But He chose a man to deliver it to men, His servant Moses. This does not mean that Moses was the originator of the law but simply the medium through whom God delivered it to men. The preposition used in the original text, *dia*, translated "by" in the King James Version, should rather be translated "through." "For the law was given *through* Moses." Moses was used by God only as an instrument. This function could have been accomplished by other men, had God so chosen.

The verb "was given" in the original Greek is *edothee*. This is in the second aorist tense and takes us back to an historical setting. The law was given at a set time by God to the Israelites through Moses. It was not a development of Moses and the prophets but came directly from God. Man's reasoning powers only led him into sin but not to develop any self-imposed punishment. That is man's nature, isn't it? You seldom hear of a man imposing punishment upon himself for some wrong that he has done. Punishment almost always has to be imposed from without. We do not like to make laws that will restrict our own freedom to do as we please. Thus the

316

law, although necessitated by man's sin, was not developed by Moses or the prophets or man in general, but by God directly and handed down through Moses.

Does this historical aorist tense of the verb *edothee* ("was given") indicate in any way that the law which God gave through Moses has been abrogated? As long as man is a sinner, God will impose punishment for his sin. God's law was given to stay. That is why we do not reject the Old Testament but, even as Christians, read it with awe and respect. In it we have the law of God, which we shall do well to study.

But what really constituted the law of God? It was divided into three parts: the ceremonial, the judicial, and the moral law. Some of the law was primarily for the nation of Israel and some of it extended to all people. We must bear this in mind if we are not to be confused.

Let us first look at the ceremonial law. This had to do with the observance of sacrifices and offerings and the different methods of purification and cleansing. Now these applied to the Jews only, up to the time of the coming of the Lord Jesus Christ, who became their fulfillment. He became the sacrifice for all men through the shedding of His blood on Calvary's cross. No more shedding of animal blood was necessary for the remission of sins. In Christ, then, we have the fulfillment of the ceremonial law. No more of that was needed for the Jews. As far as the gentiles were concerned, we believe this never applied to them, for the following reasons:

1. Because it was commanded in Exodus 34:23, 24 that those who were under the ceremonial law should go to Jerusalem three times a year. It is apparent that this was possible only for those who were within traveling distance of Jerusalem, the Israelites.

2. Because only those sacrifices offered in the temple at Jerusalem were acceptable to the Lord, and no others. Actually, even the Jews of our present day who are scattered around the world if they wished to adhere strictly to the ceremonial law could not do so, being far away from Jerusalem.

317

3. And finally because the ceremonial law was not forced upon the heathen who were converted to monotheistic Judaism.

Therefore we conclude that the ceremonial law actually never applied to the gentiles, and as far as the Jews are concerned it found its fulfillment in Jesus Christ. All these sacrifices and ablutions for the Jews were a foretaste of the coming of the Messiah. The ceremonial law represented simply a faint tracing of Christ's coming. These Jews were like people living in the night. Such people cannot see the sun, although the sun is in existence, because it is on the other side of the hemisphere. Yet, although not fully apparent, the sun is seen at night through the light reflected on the stars. Thus Paul tells us that "Christ is the end of the law" (Rom. 10:4). The word "end" in Greek is *telos,* which in this instance could very well be translated "fulfillment, goal." Christ was that to which the ceremonial law was leading. Just as the first tracing on a paper leads to the final and perfect drawing, so all these early sacrifices were replaced by the shed blood of Christ.

Now as far as the judicial law is concerned, we have to remember that in this were contained the civil laws for the government of the Jewish State. Naturally, these laws were not binding upon any other nation. Israel was a theocracy, and God gave this nation particular laws for their government. Even for the Jews outside of the State of Israel this law was not binding, nor is it binding today; although there may be a tendency toward at least a partial practice of this theocracy in the present reestablished State of Israel.

Then finally we have the moral law, which is mainly contained in the Ten Commandments. Now these were promulgations of general principles affecting all people everywhere. These moral principles still hold. Even we as Christians dare not worship any but the one true Lord and God of Israel and the whole world. We are not to make graven images to worship them. We are not to take the name of the Lord in vain. We are to remember the day of the Lord to keep it holy. We are to honor our parents. We are not to

318

kill. We are not to commit adultery. We are not to steal. We are not to bear false witness. And we are not to covet. The Lord Jesus never taught us to do anything contrary to these commandments. But our basic and motivating attitude toward these moral commandments of God ought to be somewhat different. For believers in Jesus Christ, the commandments do not constitute a covenant of works. By doing all that the commandments say, we could never attain heaven. The keeping of the commandments for the Christian is merely a by-product, a result of his belief in Christ. If these commandments were to be a means of salvation, the breaking of any of them would be calamitous, depriving a person of the desired salvation of his soul. But the believer is liberated from the penalty and condemning power of the law. Why? Because "Christ hath redeemed us from the curse of the law, being made a curse for us" (Gal. 3:13). "There is therefore now no condemnation to them which are in Christ Jesus" (Rom. 8:1). The Lord Jesus bore our condemnation, and by receiving Him we are free of the condemning power of the law, but in this we still do not violate the law, for in Christ we have the fulfillment of the moral law of God.

However, we are not to think that, because we are Christians and not under the penalty of the law, we can do as we please. As William Barclay says, "The Jew aimed to satisfy the law of God, and to the demands of law there is always a limit. The Christian aims to show gratitude for the love of God, and to the claims of love there is no limit in time or in eternity. Jesus set before men not the law of God, but the love of God. Long ago Augustine said that the Christian life could be summed up in the one phrase: 'Love God, and do what you like.' " (*Gospel of St. Matthew*, Vol. 1, The St. Andrew Press, Edinburgh, 1958, p. 129.) When we love God, we shall worship Him alone, we shall not have other gods imaginary or graven, we shall not use His name in vain, we shall keep His day holy. When we love Him, we shall love our neighbor as ourselves, and therefore we shall honor our parents, we shall not kill, we shall not commit adultery, we shall not steal, we shall not bear false witness, we shall not covet. Is the Gospel any less than this? No, it is far more.

319

CHAPTER 73

HOW CAN WE BECOME GRACIOUS AND TRUTHFUL?

"For the law was given by Moses, but grace and truth came by Jesus Christ" (John 1:17).

How is the Gospel better than the law? The contrast between law and grace is tersely put in the verse from an old book, which runs this way:

"Run, John, and live, the law commands,
But gives me neither legs nor hands;
Yet better news the Gospel brings—
It bids me fly, and gives me wings."

"For the law was given through Moses; grace and truth came through Jesus Christ" (John 1:17, literal translation). Moses was not the personification of the law, but Jesus Christ was the personification of grace and truth. God gave Moses the law on stones, and stones express no feeling, no tenderness, no pity, no forgiveness. The law tells us what we ought to be, but it does not help us to do anything about it.

The law says: This do, and thou shalt live.
Grace says: Live, and then thou shalt do.

The law says: Pay me what thou owest.
Grace says: I frankly forgive thee all.

The law says: The wages of sin is death.
Grace says: The gift of God is eternal life.

320

The law says: The soul that sinneth it shall die.
Grace says: Whosoever believeth on Jesus, though he were dead, yet shall he live; and whosoever liveth and believeth on Him shall never die.

The law pronounces condemnation and death.
Grace proclaims justification and life.

The law says: You make a new heart and a new spirit for yourself.
Grace says: A new heart will I give you, and a new spirit will I put within you.

The law says: Cursed is every one that continueth not in all things which are written in the Book of the Law to do them.
Grace says: Blessed is the man whose iniquities are forgiven, whose sin is covered; blessed is the man to whom God will not impute sin.

The law says: Thou shalt love the Lord thy God with all thy heart, and with all thy mind, and with all thy strength.
Grace says: Herein is love, not that we loved God, but that He first loved us, and gave His Son to be the propitiation for our sins.

The law speaks of what man must do for God.
Grace speaks of what Christ has done for man.

The law addresses man as part of the old creation.
Grace makes a man a member of the new creation.

The law bears on a nature prone to disobedience.
Grace creates a nature inclined to obedience.

The law demands obedience by the terrors of the law.
Grace beseeches men by the mercies of God.

The law demands holiness.
Grace gives holiness.

The law says: Condemn him.
Grace says: Embrace him.

The law speaks of priestly sacrifices offered year by year continually, which could never make the comers thereunto perfect.
Grace says: But this Man (Christ), after He had offered one sacrifice for sins forever, by one offering hath perfected forever them that are sanctified.

The law declares that as many as have sinned under the law shall be judged by the law.
Grace brings eternal peace to the troubled soul of every child of God, and proclaims God's truth in defiance of the accusations of the calumniator. He that heareth My word, and believeth on Him that sent Me, hath everlasting life, and shall not come into judgment (condemnation), but is passed out of death into life.

— *The Evangel*

Again in this verse we have "grace and truth" linked together as in verse 14. The Lord Jesus Christ did not come merely to show grace to us. He could not have done so unless God's holiness and justice were satisfied. The Lord Jesus Christ could never have forgiven us if He Himself had not paid the penalty for our sin. In "truth" we find the idea of justice embodied. Truth is the basis of justice. No justice could be rendered without the truth about a case having been established first. This is what truth involved in Christ. The truth of the matter was that He found us guilty of sin and disobedience. None of us could keep the law in its entirety and thus satisfy the holiness of God. Therefore the penalty for our sin was death. But we are the ones who must die. Instead of our dying, however, the Lord Jesus Christ ascended the cross after having descended from heaven. He paid the penalty so that we might go free if we accepted His sacrifice and work. Therefore the real contrast to the law given by Moses is not grace alone, but grace and truth. As far as Christ is concerned, truth preceded grace, but in

322

His relationship and offer to us He puts grace first.

The verb that is used in this second clause of verse 17 is *egeneto*, "came or became." "Grace and truth came through Jesus Christ." The law "was given" through Moses, but grace and truth "came" through Jesus Christ. You say, What difference is there between these two verbs, "was given" (*edothee*) and "came" (*egeneto*)? The same verb *egeneto*, "came or became," is used in verse 14 in the clause, "And the Word became flesh." In verse 14 it indicates that the eternal Word began His human existence at Bethlehem. He became man of His own power and volition.

Now we have two characteristics spoken of, grace and truth. In the Greek text the definite article *hee*, "the," appears before both "grace" and "truth" (*hee charis* and *hee aleetheia*). John is not speaking here of just any kind of grace and truth but of "the" grace and "the" truth. Grace and truth in Jesus Christ are specific, definite, and exclusive with Him. Jesus Christ did not simply teach us grace and truth—how to be gracious and truthful—but He became the grace and the truth to us. This is why, when we say "I have known the truth," it is the same as saying "I know Christ." To say "I have experienced grace, the grace of God," is the same as saying "I have experienced Christ." Christ's incarnation meant grace and truth, the grace and the truth of God for man.

In this connection, in verse 17, we could very well say that truth not only infers the justice of God which Jesus Christ satisfied through His death on Calvary, but also refers to the life which the Christian lives after he experiences the grace of God in his life. Once a person experiences the forgiveness of Christ inherent in His grace, his life becomes the life of Christ, which is truth. We become truly truthful after our sins have been forgiven. True and real life can be experienced by man when He who is the grace and the truth comes to indwell us. You see, grace is different from the law of Moses, because it does not simply proclaim the punishment and reward of sin but enables us, once our sins have been forgiven, to overcome them. Only a forgiven man can be a true saint of God.

323

A Buddhist monk in Ceylon, who was acquainted with both Christianity and Buddhism, was once asked what he thought was the great difference between the two. He replied, "There is much that is good in each of them, and probably in all religions. But what seems to me to be the greatest difference is that you Christians know what is right and have power to do it, while we Buddhists know what is right but have not any such power." And this is true, because no other religion has as its founder God, who became man, and in becoming man incarnated the grace and the truth of God. When Christ, then, becomes our life, we cannot but be full of grace and truth. It is not our grace and truth but His, for He dwells within.

But a man may say, "Can He make something out of my broken and sinful life?" In an English cathedral there is an exquisite stained glass window, which was made by an apprentice out of pieces of glass which had been rejected by his master; and it was so far superior to every other in the church that the envious artist killed himself with vexation. The law had nothing but punishment for the sinner. But the Lord Jesus Christ has grace, because He paid the penalty of sin Himself; and He produces out of the most broken and sinful life the most beautiful and wonderful creation—a new creature, a new child, a child of God, a saint. As others look at what Christ can do with a broken life, they cannot but stand amazed at the One who did it all and say, "This is indeed God." And He is. That is why He can recreate man. This is what John has endeavored to prove in the first 18 verses of his Gospel, the most exquisite and explicit passage on the person of Jesus Christ ever written.

BIBLIOGRAPHY

Arndt, W. F., and Gingrich, F. W., *A Greek-English Lexicon of the New Testament and Other Early Christian Literature.* Chicago: University of Chicago Press, 1952, pp. 353, 465, 575-6, 590, 636.

Barclay, William, *Gospel of Matthew,* Vol. I. Edinburgh: The Saint Andrew Press, 1958, p. 129.

Chrysostom, "Homily II" (Hebrews 1:3), *A Select Library of the Nicene and Post-Nicene Fathers of the Christian Church,* Vol. XIV, Philip Schaff, editor. Grand Rapids, Michigan: Wm. B. Eerdmans Publishing Co., 1956, pp. 370-2.

Cremer, Hermann, *Biblico-Theological Lexicon of New Testament Greek.* Edinburgh: T. & T. Clark, 1954, pp. 114, 236, 573, 728, 866-7.

Demetrakou, D., *Mega Lexikon Olees Tees Hellenikees Gloosees (Great Lexicon of the Whole Greek Language),* Vol. II. Athens: Demetrakou, 1954, pp. 1009-10.
—*Ibid.,* Vol. VI, p. 4741.

Fairchild, Frank M., see Goodchild, Frank M.

Godet, F., *Commentary on the Gospel of John,* Vol. I, third edition. Grand Rapids, Michigan: Zondervan Publishing House, p. 264.

Goodchild, Frank M., *Can We Believe?* New York: Fleming H. Revell Co., 1926, p. 34.

Jelf, William Edward, *A Grammar of the Greek Language,* Vol. II Syntax. London: John Henry and James Parker, 1861, pp. 58, 69-71, 123-4, 289.

Liddell, H. G., and Scott, R., *A Greek-English Lexicon.* Oxford: Clarendon Press, 1958, p. 1345.

Liddon, H. P., *The Divinity of Our Lord and Saviour Jesus Christ.* London: Longmans, Green, and Co., 1890, pp. 19-21.

Lightfoot, Joseph Barber, *Saint Paul's Epistles to the Colossians and to Philemon.* Grand Rapids, Michigan: Zondervan Publishing House, pp. 147, 156, 257-73, 403-4.

Mackay, W. P., *Grace and Truth under Twelve Aspects.* Edinburgh: John H. Bell, 1903, pp. V-VII.

Matheson, George, *Searchings in the Silence.* London: Hodder and Stoughton, pp. 137-8.

McPherson, G. W., *The Modern Mind and the Virgin Birth.* Yonkers, New York: Yonkers Book Co., 1923, pp. 20-2.

Nestle, Eberhard, *Introduction to the Textual Criticism of the Greek New Testament.* London: Williams and Norgate, 1901, p. 285.

Robertson, A. T., *A Grammar of the Greek New Testament in the Light of Historical Research.* New York: George H. Doran Co., 1923, pp. 535, 586-7, 591, 624-6, 767-8, 794, 829, 834, 891-4, 896, 1181.

Tertullian, "On the Flesh of Christ," *The Ante-Nicene Fathers,* Vol. III. Grand Rapids, Michigan: Wm. B. Eerdmans Publishing Co., 1951, pp. 537-8.

Westcott, Brooke Foss, *The Gospel According to St. John,* Vol. I. Grand Rapids, Michigan: Wm. B. Eerdmans Publishing Co., 1954, p. 16.

Winer, G. B., *A Treatise on the Grammar of New Testament Greek,* Edinburgh: T. & T. Clark, 1882, p. 429.

Zodhiates, Spiros, *God Becomes Man* (now included as part of *Was Christ God?*), pp. 47-52.

—*God in Man* (Now included as part of *Was Christ God?*), pp. 73-7.

326

I

INDEX OF SUBJECTS

II

INDEX OF ENGLISH WORDS

329

III

INDEX OF GREEK WORDS

Index of Greek Words

Greek	English	John	Page
haima	blood	1:13	246, 258
(haimatoon)			
hamartia	sin	1:5b	160
hekastos	each	1:7c, 8	185
hina	in order that	1:7a, b	180
ho (ton, hee, hoi,	the	1:1c, 2, 5a, 10,	8, 51, 97
tois, tou, too,		11, 12, 13a, d,	98, 119, 203
tees)		15c, 17, 18a	214, 225, 226
			242, 269
			288, 323
hora-oo	see	1:18a, b	15-17, 22
(heooraken)			
hos (hoi)	who	1:13, 18c	26, 253, 257
hosos ·	as many as,	1:12	216-218
(hosoi)	all who		
hoti	that, because	1:16	295, 313, 314
houtos (touto)	this	1:1a, 2	56, 118
huios	son	1:12b	242, 243
idios	one's own	1:11	207, 208, 212
(idia, idioi)			214
Iooanees	John	1:15	275
kai	and	1:13	253
kakos	bad	1:5b	160
(kaka)		(Isa. 45:7)	
katalambanoo	seize, comprehend	1:5, 11, 12a	162, 163, 213
(katelaben)			220
kolpos	bosom	1:18c	27
kosmos	world	1:10	203, 204
krazoo (kekragen)	cry	1:15a, b	282-284
lalia	speech, utterance	1:1a	52
lambanoo (elaben,	take, receive	1:11, 12, 16a, b	213, 220, 221
elabon,			230, 303-305
elabomen)			
legoo (legoon)	say	1:15a, b	285
logos	word, reason,	1:1a, 14a, 18b	21, 37, 39-43
	intelligence		47, 51, 52
			54-57, 59-61
			63, 65, 66
			68-71, 73-75
			78, 87, 95
			98, 106, 121
			126-129, 142
			188, 203, 211
			249, 251, 257
			270, 285, 293

Greek	English	John	Page
luchnos	hand lamp	1:7c, 8; 5:35	187
marture-oo	witness, to	1:7a, b, 15	180, 275
(martureesee,			
marturei)			
martus	witness	1:7a, b	182
meta	with	1:1b	71
monogenees	only begotten,	1:1a, 18	18, 20, 21
(monogenous)	only one born,	(Luke 8:42)	25, 27
	unique, of the		32, 46, 50
	same nature,		68, 87, 88
	related		93
monos	alone	1:18b	21
nomos	law	1:14c	110
oida (eidenai)	know by reflection	1:10	204
opisoo	behind, after	1:15c	288, 290, 292
ou, ouk	no, not	1:10, 11, 12	204, 212, 215
oudeis	no one, not one,	1:5a, 18a	12, 13, 158
(oudemia)	no man		
para	beside	1:1b, 14; 17:5	71
paralambanoo	welcome, receive	1:11, 12	213, 215, 220
(parelaben,			
parelabon)			
parthenos	virgin	1:13a	259
pas (panta, pan,	every, all	1:3a, 7c, 8, 9b,	123-125, 200
pantes, pantas)		6a, 10	203, 302
pateer (patros)	father	1:14	87
phainoo (phainei)	shine, to	1:4b, 5a	155-157
phengos	luminary	1:4b	153
pheroo (pheroon)	bear, carry	1:10	203
phoos	light	1:4b, 7, 8, 9b	150-153
			181, 193
phootizoo	light, to	1:9b	193-195
(phootizei)			197, 198
pisteu-oo	believe	1:7c, 8, 12c	186, 225-227
(pisteusoosin,			
pisteuou-si			
pisteusasi,			
pisteuein)			
pistis	faith	1:12c	227
pleerees (pleeree)	full	1:14c	114, 115
pleerooma	fullness	1:16	300
poopote	ever, at any time	1:18a	17
presbus	ambassador	1:6a	171
prootos	first	1:15c	292, 293

Index of Greek Words

Greek	English	John	Page
proototokos	first-born	1:1a (Col. 1:15, 18)	46, 47
pros	toward	1:1b, 2	71, 72, 119
proteros	prior	1:15c	292
rheema (rheemati)	word	1:10 (Heb. 1:3)	203
sarx	flesh, human nature	1:14a	63-65
skeenee	tent	1:14b	74
skeenooma *(skeenoomati)*	tent, abode, dwelling	1:14b (II Pet. 1:13, 14)	75, 80
skeeno-oo *(eskeenoosen)*	tent, to	1:14	74, 75, 80
skotia	darkness	1:5a, b (I John 1:5)	158-160 161
skotos	darkness	1:5a (I John 1:5)	158, 159
stelloo	send	1:6a	171
sun	with	1:1b	71
sunisteemi *(sunesteeken)*	cohere	1:10 (Col. 1:17)	203
teknon (tekna)	child	1:12b	241-243
telos	goal	1:17a	318
theaomai *(etheasametha,* *theasthai,* *tetheamai)*	behold, gaze upon	1:14, 32, 38; 4:35; 6:5; 11:45 (I John 1:1; 4:12, 14)	83, 84, 86
theios	divine	1:1c	100-102
theiotees	divinity	1:1c (Rom. 1:20)	101
theleema *(theleematos)*	desire	1:13 (I Cor. 7:37) (Eph. 2:3)	263
theloo	wish, will	1:13	264
theos *(theon,* *theou)*	god	1:18a	6-8, 12, 18 26, 98, 101-102 119, 242, 269
theotees	deity, godhead	1:1c (Col. 2:9)	101, 102
tiktoo (tiktein)	bear, i.e., children	1:12 b	241, 242
zooee	life	1:4	139-141 146, 149